THE ORIGIN OF
EVERYDAY MOODS

THE ORIGIN OF
EVERYDAY MOODS

Managing Energy,
Tension, and Stress

Robert E. Thayer, Ph.D.

OXFORD UNIVERSITY PRESS
New York   Oxford

Oxford University Press

Oxford   New York
Athens   Auckland   Bangkok   Bogotá   Bombay
Buenos Aires   Calcutta   Cape Town   Dar es Salaam   Delhi
Florence   Hong Kong   Istanbul   Karachi   Kuala Lumpur
Madras   Madrid   Melbourne   Mexico City   Nairobi   Paris
Singapore   Taipei   Tokyo   Toronto

and associated companies in
Berlin   Ibadan

Library of Congress Cataloging-in-Publication Data
Thayer, Robert E.
The origin of everyday moods : managing energy, tension, and stress
/ Robert E. Thayer.
p. cm.   Includes bibliographical references and index.
ISBN 0-19-508791-7
ISBN 0-19-511805-7 (Pbk.)
1. Mood (Psychology)   2. Affect (Psychology)   I. Title.
BF521.T47   1996
152.4—dc20   95-36962

1 3 5 7 9 10 8 6 4 2

Printed in the United States of America
on acid-free paper

PREFACE

Over two decades ago, my biopsychological research began to take shape and yield a picture of important relationships between mood and major biological functions of the body. Among other things, it became increasingly clear that everyday moods are closely related to often overlooked biological variables—sleep, health, physical fitness, daily cycles, exercise, and nutrition—as well as to the more commonly described variables of stress and cognition. In particular, I found that central feelings of energy and tension, in different combinations, underlie most of the moods we experience each day. Moreover, it became clear that these feelings are the subjective indications of wide-ranging arousal systems in the body.

These relationships were described in my earlier book, *The Biopsychology of Mood and Arousal* (Oxford University Press, 1989), and the supporting scientific literature up until the end of the 1980s was analyzed there. That book only suggested some of the ways my theory of everyday moods could provide insights into how we might regulate our moods. But my university students were ever insistent on exploring those practical applications, and even though I tended to focus on the more scientific theoretical implications of mood and behavior, I found myself attending more and more to the practical benefits of my work.

I have been reminded often that, in addition to my students, the general public is very curious about the nature of mood and any practical information on the topic. Since the mid-1980s, when our research became widely available, writers in the popular press have often approached me with questions about how our scientific findings can be applied to an array of practical problems. Public interest peaked at the end of 1994, when my research team published our findings on how people from many backgrounds manage their bad moods, revealing what works best and what doesn't work. This publication produced an immediate avalanche of newspaper, television, and radio reports, followed a few months later by more extended articles in many national magazines.

All of this interest should not go unmet, I was told by my students and colleagues, and by my editor at Oxford Unversity Press. There are so many practical implications, things that can provide immediate help for many people, that a straightforward book should be written that presents the theory for the general public. After beginning work on this, however, I saw the potential to expand much of the theory into previously unexplored areas. For example, dieting and, in general, the management of food and exercise are urgent problems for many people. How can the theory be most directly applied in these areas? Also, the implications of previously published findings on how people self-regulate bad moods were not developed extensively, and this book offered the possibility to do that. Finally, since this is one of the most active scientific areas and interesting new findings are continuously being published, it became apparent that the present study should update the most important findings since my previous one.

This book began as a simple exposition, but gradually developed into a more extensive treatment of everyday moods that I hope adds an important new theoretical framework to our understanding. Since these kinds of concepts involve technical issues that must be addressed for those readers who want to know about such matters, an extensive section of notes was developed in which such things are discussed without interfering with the easy flow of ideas. My students helped me greatly in writing this book. I was able to draw on their personal experiences to illustrate many of the concepts presented here. Several of the short case studies are from my students' personal experiences.

I wish to thank many people who have generously given their time and evaluated the ideas and early drafts of this book. First, I am very grateful to my close friend and colleague Retha Evans, who not only offered a good sounding board and intelligent discussion of many of the concepts as I was developing them, but patiently and competently read and critiqued each chapter. She also helped greatly in the final editing of the book. It is extraordinarily helpful for a writer to have a trusted other such as I did, who could read and provide valuable feedback on the communication of complex ideas. As any writer knows, it is too easy to go astray and produce incomprehensible prose.

I also owe a great deal to Joan Bossert, my editor at Oxford University Press. She early saw the value of this kind of book and encouraged me to write it. After I finished an early draft, she patiently edited it, not only suggesting word and sentence changes, but providing detailed questions about concepts that were unclear as well as suggestions that would add to the usefulness of the final work. This help was invaluable. I especially appreciated her ready encouragement because it is much too easy for a writer to become discouraged at times, even if he believes in his work.

My two daughters, Leah and Kara, also helped me a great deal in lengthy discussions, not only while I was writing the book, but in earlier years while many of these ideas were being formulated. Kara especially was interested in these ideas, and she had much to add whenever we discussed them. In addition, she provided helpful comments on one chapter of this book. Others who read and gave me useful comments on portions of the book include the distinguished physiological psychologists Robert Stelmack, Alexander Beckman, and Kenneth Green. A number of others read portions of the book, but I wish to thank in particular Ruth Stewart and Nancy Voils. I am very grateful to all these individuals, but of course none of them should be held responsible for any errors that remain—these I clearly made alone.

I also wish to thank my students past and present who contributed immeasurably by listening to, discussing, and challenging my ideas, therefore making them much more sound. I am especially grateful to the individuals whose cases I described in this book because they gave personal relevancy to what otherwise might have been abstract ideas. Although they remain anonymous, their contributions are important and appreciated.

A number of students and colleagues have helped me greatly over the years on the research that is so much a part of this book. In particular, I want to thank former students and fellow researchers Mary Ann Cejka, Bonnie Shrewsbury, Janet Metz, Kimberly Mercer, Don Peters, Paula Takahashi, Angela Birkhead-Flight, Faye Docuyanan, and especially Tracey McClain, who served as project manager in the studies of how people self-regulate their negative moods. In that research my friend and very able colleague J. Robert Newman contributed immensely to the final product, particularly in the analyses, interpretation, and writeup of the findings.

Long Beach, Calif.   R. E. T
January 1996

CONTENTS

PART ONE

The Origin of Moods

1

Mood and Its Meanings

Everyday moods are so ephemeral and illusive that it seems impossible to know where they come from, why they occur, and, perhaps more important, what we can do about them. But these daily variations in our feelings are actually easier to understand and manage than most people realize.

Our moods are important for many reasons. For example, a good mood can help us carry out a disagreeable task—it has a way of improving our outlook. Even an unpleasant social interaction can be tolerable if our mood is positive. On the other hand, if we are in a bad mood, an activity that usually is very pleasant, one that otherwise gives us great enjoyment, can be boring and uninteresting. When our mood is low, even the most positive events become meaningless.

If we think of our moods as emphasizing meaning and enhancing or reducing the pleasure in our lives, we can understand how central they really are. In this respect, they are more important than daily activities, money, status, and even personal relationships because these things are usually filtered through our moods. In many ways, our moods are at the core of our being.

Where do these moods come from? Many people believe that our activities, relationships, successes, and failures create our moods. But that's only partly correct, as will become apparent throughout this book. Health, sleep, food, amount of recent exercise, and even time of day are very significant as well. Moods are general indexes of both physiological functioning and psychological experience. Mood is something like a clinical thermometer, reflecting all the internal and external events that affect us.

In these pages I explain how natural biological rhythms are central to the experience we call *mood*. In some respects my explanation counters the commonsense notions of what mood is. Most people and even scientists think of moods as psychological reactions to events. Although scientists are usually aware that mood is also influenced by natural biological events, psychological causes often take center stage, and these other influences are never explored.

A new model is offered in this book. Recent scientific findings make it increasingly clear that everyday moods are biopsychological in nature—in other words, they are a mixture of many biological and psychological influences. Not only are they affected by events, but they also change with the body's rhythms and conditions. They are crucial indicators of how we are functioning at any moment. According to this model, mind and body are not separate, and our moods are windows to the state of both. In this explanation of moods, the psychological bases aren't left out but are simply integrated with physical and biological bases.

We continually sense our moods and often unconsciously try to improve them. Scientists refer to this as the *self-regulation of moods*. Eating sugary snacks is an example of an attempt to feel better, or to regulate mood. Many other behaviors have the same function. When in a bad mood, some people seek social interaction; others try to control their thoughts; and still other people avoid social contact. We attempt to self-regulate our moods in many different ways. In the case of alcohol and other drugs, it has become common to speak of people self-medicating a negative mood. But many kinds of behaviors have exactly the same kind of "self-medicating" function.

Unfortunately, in the long run, these self-regulating activities aren't always beneficial. They may work temporarily, which is why we use them. But over time, quick-fix behaviors are not successful. Over-eating, excessive drinking, smoking, and illegal drug use are just some of the dysfunctional methods that people choose. And such self-regulating activities—too much TV viewing, isolating oneself, and even coffee drinking—can lead to bad moods.

The psychology of how people self-regulate their moods—with good and bad effects—is one of the principal subjects of this book. Our most recent research has identified what most people do to change their bad moods and how they try to sustain and improve their good moods. Moreover, I believe we have discovered what works and what does not. Although bits and pieces of this research have been widely reported in the popular press, our conclusions are more extensive and more complex.

In this book, we explore normal daily moods and also touch on more extreme mood states such as depression. We look at these moods in personal cases and make sense of recent scientific find-ings—in particular, the ways in which moods and other behaviors influence one another, how these normal daily moods are created, how they affect our lives, and how they can be regulated.

What Is Mood?

We can think of mood as a background feeling that persists over time. Usually our moods are subtle, but sometimes they can be intense and overwhelm us. Moods are not the same as emotions, but they do have a great deal in common with them. Moods are sometimes defined as less intense and longer lasting than emotions, although this lower intensity isn't true in the case of a serious depression. Unlike most emotions, moods don't seem to have an identifiable cause. That is, there usually isn't an obvious cause-and-effect relationship between our moods and events. This isn't true of emotions.[1]

Although moods are usually regarded as a kind of emotional reac-tion, some scientists also include cognition in this definition. For example, we speak of a person as having a contemplative or thoughtful mood, a mood that doesn't seem to have an emotional quality. In another sense, the term *mood* is sometimes used as a disposition to do something.[2] "I'm in the mood for some ice cream," is an example. Described in this way, moods indicate a greater tendency to do certain things. Although they are not the direct cause of a particular behavior, moods increase the likelihood that the behavior will occur.

Most of us would agree that moods are either positive or negative. Although not all scientists accept this good–bad dimension as central to mood, any general scientific theory of mood must account for the positive or negative feelings that moods produce. In fact, an influential theory, which we will discuss shortly, defines all moods as either positive or negative.

Moods are usually conscious, which is one of the reasons that we talk about them as feelings. Indeed, people can evaluate their moods, especially when prompted by relevant questions. Accordingly, almost all scientific research on mood includes inventories that people can use to rate their moods. And yet people who seek guidance from psychotherapists, and many who do not, are often not aware of their moods or find it difficult to describe them.

Both professionals and laypeople sometimes infer a person's mood from behavior, posture, and other physical signs such as tone of voice, slowness of response, and slumped shoulders. A relaxed person who stands tall with shoulders back and head held high looks not only confident but also positive about life—in other words, in a good mood.

In extreme forms, some moods are unmistakable. Depression, for instance, can be a compelling, driving, gnawing sense of hopelessness and despair, laced with a heavy mixture of fatigue and anxiety. But in its milder form, this negative mood may simply be manifested as a pattern of tiredness and fatigue mixed with some tension. Researchers have found that such feelings are closely associated with pessimistic and sad thoughts. When a person experiences persistent tension and fatigue, with no apparent physical cause, depression is often the problem.

Various terms are used in the scientific literature to refer to moods. *Affect*, for example, is a term that many biological and behavioral scientists use to indicate mood. Affect has a certain surface quality or immediacy associated with it. Clinicians may also refer to a patient's *affect level*, indicating observable emotional reactions such as crying.[3] But when research psychologists measure affect with various scales, *affect level* usually refers to ratings of immediate feelings that the subjects make themselves. *Feelings* and *feeling states* are other terms often used synonymously with mood.

Our understanding of mood was advanced considerably in 1985 when a landmark paper was published by two psychologists, David Watson and Auke Tellegen. They combined the separate analyses of many of the best studies up to that time, using a mathematical technique called *factor analysis*. This technique identifies a few common factors or dimensions that account for a large number of variables. Although Watson and Tellegen studied hundreds of apparently different moods, using self-ratings in previous mood research, they found that most of the mood variations could be explained by just two factors or dimensions, which they labeled *positive affect* and *negative affect*.[4]

The mood dimension called positive affect is associated with many feelings. For example, a peppy mood often is moderately correlated with elation, enthusiasm, strength, and activity. And it is the approximate opposite of feelings such as drowsy, dull, sleepy, and sluggish. Negative affect is described by adjectives like distressed, fearful, hostile, jittery, nervous, and scornful. And these are the opposite of such feelings as calm, placid, and relaxed. What is particularly interesting for this book is that in Watson and Tellegen's research, feelings related to energy were central to positive affect and feelings related to tension were central to negative affect.

Watson and Tellegen's factor analytic study is important for another reason. It indicates that only a few moods seem to account for a large number of feelings. In other words, our many feelings—which might be identified as separate moods—are variations of just two, or at most a few, basic moods. We experience a wide array of moods because our associated thoughts determine how we interpret basic biological processes.[5]

Rather than considering positive and negative affect as the central dimensions of mood, I believe that energy and tension are central components of what we experience as mood. Thus, a complex mood such as depression really indicates low energy and moderately high tension, accompanied by a host of associated thoughts (e.g., hopelessness, low self-esteem). Similarly, optimism is probably associated with a pattern of higher energy and somewhat lower tension. Happiness involves relatively high energy and either moderate or low tension. Other complex moods can be described in the same way. In each case, the basic mood patterns interact with relevant thoughts to produce the states that we identify as moods.[6]

2

A Theory of Mood

We can think of the body as having at least two general arousal systems involving many closely interrelated physiological and psychological processes. These range from simple metabolic processes and elemental biochemical reactions to more complex psychophysiological systems—the cardiovascular, respiratory, skeletal–muscular, and endocrine. The brain is certainly involved, with its neurotransmitter and neuromodulatory biochemistry, and on a conscious level are thoughts, what scientists call *cognitive processes*.

Because of the complexity and limitations on research with humans, scientists still don't fully understand the physiological causes of mood. But on the level of conscious awareness, mood processes are more obvious. For example, we can identify positive and negative moods, and we can see how all of us—consciously or not—regulate our moods.

In this book, using mood as an index, we will concentrate on the feelings we experience when these major arousal systems are at work. To begin, it is essential to see that moods are not solely mental reactions. When, for example, you feel tired, it is difficult to separate how your body feels (run down, hungry, in need of sleep) from how your mind feels (edgy, distracted, "brain dead," to use a popular expression). What I hope this book will show is that it is impossible to disentangle the mental and bodily states because physical and cognitive reactions are closely interrelated through both cause and effect.

A question that I am frequently asked is What is the physiological cause of moods? That is, is there some master physiological or biochemical system that affects how we feel? The popular notion is that someday we will understand the master system and be able to develop a magic pill that we can take to remain in a good mood forever, with little or no effort.

Currently, the best answer about the physiological cause of moods is that there is no single cause, that what we experience as everyday moods are the conscious representations of our body's general arousal patterns. There is a lot of media coverage about endorphins and other neurotransmitters of the brain, but there is little certainty about these things (see Chapter 8). Endorphins do appear to be important elements of some pleasurable experiences, but right now the evidence about this still is unclear. On the other hand, the high energy associated with good moods probably is related to many different kinds of physiological processes, all operating simultaneously.

This tendency of the body to operate in holistic patterns has an important implication. Because one bodily system affects another, when we consider self-regulation of mood, we will find that controlling one aspect of arousal produces other changes throughout the body. For example, if we reduce muscular tension by stretching or doing yoga, we often will experience an elevation of mood. Similarly, a short brisk walk that increases heart rate usually increases feelings of energy as well. Or if we can control our thoughts so as not to think about a problem, we will experience reduced muscular tension.

Over the years, I have devised a vocabulary to capture how many of my students and experimental subjects describe their moods. I plot four states on two arousal continuums: *calm-energy*, *calm-tiredness*, *tense-energy*, and *tense-tiredness*. The two arousal continuums range from energy to tiredness and from tense to calm.

Calm-Energy

As an example of how these arousal systems operate, consider Jane Jones who is in a good mood. In the middle of the day, say around noon, she is working at her desk. She is healthy, and she has eaten a nutritious breakfast. Her heart rate is relatively high in relation to the normal daily variations of this kind of activity. Her respiration rate also is somewhat elevated, and her metabolism is relatively high. Jane's thoughts are focused fully on her work, but she feels no urgency, just a quiet and relaxed attention.

Let us turn to Jane's feelings. She might describe them as energetic, peppy, and vigorous. An introspective person might also describe other feelings, perhaps confident, sociable, and maybe even happy. In addition, if Jane thought about it, she might also say that she feels calm, quiet, or placid. If someone asked her, she might say, "I'm feeling good today." This is the state I call *calm-energy*. In my view, it is an ideal that most of us would like to achieve, a state that all of us would describe in positive terms.

But the conscious experience of calm-energy cannot be separated from the associated physiological processes taking place in the body. The idea that the body and mind are different entities cannot explain mood. Just as the heart and lungs have a particular biological function, so do moods. Moods provide vital information about the state of one's body and the danger or safety of one's surroundings. Although the two functions are somewhat different, both are biopsychological in nature.

Calm-Tiredness

To develop this point a bit further, let us consider Jane at another time of day, say 11:00 P.M., just before she goes to bed. Now her cardiovascular system is operating at a lower level of activation; her respiration is reduced; and her metabolism is decreased. Work isn't the focus of her thoughts now. Perhaps she is reading an enjoyable book, or listening to some quiet music. Maybe she is occupied with an undemanding hobby. In any case, her thoughts are not on the major or even minor problems of her life.

Jane's feelings now are also different. She still may say that she is in a good mood but use different adjectives to describe these feelings. Perhaps these terms would be tired, sleepy, or drowsy. As at noon, however, calmness prevails. This good mood isn't quite as intense as the one felt at noon, and Jane wouldn't give it as high a rating. But it is good, nonetheless. I call this state *calm-tiredness*.

Tense-Energy

Tense-energy, another of the four basic moods, is one that some may say also is positive, though it is definitely not calm-energy. In this example, at around noon Jane again is working, but now she has a deadline to meet. Her boss is waiting impatiently, and Jane senses that her job rating will rise if she finishes this project quickly and well. She clearly feels a sense of urgency.

The internal environment of Jane's body is similar to the first example, of calm-energy. Her cardiovascular system is activated, and her metabolism and respiration have increased. Each of these physiological systems may be at roughly the same level of activation as they were in the first example. But level of arousal isn't what is important here. In fact, it would be difficult for a physiologist to detect any real differences among many of the body's major arousal systems. For instance, in a state of tense-energy, adrenalin levels may be high, but that also could be true with calm-energy. Adrenalin does more than just mediate stress and anxiety; it is a hormone that regulates blood glucose, heart rate, and metabolism, among other functions.

In a state of tense-energy there would be certain physiological differences from those of calm-energy. In tense-energy, the skeletal muscles probably are tight rather than operating smoothly to perform various motor functions. This muscle tightness can be detected in the jaws, shoulders, neck, or back.

From an evolutionary perspective, it is almost as though Jane is prepared for some violent action. The famous physiologist Walter Cannon called the subsequent action she is preparing for *fight or flight*, although neither fight nor flight is relevant here. Instead,

Jane is showing a muscular freeze reaction. That is, even though her skeletal–muscular system is prepared for fight or flight, no significant action is occurring. This skeletal–muscular tightness is important, however, as we will discover in a later discussion of the evolutionary biology of this state of tense-energy. Such reactions in people who are anxious, tense, or nervous have certain evolutionary origins. Their primary biological function is preparation for an emergency.

Jane's thoughts also are different here. She is concentrating on her work but not fully, as she was in the first example. Rather, she is slightly distracted, almost as though her thoughts were scattered. This is troubling because in this job Jane should be totally focused. But as she works, she keeps thinking about the time. Although she is thinking fast and may be enjoying what she is doing, her eyes are on the clock.

Next let us consider Jane's feelings, her mood. To many people, these might not be bad feelings. At this moment, Jane might say that she has feelings of energy, pep, and vigor, just as in the first example. But now she has an added sense of tension, jitteriness, a kind of intenseness that was not present with calm-energy. A clinician might even describe these feelings as low-level anxiety, but I call this state *tense-energy*.

Tense-Tiredness

Just as calm-energy and calm-tiredness are related, there is another mood related to tense-energy, a distinctly bad mood. I call it *tense-tiredness*. It occurs when resources are depleted, when an individual is used up, so to speak. When fatigue is mixed with nervousness, tension, or anxiety, it produces a state that is definitely unpleasant.

Suppose that Jane has been working feverishly all day and that it is now late in the afternoon. She didn't sleep well the night before. Her food for the day consisted of some doughnuts, lots of coffee, and maybe a quick sandwich gobbled down in a few bites. And she certainly didn't get to the gym. (A person who often finds herself in this state probably seldom gets to the gym.) Asked about her mood now, Jane would say, "Bad!"

This tense-tired state is an interesting one in the sense that it's not just a bad mood. It's also the mood that often underlies depression. In addition, it's not just a set of feelings; thoughts usually accompany it. These are negative thoughts about oneself, including low self-esteem. If they enter one's mind, personal problems will loom large, perhaps even seem insurmountable. The future looks bad. In the middle of the afternoon when the job demands more attention, these thoughts about one's life condition may be minimal. But the negative thoughts arising from this tense-tired state are well known to the person tossing and turning in bed, trying to get some needed sleep. They also are familiar to the individual who awakens at 3:00 A.M., and surveys his or her life, only to conclude that it's a mess. Tense-tiredness is not a pleasant mood.

The differences among these four moods often are not well understood. When I talk to my university students or to lay audiences, I find that many have a difficult time understanding the difference between calm-energy and tense-energy. Frequently they don't understand *calm*-energy, as they believe that whenever they are energetic, there is a slight edge associated with it. (I would call this tension.)

People who regularly exercise or meditate, however, understand this difference. They know what calm-energy feels like, and though they have energy, they don't feel a bit tense. Some of these people have taken stress management training or are athletes. In any case, you can usually remember a time—perhaps when you were a child or much younger or fitter—when you felt alert, boundless, with no "edge." This is calm-energy.

Because I view calm-energy as the optimal mood, I shall refer to it frequently in this book. But to conclude this description of calm-energy, let me share an observation. It seems to me that calm-energy is foreign to many Westerners, but not to those of other cultures. For example, most of us are familiar with some ideas of Zen. The Zen master Shunryū Suzuki said this about the calm state I am attempting to describe: "Calmness of mind does not mean you should stop your activity. Real calmness should be found in the activity itself. It is easy to have calmness in inactivity, but calmness in activity is true calmness."[1] This sounds very much like calm-energy.

Mood as a Biological Rhythm

To understand the biological rhythms of mood, it is necessary to start with the daily rhythms of energy, as they are essential to understanding mood, especially mood management. Think of how energetic you feel at this moment. You might rate yourself on a 5-point scale, ranging from extremely to not at all. If you make this kind of self-rating once an hour—from the time you wake up until just before you go to sleep—a pattern will emerge.

In several studies, my colleagues and I have asked participants to make these kinds of systematic self-ratings. For example, in one study, we asked 18 volunteers to rate themselves on six typical days over a three-week period. These were days on which they awoke and went to sleep at approximately the same time and on which they engaged in normal routines.[2]

To get reliable results, it is best to rate yourself for at least three days. But even the ratings for one day will give you a rudimentary idea of your energy pattern. Averaging the results of such ratings and plotting them over all your waking hours will give you a good indication of the *circadian*, or daily, rhythm of your energy. Energy levels are higher or lower at approximately the same times each day. Interestingly enough, natural rhythms have been found for virtually every biological function studied over time—heart rate, respiration, blood-sugar level, norepinephrine, and many more. Moods are no exception.

These patterns form what chronobiologists often call *endogenous biological rhythms*. They are considered internal, or *endogenous*, because they are largely influenced by bodily processes that are established by a kind of biological clock. The endogenous nature of these rhythms and how they make us feel more or less alert and energetic become obvious when we fly across time zones. Flying from California to New York or from California to Europe results in disruptions of these rhythms that we commonly call *jet lag*. Our internal rhythms are disrupted because we are now encountering hours of light, darkness, sleeping, waking, and eating that are very different from those our body is used to.

Energy levels slowly rise to their highest level (their *acrophase*) sometime in the first third of the day, around noon or 1:00 P.M. Then they drop in the mid-to late afternoon, reach a subpeak in the early evening, and decline until sleep. Energy is lowest just before sleep, but for most people it also is low at awakening, even if they have had a good night's sleep (see Figure 1).[3] As we begin to consider strategies for managing moods, it will be important to learn to detect these slow and gradually rising or falling changes in energy.

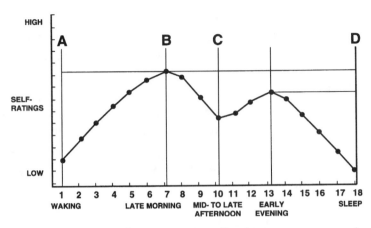

Figure 1   Theoretical representation of endogenous energy cycle

I have been speaking here about rhythms during waking, or *diurnal* hours, but a 24-hour, or *circadian* rhythm extends into the sleeping period as well. We know this because people who are kept awake so that scientists can study the effects of sleep deprivation continue to grow sleepier until the middle of their customary sleep period, usually 3:00 or 4:00 A.M. Then they gradually become more alert. At their normal waking time the next morning, they often feel almost as alert and energetic as usual. The loss of sleep hits them later in the day, often in the late afternoon and evening. As we will discover, the point at which sleep loss has its greatest impact is important because it is also the time when people's moods are often at their lowest ebb.

Although on average, people's energy reaches a peak in the late morning or early afternoon, there are many individual differences. So-called morning people may experience their peak soon after awakening, and evening types may not reach their acrophase until later in the day. (It is interesting that introverts experience their energy peak earlier in the day and extraverts, later in the day.)

Vulnerability to Tension, Nervousness, and Anxiety in the Circadian Energy Cycle

Tense-tiredness is most likely to occur when energy is low. Our research shows, for example, that late afternoon and evening are times when people are most likely to feel tense-tired. For the average person, around 4:00 P.M. and 9:00 to 11:00 P.M. are vulnerable periods

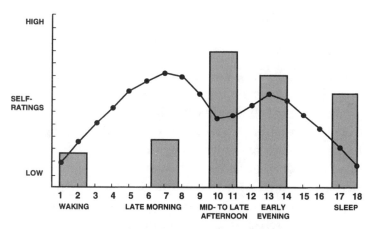

Figure 2 Theoretical representation of tension effects (darkened bars) during times of stress in relation to endogenous energy cycle

(see Figure 2). Just after awakening is another time when people's energy is low and they also may be vulnerable to tension. Some clinicians regard anxiety at morning awakening as an indication of one kind of depression. (Tense-tiredness is a characteristic arousal pattern of depression.) But even though their energy level may be low, many people do not experience this morning anxiety.

Furthermore, not all people are vulnerable to tension during the late afternoon and evening. As I have already mentioned, individual differences are often quite pronounced. We have observed hundreds of different, widely varying energy cycles in our studies. Some people find afternoon to be their most energetic period of the day, and others feel only a slight decline in energy in the evening. Instead, these night people usually experience low-energy levels at different times of day.

Since there are so many differences among people, general principles of mood functioning must be personally tailored. One of my students' favorite activities is establishing their "best" and "worst" hours of the day. Each student does this by systematically self-rating energy and tension every hour for three to six typical days. These patterns of energy and tension levels are then used to establish the best and worst hours.

The worst hours occur during patterns of relatively high tension and low energy, or tense-tiredness. Conversely, the best hours come during patterns of high energy and low tension, or calm-energy. Some people also like high energy and high tension, or tense-energy. Later, however, we will discuss why tension over long periods of time can damage mood, even though some people may seem to feel energized and empowered.

Many negative psychological reactions can occur during naturally low energy periods of the day if there are chronic stressors or problems in a person's life. Without stress however, low energy may produce a rather pleasant state of calm-tiredness. But during periods of stress, low energy can result in low self-esteem, unrealistic concerns about personal problems, feelings of depression, and many other negative reactions. I am convinced that the general principle underlying many of these reactions is increased vulnerability to tension, a condition that leads to tense-tired mood patterns.

Insignificant hassles or minor stressors can have their greatest impact at these tense-tired times of day. That is, a small problem that at another time of day goes unnoticed may explode into a major conflagration during these times, or an unimportant dispute with coworkers or a family member may escalate into a full-blown fight. Observant parents of small children know this phenomenon well. When children are tired, they cry easily, and everything bothers them. In all these cases, the principle is the same. A decrease in energy leaves an individual vulnerable to greater tension, and this tense-tired state predisposes a wide array of negative reactions.

The degree to which these tense-tired times of day are basic to some of our most elemental ways of viewing the world was evident in a series of experiments that my students and I conducted. In one experiment a small panel of volunteers agreed to a rather arduous procedure involving many self-ratings over 10 typical days in a 3-week period.[4] The participants knew nothing about our hypotheses, but agreed to participate because of the promise that they would learn more about themselves.

All the subjects in this experiment had in common a personal problem that was unremitting, the kind of difficulty that doesn't go away in one day. For example, one slightly older woman was in the midst of a difficult marital separation; another young woman was in the center of severe parental discord; and a third had an unyielding weight problem. These problems were the kind that the subjects repeatedly thought and worried about.

The experiment involved five ratings a day of how serious the problem appeared, with each judgment made only at the moment of the rating. The participants also rated their current energy and tension levels. On each of the 10 days, the ratings were made just after awakening, in the late morning or early afternoon, in the late afternoon, and just before sleep at night. The other rating was made following a brisk 10-minute walk at a time of day at least an hour and a half away from the other four ratings. Each subject was carefully instructed to think only about the problem and his or her current mood level at the moment of the rating.

The results were fascinating and illustrated very well the principles I have just described. After averaging the ratings over all 10 days, the same problem was rated as more serious in the afternoon than in the late morning, a statistically significant difference. Furthermore, regardless of the time of day, the problem always was rated as more serious if the person was in a tense-tired mood and less serious if in a calm-energetic mood. But these differences were subtle and showed up only when we averaged the ratings over all 10 days, probably because on any one day something unusual may have occurred. But on average, the differences were quite apparent.

In research like this, of course, a scientist must consider several interpretations. (I also discuss many technical issues and methodological problems in the notes to this book.[5]) Aware that there could be other interpretations, we decided to conduct two other experiments with somewhat different procedures, but we still obtained essentially the same results.[6] This research, therefore, is a good indication that the way we look at our problems is related to our moods.

Think about this for a moment: The problem did not change; the only different variable was the person's mood. If the way that we look at our problems can vary with time of day and with naturally occurring mood cycles, then we may question what is real about these problems. Are personal problems as fleeting as our moods?

The results of our studies should not be surprising to most people. I first started to do research on this topic when I found myself in similar circumstances. I noticed that when I thought about a problem late at night or when I was tired and slightly tense, the problem often appeared very serious, even insurmountable. But when I thought about the same problem the next morning when I was more energetic, it didn't seem so serious. Many of my students have had the same experience. So when judging the severity of problems, this should illustrate how important it is to consider the time of day and energy level when evaluating problems.

Why should problems appear more serious when you are tired than rested? I believe that it may have something to do with simple feedback loops involving moods and thoughts.[7] For example, when you think about something that you must do in the future, a key piece of information is your energy level at the time you must perform the task. Since personal problems are often associated with ongoing and future requirements, energy level becomes an important element in assessing the problem. But because *future* energy levels are difficult to determine, you usually use your *current* energy level as the best indication of your future energy resources. Therefore, if you are tired, you probably will conclude that you lack the energy to tackle the problem and so it will appear insurmountable. Clearly, there is an error in logic here. But it is an easy one to make, and the feedback loop involved probably circles so rapidly that you are scarcely aware of it.

Interestingly enough, the same kind of error can be made in reverse: Future activities that will require a good deal of energy to accomplish may be judged too optimistically if the judgment is made during a period of unusually high energy. Thus, you may plan to do something when you are energetic but may be too tired to do it when the time comes. Again, your current energy level is incorrectly influencing your judgments about your ability to muster enough energy and commitment for the future task.

This error in logic has a number of practical implications. If the time you usually take stock of your life and make your plans for the future is late in the evening or at some other low-energy time, you may take a pessimistic view, compared with someone who thinks about such problems during periods of middle or high energy. On the other hand, thinking about your life only at high-energy times can also lead to unrealistic judgments.

A related implication is that you may make plans in a high-energy period but fail to carry them out when the time comes and you feel less energetic. This in turn can lead to a sense of failure and depressing thoughts that you are unable to manage the commitments you have made. The best course is always to be aware of the way that current energy levels may influence your thoughts about future problems and demands.

3

Moods as Barometers of Well-Being

Our energy level tells us a great deal about our body's overall well-being. Tension level also is important. And the combination of energy and tension, together with the thoughts they influence, produce what most people call moods. In fact, our moods are infallible indicators, or barometers, of our most basic functions at any given moment. For example, our feelings about how energetic or how tired we are convey vital information about our physical and psychological health, as well as our readiness for action or our need for rest and recuperation. Tension and calmness, on the other hand, are signals indicating how safe or threatened we feel, both consciously and unconsciously.

In this chapter, I discuss what determines our sense of energy and tension, and from this a much better picture should emerge of how both psychology and biology produce moods. A word of caution is necessary at this point. Scientists argue incessantly about these matters, and our evidence is not complete. Thus a great number of claims are made without any firm basis, particularly about energy—a topic near and dear to health-conscious Americans. People in sales are quite aware of the importance of this feeling: If it could be bottled, packaged, or taught, someone could make a lot of money. Indeed, everything from ginseng to vitamin E has been touted as an energy booster. There is even a car named Vigor!

But is there any scientific evidence concerning what causes fluctuations in energy and tension? Tense feelings—including anxiety, fear, and nervousness—have a long history of study in psychological science and clinical practice, so our understanding of tension is fairly good. But what about energy feelings, the central elements of good moods? Energy has been studied much less. Although we don't know all the determinants of energy feelings, we do have some good indications of what causes the greatest changes in these subjective states. For example, the circadian rhythms of energetic arousal that we described earlier produce some of the most obvious variations in how energetic we feel, and these variations occur daily. But there are a number of other important influences as well.

Exercise

Along with circadian energy rhythms, exercise has a significant influence on energy level. Research has shown that moderate exercise tends to increase energy but that strenuous exercise temporarily decreases it. I am not speaking here of the kind of energy increase that comes from physical conditioning that follows from a lengthy program of exercise. That certainly occurs. Instead, I am referring to the *immediate* effects of the exercise.

The idea that moderate exercise enhances energy while the exercise is occurring may seem paradoxical, as we usually think of exercise as leading to fatigue. But a significant body of scientific evidence shows, with a fairly high degree of certainty, that the immediate effect of moderate exercise is increased energy.[1]

This phenomenon can be observed most readily under certain conditions. For example, if after sitting for a while, you get up and slowly begin to walk, your feelings of energy will start to rise. As you walk a bit faster, your energy will rise correspondingly. But don't expect dramatic changes in how you feel; they are subtle, and it takes a good self-observer to recognize them. With practice in self-observation, however, fluctuations in energy levels become quite clear. Indeed, these changes in feelings are so predictable that it is as though the subjective energy response is somehow integrally tied to basic movement. And as I will show later, that is likely to be the case. Movement and feelings of energy are integrally associated through a common biological system.

Naturally, there are some limits to this phenomenon. For example, if you are sick, very tired, or perhaps in pain that is brought on by the movement, then energy is not likely to be the primary response. Nor will the same increase in energy occur at all times of day. But surprisingly, this relationship between moderate exercise and increased energy readily occurs in most people and settings.

This association between walking and energy came to my notice almost by accident. I had been searching for a method of producing activation in an experiment, something that could be used in natural settings to create a state of general bodily arousal. Walking seemed the perfect activity, and so I chose 10 minutes of brisk walking because it fit nicely into most people's schedules, and caused little disruption in their lives. In the first experiment, I devised a procedure that included disguised experimental and control conditions and university students as subjects, with appropriate measures of mood before and after the exercise.[2] The experimental group walked with me around the campus, and the control group sat quietly and read whatever materials they had brought with them. The change in mood using this procedure was unmistakable. Energy enhancement was the primary mood response, a measurable and statistically significant effect.

Between that research conducted in the late 1970s and more recent experiments, the effects of short brisk walks have been systematically investigated in a wide variety of ways, by both myself and others.[3] We have learned, for example, that 15 minutes of walking produces slightly more energy than 5 minutes does but that even 5 minutes of brisk walking has a significant effect.[4] One of the most interesting findings was from a study of how long the enhanced energy lasted following a 10-minute walk.[5] We took mood measures at 30, 60, and 120 minutes after the walk and found the greatest effect at 30 minutes (20 minutes after the walk) but still a statistically significant effect at 60 minutes. Even at 120 minutes a weak energy increase was still evident. From our research and similar experiments by others, a conservative estimate is that 10 minutes of brisk walking enhances energy for 30 to 90 minutes afterward.

In 1988 I was invited to deliver a keynote talk to the National Press Club in Washington, DC, as part of the ceremonies for National Walk Week.[6] From that talk, the media became interested, and since then the results of my research often are cited in health-science reports. Such articles usually end with summary prescriptions for helping yourself when you are feeling down. The short brisk walk is suggested as a sure method. I am convinced that the reason it has remained popular for these many years is that it works!

Although walking has been our preferred method of producing the general effect of increased energy, various kinds of moderate exercise work in the same way. Energy enhancement is the primary effect; tension reduction is a secondary effect (usually present but not always); and general elevation of optimism is a tertiary effect. The increased optimism is much more subtle than the energy increase, but it was reliably observed in more than one experiment. Vigorous exercise, on the other hand, produces different results. An hour of aerobics, for example, is not likely to result in immediate energy increases; instead, fatigue is the likely result. But vigorous exercise is more likely to reduce tension than moderate exercise is.[7]

I am convinced that there is also an energy response to vigorous exercise. It begins in the exercise's initial phases, often with a substantial increase in energy sometime after recovery from the exercise, generally an hour or more after 45 minutes of vigorous aerobic exercise. This delayed energy response has not been scientifically documented at this time, but I have systematically collected reports by my students who regularly practice aerobic exercise, and the delayed energy response is a common observation.[8]

In the late 1970s when I first started my research on the relationship between moderate exercise and feelings of energy, there was hardly any other research available. But now the relationship between exercise and mood has become a popular research topic. Some of the best research is being done by exercise physiologists who carefully grade the exercise workload with measures such as degree of oxygen consumption or VO_2max (a measure of physiological function roughly correlated with different degrees of maximum heart rate).[9] Although

I have only briefly summarized the results here, many variables must be considered for the best predictions. These include the person's physical condition, nutritional status, health, age, and time of day. For the best predictions, a kind of calculus equation is necessary, using several simultaneously changing variables.

The effects of different degrees of exercise on mood are important to practical applications. One of the best ways of dealing with persistent negative moods, including depression, is regular exercise. In addition the level and type of exercise need to be considered, as will become apparent in later sections of this book.

Food

I am convinced that mood is closely tied to food intake, although this relationship is difficult to demonstrate experimentally. At best, the scientific evidence is mixed. The difficulty occurs because food effects are very subtle and can easily be overridden by other influences. Nonetheless, most of us have a sense of this association that is based on much experience, and this sense is not likely to be wrong.

The basic biological relationship between food and mood can be viewed most clearly in the context of nutritional extremes. Extreme food deprivation, for example, substantially influences energy level. Perhaps the best scientific evidence of this comes from a large research project on semistarvation conducted in 1944 by the Selective Service Administration and the University of Minnesota.[10] As part of the war effort, conscientious objectors volunteered to undergo nine months of severe food restriction while scientists systematically studied their physiological and psychological reactions.

Striking physiological changes were associated with increasing emaciation, and energy level was severely reduced. Of the extensive and regular mood measurements that were taken between deprivation and control conditions, feelings of tiredness changed the most. The participants commonly reported that they no longer chose do anything that required energy.

These controlled experimental results are consistent with numerous observations of populations undergoing involuntary famine because of war or general environmental conditions. For instance, in Somalia before the United Nations intervened, the starving population became more and more lethargic, and they didn't have enough energy to plant crops or to tend farm animals. In this respect there is little question that food restrictions have a substantial effect on mood.

Although extreme nutritional conditions definitely show a relationship with mood, people who experience more normal nutritional variations may hardly notice the mood effects. Nevertheless, it is likely that our mood changes at least a little when we miss even one meal. We may feel a slight decline in energy and a small amount of tension.[11] This tense-tiredness is an unpleasant mood that can lead to all kinds of undesirable behaviors, as we shall see in later chapters.

Most people are convinced that there is a mood effect from food, and there are well-established beliefs regarding this.[12] Whenever I talk to lay groups, food and mood questions are among those most frequently asked. Any local library or bookstore has many books devoted to the topic. Because food is used as a mood regulator, it in turn can lead to overeating. Therefore, mood is directly relevant to dieting, and vice versa. Are these beliefs about food and mood all in the minds of the believers, as some scientists would have us assume? I think not, although the relationship is very complex.

There is so much talk about the relationship between food and mood that one would think there have been a huge number of scientific studies. But one of the most interesting things about the scientific literature concerning food and mood is how little there actually is. I'm not talking about the physiological effects of different foods but rather about the mood effects. Some research has been done on sugar and mood, but little research has been done on such questions as the immediate mood effects of eating fruit instead of candy, or different kinds of complex carbohydrates, or various relative mixtures of fats, proteins, and carbohydrates.

Why has there been so little scientific research on a topic of such great general interest? I think the reason is that normal people who are eating regularly experience only slight mood effects from food. In fact, these effects are so subtle that they are difficult to capture in traditional scientific studies. Thus a particular kind of research design is necessary to assess these reactions, one that is almost never used. In my view, food influences on mood must be studied over many occasions, and the results averaged. It may also be necessary to do this research in the natural environment in which the subjects are eating different foods on a regular basis.[13] Incidentally, anyone can do this kind of self-study using a technique that I describe later as systematic self-observation.

Another problem with the existing food research is that mood effects often are different immediately after eating a particular food than they are an hour later. This is an important point to bear in mind for those trying to understand their own reactions to food. Good research should focus on both the immediate effects of food ingestion and the effects after 30 minutes, 1 hour, 2 hours, and so on. The delayed time effects are important to understanding the way that people use food to regulate their moods. Unfortunately, scientists do not often use the kind of research design that might obtain these results, probably because studying food–mood associations in these ways allows only imperfect control over the study subjects' expectations concerning food effects (i.e., blind or double-blind experiments are difficult or impossible).[14]

Taking into account these limitations, in 1987 I published one of the first studies of the immediate mood effects of eating a sugar snack.[15] I studied mood changes in subjects over 2 hours after they ate a standard-sized candy bar. I made these comparisons on many occasions over 3 weeks and averaged the results. From these extended observations, I found that eating a candy bar produced a number of statistically significant results. The immediate reaction was an increase in energy—no surprise to anyone who eats a candy bar as a pick-me-up. This immediate increase in energy is consistent with what we know about metabolism, that when we consume food our metabolism and catecholamine activity, two physiological changes associated with bodily arousal, increase.[16] But even though the candy increased energy initially, after an hour, energy dropped below the levels present before the candy was eaten. The obvious implication of this effect is that someone who eats sugar for a boost may find that in an hour or two it will have the opposite effect. Although it is possible to observe this drop if we watch ourselves carefully after a sugar snack, most people remember only the initial boost.

Another significant result occurred after the sugar snack: an increase in tension one hour after the candy was eaten. These results were consistent with popular beliefs that sugar makes people tense and jittery, even though some scientists question this effect.[17] Unfortunately, a single study with results like these cannot be definitive, and so we must await further research for confirmation. Nonetheless, the tension effect that we found was a reliable one and quite interesting.

Why would tension levels increase an hour after eating candy? Fatigue may well be the primary effect some time after sugar is eaten.[18] Increased tension may result when the tired person must continue to tackle demanding daily activities. We conducted a study that suggested this.[19] Compared with control subjects who ate nothing, experimental subjects who ate a standard-sized candy bar reported greater tension within an hour when faced with a difficult computer task. But when the computer task was easy, the candy did not produce increased tension.

If sugar does have an effect on energy and tension, it could explain why people who eat lots of sugar find themselves in a cycle that leads to drops in energy and increased nervousness, which in turn motivates further sugar snacking. This is consistent with studies demonstrating that negative moods and emotional upsets can stimulate cravings for particular foods (see Chapter 11). This is a complicated issue. A moderate amount of tension may increase food craving, and yet high levels of tension can make a person avoid food and thus lose weight. For example, people who are going through a painful marital separation often suffer a large weight loss.

The complex energy and tension effects from sugar also could explain results from research by Larry Christensen and his colleagues at Texas A&M University. Their research showed that diets from which sugar has been eliminated lead to decreases in depression, and depression is part of the state I define as tense-tiredness.[20] The reduction in depression that Christensen found wasn't true for everyone, but it was particularly evident for some people.

Some of the best evidence of the relationship of food and mood comes from studies of people on diets and those with various eating disorders. A number of studies have shown that for these people, negative emotions trigger eating.[21] You may have noticed yourself wanting to eat when you were feeling depressed or upset. If food is the natural response to negative emotions, then it must have an effect on those emotions and moods. In my view, this is very persuasive evidence of a relationship between food and mood.

Although there is likely to be a connection between food and mood, the effects of food are complicated, as we can see from research with certain distressed groups.[22] Hypoglycemics, for example, have much stronger mood reactions to sugar than do people with normal sugar metabolisms. When their blood glucose is not adequate, hypoglycemics experience substantial drops in energy and increases in tension; that is, tense-tiredness is the clear effect of hypoglycemia.[23]

Similarly, food allergies or intolerances also seem to produce substantial mood changes.[24] Mood associations with food, particularly simple carbohydrates, also are apparent from scientific reports of food cravings among various other subgroups, including women suffering from premenstrual syndrome (PMS) and people experiencing seasonal affective disorder (a form of depression often attributed to a lack of sunlight).[25] In addition, those with eating disorders and even regular dieters may experience unique mood effects from food variations.[26] In sum, food and mood are undoubtedly connected, although the relationship is quite complex.

Health and Illness

The biological bases of mood are certainly clear from the research on daily cycles, exercise, and food, but nowhere is this biological association more evident than with health and illness. Healthy people feel more energetic than sick people do, and a good deal of indirect, but fairly convincing, evidence supports this observation. A wide variety of illnesses are associated with decreased energy, and higher energy levels generally are a mark of good health. In fact, the chief complaint that physicians and nurses hear is that the patients are fatigued and lack energy. This was apparent, for example, in one study of 500 medical patients seen in a general medical facility in the Boston area.[27] Thirty-seven percent said that they had been very tired, often for months before seeking treatment.

Other research supports the finding that many illnesses lead to decreased energy levels. A good study that shows this relationship was carried out by Jane Dixon and her associates at Yale University, who assessed the health status of more than 300 nurses.[28] The results showed that energy level had the highest correlation with general health status. Moreover, energy was the best predictor of both physical and psychological health over time.

Studies of physical conditioning and energy lead to the same conclusions. Maximal health is associated with increased energy. To use just one example, in a study of physical conditioning carried out on sedentary, mildly obese women, which used moderate exercise as a factor, energy increases were significantly associated with improvements in cardiovascular fitness.[29] The greater the increase in fitness is, the greater the energy will be. In this study, the women briskly walked for 45 minutes five times a week for 15 weeks. In addition to feeling more energetic, they also felt less tense.

Although this relationship between health and energy is so obvious that it is hardly debatable, energy may be related to health in another way—but in this case the evidence is not nearly as clear. It is quite possible that declines in energy may signal physical illness, sometimes far in advance. Changes in energy level appear to represent something like an early warning system of impending physical illness. Again, we can think of our energy-related moods as an index of our general condition, but in this case as predictors of physical illness in the future.

Although this conclusion must be regarded as a hypothesis that requires further testing, a number of intriguing studies support this idea. For example, the study described here that took place at a general medical facility showed that fatigue often occurred months ahead of a visit for treatment. Other support comes from a number of studies of particular kinds of illness, as well as studies of immune-system functioning.

In one piece of research on middle-aged people who suffered from migraine headaches, the researchers found that they could predict headaches by feelings of fatigue from 12 to 24 hours before the actual headache.[30] Another study of epileptic seizures showed that mood often enabled sufferers to predict their own condition on the day before the seizure.[31] And in a study using a double-blind procedure (in which neither the subject nor the experimenter knew the hypothesis being tested), mood—including feelings of depression—varied with exposure to allergic-producing substances.[32]

We can look at this presumed relationship in another way. Several studies have now shown an association between our moods and how well our immune system responds. Because an impaired immune system is a likely precursor to illness, we can consider this problem from a different angle. For example, one set of researchers studied the immune responses of 98 men who had recently experienced a death or serious illness in the family.[33] Those men scoring highest on a depression checklist showed significantly less lymphocyte responsiveness, an indication that their immune system was impaired.

In one of the most convincing studies of this relationship, research-ers at the State University of New York collected data from medical students over eight weeks using IgA, an index of immune-system func-tion taken from saliva.[34] Ratings of mood on each day of testing showed that the immune-system response was lower on days of strongly negative mood and higher on days of strong positive mood. Thus, it is likely that those in a negative mood were more vulnerable to illness and those in a positive mood were more resistant.

Even though this kind of evidence is not proof that mood predicts physical illness, the possibility definitely exists. We do know that en-ergy level is an index of well-being—at least in the limited sense of its immediate association with illness and health and how we perceive those states—and it may predict future illness as well.

Sleep and Wakefulness

Sleep must be considered in any assessment of energy level. Poor sleep leads to substantial declines in feelings of energy during waking hours. Earlier I stated that energy follows an internal biological rhythm, with peaks and troughs at predictable times and the greatest shift downward occuring at normal sleeping times. If sleep is dis-turbed or displaced during that period, changes in mood will inevi-tably follow. This phenomenon is familiar to any traveler who has crossed several time zones and experiences tiredness and a lack of energy, often for days afterward.

Although the relationship of sleep to internal circadian rhythms is not usually questioned, the effects of moderate sleep loss on daily energy levels are often challenged or disregarded. For example, some scientists and many laypeople dispute the idea that mood is directly related to sleep, although this position has always seemed indefensi-ble to me.[35] Most people do not get enough sleep, and their energy level certainly is affected by this lifestyle choice. These views are sup-ported by many sleep scientists, as evident from a national study.

The National Commission on Sleep Disorders Research compiled an exhaustive review and concluded, "One thing is absolutely certain in America: The quality and quantity of sleep obtained are substan-tially less than the quality and quantity needed. . . . A convincing body of scientific evidence and witness testimony indicates that many Amer-icans are severely sleep deprived and, therefore, dangerously sleepy during the day."[36] In fact, the commission found that a range of sleep disorders affect as many as one-third of all American adults, and in relation to these direct effects, it also pointed out that sleep disorders are associated with many mental and substance-abuse disorders.

Certainly, everyone would agree that severe sleep deprivation results in persistent tiredness. But just how much sleep is necessary for energy levels to remain normal during regular waking hours? According to the Sleep Disorder Commission, "Evidence, to date, suggests that the vast majority of adults need a nightly average of at least seven hours of sleep to avoid the consequences of sleep deprivation; many individuals require more than eight hours of nightly sleep."[37]

Based on informal studies done by my students, I certainly would agree with these conclusions. In a class that I sometimes teach, students keep a stress journal over a number of weeks, recording their daily mood levels as well as the influence of variables such as the previous night's sleep. These journals show not only that sleep loss affects mood (and thus energy and tension) but also that a variety of other negative effects subsequently emerge that are associated with higher stress levels.

Although this evidence is fairly clear, many people—perhaps most—seem unaware of their sleep deficit. Rather, they regard sleep as expendable, as an activity that can be shortened with few consequences. However, it has been shown that negative mood states are inevitable consequences of sleep deficits.

The relationship between mood and sleep is not clear-cut. In Chapter 6 we look at what happens to mood when a person becomes exhausted. Here, a different kind of mood effect is created. In addition, a number of studies have now demonstrated that one night of sleep deprivation or several nights of substantial but not complete deprivation can lead to a temporary remission of depression.[38] As with other factors affecting mood, individual differences must be taken into account, in this case, whether the person is depressed.

Mood, and especially energy level, is affected by the major biological influences associated with exercise, food, health, and sleep. Although these factors are often forgotten in analyses of mood, they nonetheless are important. In the next chapter we look at another major influence on mood, thoughts. In this case we will see that tension, rather than energy, is the primary mood effect.

4

The Relationship Between Mood and Thoughts

Viewing cognitive or thinking processes as all-powerful controllers of behavior has lately been popular and scientifically fashionable.[1] Many people believe in the power of positive thinking, and in many respects this is an important element of applied cognitive psychology.[2]

Thoughts are likely to influence mood in a complex way. They affect energy levels only to a limited degree, although they probably have a substantial effect on tension. Thoughts have less influence over energy level, for example, than do the other biological factors we discussed in Chapters 2 and 3, namely, time of day, diet, health, and sleep, which account for the most frequent and dramatic energy changes we perceive. But stress also affects mood, and the main mood effect of stress is increased tension. Tension can be magnified or diminished by our thoughts, and moderate but persistent stress can deplete our resources and alter our mood. In these cases, we feel our energy level decline, probably as a secondary effect of tension. High levels of tension are associated with reduced energy (tense-tiredness). This inverse relationship between energy and tension is an important element of the larger theory of how normal moods operate, and I discuss it more extensively in Chapter 6.

Having said this, let me complicate the picture by stating that energy changes do occur following thought-related things such as a pleasant surprise, a compliment, an interesting conversation, or even a visit to a museum. Clothing and other personal characteristics also can affect mood, probably through energy changes. Clothing effects are likely to occur through enhanced self-esteem, which is positively correlated with energy.[3] When we notice how nice we look, receive compliments from others, and think that we fit the cultural ideal of beauty, our self-esteem rises. Of course, our assumptions may not be correct, but that isn't as important as what we perceive as correct.

Although thoughts have a moderate effect on energy, they have a much greater effect on tension. And because many complex moods are combinations of energy and tension, in this respect thoughts do influence moods substantially. Our thoughts can affect tension because in a tense state we perceive danger, threat, or stress, and in most cases, our reactions to stressful circumstances are based on our interpretations, judgments, or appraisals of current conditions. These so-called cognitive responses occur in the face of danger, and in turn activate the stress response.[4]

Modern scientific analyses of stress are well understood.[5] Research has delineated the way that humans—and other animals too—deal with subtle and more serious threats. The process involves complex interactions of past experiences with the threat, decisions about how threatening the circumstances are, anticipations of further threat, and planning on several levels what should be done. A host of cognitive actions take place between threatening circumstances and the tense reactions that they produce; tension is clearly dependent on thoughts.

Although tension is most often based on a conscious appraisal of some sort of danger, there probably are times when this occurs with little or no conscious awareness of the danger. For example, internally generated pain or allergic reactions appear to produce a state of tension.[6] So if you wake up with a toothache, the muscles in your shoulders and neck may already be tight, producing the characteristic feelings of tension. This tension has little to do with conscious cognitive interpretation, however.[7] Tension is a primitive elemental biological reaction to real or imagined danger. Even though cognitive interpretation is often at the base of this reaction, the body appears to have an internal sensing system to alert us by means of a general tension response when there is danger, either consciously or nonconsciously judged.[8]

Mood and Thought Congruence

As we have seen, the body operates in general, integrated patterns; that is, what happens to one bodily system affects the others. This principle also applies to moods and thoughts, and so when you are in a negative mood, your thoughts tend to be negative as well. Similarly, positive, optimistic thoughts accompany positive moods. In other words, moods and thoughts are congruent.[9]

This relationship can be quite maddening to someone who is depressed. With milder depression, the negative thoughts may not be that insistent. But when we are mentally idling, so to speak, we invariably find ourselves thinking about negative aspects of our lives. This is why some people seem overly pessimistic, which could be an indication of mild depression.

With deeper depressions, negative thoughts intrude into consciousness both insistently and constantly. Positive thoughts are scarce unless they are consciously forced, and as soon as depressed people stop forcing themselves to think positively, their negative thoughts reappear. From the principle of mood congruence, we can see why depressed people continuously think about how inadequate they are, how bad their life is, and how unpromising their future is likely to be.[10]

As negative as this mood congruence can be for a depressed person, the same principle can result in a positive outcome. Cognitive therapies employ this idea, that if positive thoughts can be generated and retained, the depression will be reduced.[11] As I show in Chapter 9, when someone is in a bad mood, a good way to change it is to control one's negative thoughts and to think positively. Unfortunately, this is not easy, and it often fails.

State Dependency

Another phenomenon, called *state dependency*, is similar to and possibly the same as the more scientifically accepted mood congruence. State dependency means that certain thoughts are linked to the states in which they first occurred. We observe state dependency most often with learning: If we learn something in a particular mood state, we will remember it better at times when we are in that mood and remember it less well when we are in a different mood. Using an old computer analogy, it is as though specific memory banks are tied to particular moods. One memory bank is attached when we are depressed, and we remember all the bad things about ourselves that we ever discovered in previous depressions. But another bank controls our memories when we are elated.[12]

State-dependent memory has been demonstrated with various psychoactive drugs and with both animals and humans.[13] The theory is that if people learn something in a particular drug state, such as one produced by alcohol, marijuana, or even nicotine, they will remember it better in that same state than in another. An amusing example of this was portrayed in an early Charlie Chaplin movie, *City Lights*. The hapless Chaplin helps a rich man and they become buddies while both are drunk. But the next morning, the rich man doesn't remember Chaplin. Once again drunk, however, the millionaire greets his friend warmly, and after a night of drinking the two collapse in the rich man's mansion to sleep it off. But the next morning the sober millionaire treats Chaplin as an intruder and orders his butler to throw him out.

Those of my students who are familiar with this scientific literature sometimes try to match their coffee drinking, smoking, or other caffeine states when they are studying and when they are taking their exams. (An interesting aside is that arousal levels such as those associated with different times of day may follow the same state-dependency principles.[14] While the evidence is meager about this, things studied at one time of day might be remembered better on another day at the same time.)

It should be apparent why the evidence of state dependency involving drugs would lead us to think about moods, as drug and mood states often seem quite similar. Though not all scientists agree, I believe that moods do produce a kind of state dependency that influences how information is stored in memory, particularly when the moods are pronounced. For example, in one National Institute of Mental Health study of cycling manic depressives, associations produced in either the manic or the normal phases were better recalled in the same phase than in the other.[15] This research is unusual, however. Because of ethical constraints, usually only weak moods are studied in scientific laboratories, and the studies offer only mixed evidence.[16]

If state dependency involving moods is a valid phenomenon, it is important what experiences a person has in a particular mood because it is these that he or she will remember. Because such experiences could be extensive and negative in longer-term depressions, this might be one reason that depressions tend to be recurrent. Whether or not this is true, however, a connection between state-dependent learning and moods would yield fascinating information about how the brain is organized and functions.

How We Assess Our Energy Reserves and Self-Regulate

Thoughts and moods interact in another, more basic way. Thousands of times a day you are confronted with tasks that require resources to accomplish, and in each case you must make a momentary evaluation of the task's requirements in relation to your resources. This rapid evaluation involves an instantaneous cognitive assessment of your current mood. Although the assessment is made so quickly that you are rarely aware of it, you nevertheless obtain information about the principal questions: Do I have the energy to accomplish this task? and Am I too tired for that?

Consider a simple matter like putting away your clothes that are strewn on a chair. Let us assume that it is late in the evening and you have worked hard that day. As little energy as dealing with the clothes requires, it still takes some. Looking at the clothes, you rapidly assess your level of tiredness in relation to going to the closet, getting out the hangers, folding or arranging the clothes, and deciding what needs to be put away and what must be put aside for washing or cleaning. For each task, or for the whole task, questions arise about your energy to do it. These aren't well-formed questions about resources and step-by-step task requirements, but in some form these kinds of questions and your answers to them will be part of your decision concerning the action.

Suppose that you decide not to put away the clothes. Even though it would take only a few minutes, it just seems too hard. What has happened here is that you made an instantaneous assessment of your energy resources in relation to the requirements of the task at hand. Although you decide not to do it and may feel guilty, the procrastination makes sense if viewed in this way.

The self-assessment is even more complex, however, than I have indicated in this example. Perhaps you have enough energy only to push your clothes aside so you have a place to sit. Or you can put away the item that will be most wrinkled, but nothing else. These decisions, which seem to come from nowhere, actually represent self-assessments of energy level and a comparison with the requirements of the task. You need not feel guilty. The seemingly slothful decision not to put away your clothes is based on an understandable assessment of your reserves and requirements. Maybe you can work up some guilt about not expending the necessary energy to complete the task, but an understanding of your energy reserves and requirements at least makes this a logical process. Such an understanding offers all kinds of possibilities about how to change your behavior in the future.

All the time as we move through the day and face various challenges, we are reacting to these changing energy levels and regulating our activities accordingly. This self-regulation is central to understanding moods and how they influence our behavior. It is an extremely subtle process, one that easily can be missed without knowing how to think about it and what to look for. Let us take another example and add a different kind of self-regulation. You are at work, and at about 4:00 P.M. your boss asks for a report that needs to be done by the end of the day. You're tired, and you have only an hour. Of course, you could work late, but you feel that your energy is completely spent. Think about this for a minute given what you now know. You could take a short brisk walk outside the office to clear your head and raise your energy level. You could get a candy bar and soda from the machine in the canteen. Or you could tell your boss that his request is unreasonable and that you need more time. (The last solution requires lots of energy reserves.)

The candy bar and Coke alternative is very attractive. It is easy, and it will immediately raise your energy reserves. And it will taste good.

But it contains all kinds of negatives, not the least of which is probable tense-tiredness before the job is finished and guilt about a broken diet. Clearly you should take a brisk walk, but it's hard to get moving. In cases like this, you must engage your thoughts in what I call *cognitive override*, in which your cognitive processes override what your body is telling you to do.

In the case of the short brisk walk, your tiredness will disappear within a minute or two after you start. But anyone who has tried to do this will realize how hard it is to override fatigue. The difficulty of beginning to exercise when your energy is low indicates how influential these kinds of cognitive "microassessments" can be. Yet it isn't impossible, particularly if you are aware of how your energy levels are affected by your activity level. The knowledge that the Coke and candy seem attractive but that the walk is better will enable you to engage in cognitive override.

It is clear that thoughts and moods form an interactive process. Based on this conclusion, you regularly engage in behaviors that directly affect your energy and tension levels, like deciding whether to work beyond your regular bedtime at the cost of adequate sleep, to exercise, to eat a candy bar, to drink some coffee, or to smoke a cigarette. In such examples, you must make decisions that will immediately influence your energy and tension states. But you seldom make these decisions without first gauging your energy and tension, and in most cases, this information about your current mood will directly determine what action you will take.

If you sense you have little energy and a moderate level of tension, for example, you may decide to eat a sugar snack, have a cup of coffee, or drink a beer. These activities, in turn, influence mood, which may then motivate you to continue the activity, increase it, or decrease it. If this interactive process is efficient and you are a good self-observer, your behavior can proceed with few problems. But often this is not the case.

Instead of having a small snack or just one alcoholic beverage, people often gorge or imbibe until they are drunk. Part of the problem is that many people are poor self-observers, which can be especially tricky if the behavior or substance has a delayed mood effect. For instance, alcohol may increase your energy quickly and reduce your tension with little or no impairment of your activities. But to continue that feeling, you may keep drinking, not realizing the delayed effects of the alcohol. The real impairment doesn't come until well after you have downed that second beer. As you begin to feel your good mood slip away, you are beyond regaining your energy. Similarly, people often choose sugar because of its immediately positive effect, and the unpracticed self-observer is unaware that just a short while later, a negative effect will set in. The secret to avoiding these traps is to become a good self-observer and to try to keep track of what you are eating throughout the day. With this information, cognitive override makes sense, and it works. (We will discuss this practice of systematically observing mood and behavior in the last part of the book.)

Requirements and Resources

Considering how you assess your energy levels throughout the day and keeping in mind that your assessments of danger will lead to tension, it should become apparent that thoughts and moods interact in another way. The momentary self-assessments of energy levels lead to more or less tension, depending on the extent of your requirements in a particular situation. When your requirements exceed your resources, you experience tension, nervousness, or anxiety. The requirements of a situation are associated with your perception of how you will be affected by the outcome of the situation and what you must do to meet the challenges. Resources are judged by your self-assessments of energy. Both the assessments of energy and the perceived requirements of the situation are cognitive processes.

Thus, for any given situation or task, you must decide what is required and whether you will be able to accomplish the task. If there is an imbalance, tension will rise, and depending on the degree of imbalance, the resultant mood may be tense-energy, in which you feel good about your reserves but uncertain of the outcome. Or your mood may be tense-tiredness in which your reserves are low and your judgment is that the outcome will be poor.

Looking at tension in this way, we can see how we may interpret a situation as dangerous if we don't have the reserves to stand up to the challenge. In other words, any situation may become dangerous when requirements exceed resources, and because resources are continually changing, danger is relative. For example, if you find yourself walking on a dark street, you may not feel in danger or tense if you view yourself as fit and fully capable of dealing with any situation. On the other hand, if your resources are low (perhaps you are tired or ill) or if the potential requirements are great (the neighborhood is associated with violent crime), then tension, fearfulness, or anxiety are likely to result.

Perhaps a less obvious point is that a potential imbalance between requirements and resources causes tension to vary at different times of day as energy rises and falls during its normal daily rhythms. If tension occurs because requirements exceed resources, then the same task or activity can lead to tension at one time of day but no tension at another. For example, driving a car in traffic may be associated with calm-energy in the middle of the morning, but the same activity may lead to tense-energy or tense-tiredness in the late afternoon. The only difference is in the person's changing resources or energy level.

Another example concerns personal interactions. Tension may not be present in a relationship with another when each person is rested, healthy, and feeling energetic. But a great deal of tension may be present if resources are low. That is, you may get along fine with your mate at most times of day but have tension-induced arguments late in the evening. The next time you find yourself in the midst of a battle with your spouse, ask yourself how tired you are and how tired your spouse probably is.

The Influence of Subtle but Persistent Moods

Moods and thoughts interact in another important way, and again, the self-regulation of subtle changes in mood is crucial. We continuously assess how we feel, but small changes may not register as dramatic enough to take notice of them. For example, you might overlook mild tension for some time and overcome it by extra effort. But in time you will eventually succumb, probably when you are particularly fatigued or during a low-energy time of day.

What this means is that subtle negative mood states can have a substantial effect on behavior if they persist. A good example of this often occurs with people on diets. They may have subtle but persistent urges to eat, their hunger probably associated with lower energy and slightly higher tension levels (tense-tiredness). The dieters may be able to withstand the food urges for quite some time. But if the urge is sufficiently persistent, eventually their resolve will weaken.

According to the principles of mood variation we have discussed, you can see exactly how that happens. The dieters may give in to their urge in the late afternoon or evening when their energy is low, or the combination of lowered energy and subsequently increased tension may break down their resolve.

The influence of thoughts in this case can be seen in the eventual breaking of the diet and then in the awareness that they weren't able to maintain their resolve. This leads to feelings of low self-esteem, including a decreased ability to withstand temptation. These thoughts about self can create even more tension, which in turn causes one to give up and to eat without restraint. Once the diet is broken, it may be a while before a new diet is begun. Exactly the same process can occur in the case of an abandoned exercise program. A temporary lapse in an exercise schedule can cause one to see oneself as incapable, which in turn leads one to give up.

Premenstrual syndrome, or PMS, offers another interesting example of how thoughts affect mood (see Chapter 5). Although a woman may experience mild tension each month because of bodily discomfort, she ignores the increased tension much of the time. But as her energy rises and falls during the day, she may feel more vulnerable to tension and become increasingly aware of it. At such times, thoughts may race through her head: "Here it is again. Month after month, this is always with me. I can never escape it." And at this point she may lash out or exhibit uncustomary anger or irritability.

In all the examples, subtle but persistent moods cause responses that are more extreme than are warranted by the initial mood. With the broken diet, it is the thought of being incapable of avoiding food that leads one to give up altogether. The same thing is true with the abandoned exercise schedule. But if you recognize that this is only a momentary lapse and that it probably occurred because of low energy levels, you can regard the lapse as simply that—a temporary depression in your energy reserves.

5

Energy and Tension Changes with PMS, Drugs, Social Interaction, Weather, and Life Events

Premenstrual Syndrome (PMS)

Premenstrual syndrome (PMS) is a controversial concept, but one that many women feel very strongly about and are very interested in. (It is also known as *premenstrual dysphoric disorder*, and *late luteal phase dysphoric disorder*.) Dozens of studies of this condition have been published in the scientific literature, the majority of which support the existence of increased tension as well as other physical symptoms appearing late in the menstrual cycle, generally just before the menstrual flow begins.[1]

One reason that PMS is controversial is that it is usually identified on the basis of retrospective reports. But studies in which self-ratings are gathered each day—particularly those studies in which participants are unaware of the purpose of the research—often show *no* increased feelings of premenstrual tension.[2] Therefore, some investigators have inferred that PMS may be a monthly excuse for stress reactions that women always have. This is akin to concluding, "It's all in their head."[3] Another reason that PMS is controversial is that many people are justifiably concerned that evidence of periodic tension states in females may be used to discriminate against them in the workplace and elsewhere. This aspect of the controversy was recently highlighted when the American Psychiatric Association voted to include late luteal dysphoric disorder in the latest (fourth) edition of its *Diagnostic and Statistical Manual of Mental Disorders*, the *DSM IV*.[4] Since this disorder as classified is often associated with depression and other debilitating symptoms, this decision appears to place women in a unique category with regard to mental disorders.

Do women in fact experience increased tension in the late luteal phase of their menstrual cycle, or is this an imaginary mood change? The question cannot be answered definitively on the basis of the current scientific evidence, which is contradictory. But my view is that PMS is not an imaginary condition, although the evidence also suggests that for most women it does not lead to work decrement or other kinds of debilitation.[5]

Various kinds of evidence support this conclusion. Most important, there is sufficient evidence, even from day-by-day studies, that many women regularly experience various unpleasant physical symptoms (cramps, swollen breasts, water retention, headaches) during this phase of their cycle. Furthermore, increased tension would be an inevitable consequence of such unpleasant physical symptoms. As we have already seen, tension is an elemental biological reaction to danger, in which the system is activated by a variety of internal conditions, even without a conscious assessment of what is happening. If physical discomfort occurs, increased tension will be the result.

But if increased tension is likely, why do many prospective studies show no evidence of mood change? Among the possible reasons for this, the most important is that the existent changes in tension are likely to be subtle, not dramatic, at least for most women. Thus, measures over one or two menstrual cycles could easily miss the subtle changes. These mood changes must therefore be assessed on multiple occasions, probably five or six cycles at least, in order to obtain reliable measurements, but such studies of multiple cycles are rare.

On the other hand, retrospective reports, though often not trusted by investigators, do have the advantage of taking into account many occasions in their conclusions. That is, a woman reporting past PMS experiences may be remembering enough occasions to increase the reliable assessment of her mood states that otherwise would be too subtle to identify in day-by-day studies.[6] Identifying increased tension also may be difficult because the tension is present for only some women or during only some cycles. This, in turn, introduces more error into the measurement process when considering women as a group.

Perhaps a personal anecdote can shed some light on the puzzle of PMS. I frequently teach a course called the Psychology of Mood to university seniors and graduate students. Each semester, the students decide on mood topics that they will investigate further, and premenstrual tension is a popular choice. Female students frequently choose PMS. They read the scientific literature and report to the class on the best studies, including studies that do and do not support the existence of PMS. These advanced psychology students have quite a sophisticated understanding of this research, and they present their findings in an evenhanded manner to the class. At the end of the semester, I have made it a point to survey the female members of the class about whether they believe that a large portion of the female population experiences premenstrual tension or whether it is "all in their head." Semester after semester, virtually every female student states that premenstrual tension is a real and valid phenomenon. Even though they are well aware of the research findings that do not support its existence, they remain convinced of it—probably because of their own experiences.

Drugs

A variety of drugs are frequently used to affect energy and tension states and thus to control moods, consciously or not. Essentially, many people use these drugs for self-regulation. The most common drugs used for this purpose are caffeine, nicotine, and alcohol. Various prescription drugs, including tranquilizers and barbiturates, also are commonly used to alter levels of energy and tension. Less common, but still widely used for these purposes, are such substances as cocaine and amphetamine. Furthermore, according to some definitions, sugar might be said to be the *most* commonly used "drug" of all.[7] The primary effect of all of them is often seen as either increasing energy or reducing tension. Although both feelings together usually are not considered, it is highly likely that these substances influence both mood dimensions simultaneously because the two moods interact (see Chapter 6).

The use of drugs to regulate mood is discussed more fully in the last half of this book. Here we will look at some characteristic effects of these various drugs in relation to the mood states that we have been considering. Although many users may be unaware that they are self-regulating, increased energy probably is the desired effect of such drugs as caffeine, nicotine, cocaine, and amphetamines, and pharmacological and behavioral studies show that these drugs do produce increased energy, alertness, and vigor.[8] Moreover, these very positive feelings are a powerful motivator for continued and addictive use.

Less understood are the energy effects of alcohol and tranquilizers. The mood dynamics associated with these two substances, and others employed for self-regulation, is often confusing because users report feeling both activated and deactivated (e.g., energized and relaxed). This has led to discussions in the scientific literature of the apparent paradoxical effects of some of these drugs.[9] But the effects aren't paradoxical at all if we think of the two basic mood dimensions as often acting reciprocally; that increased energy reduces tension, or reduced tension increases energy.

To see the dynamics of these apparent paradoxes, consider nicotine, a drug that increases central nervous system arousal.[10] Even though smoking one cigarette may raise the heart rate as much as 40 beats per minute, nicotine is often used as a relaxant.[11] Thus, smoking appears to both activate and deactivate a person simultaneously. The paradox is resolved, however, if we assume that the activating effect primarily concerns energetic arousal. Moreover, if the relaxant effect involves skeletal–muscular relaxation—a response for which there is some evidence—then reduced tension also may be a result.[12] Thus calm-energy is temporarily generated by nicotine. Because a person is both activated and relaxed at the same time in this state, it is no wonder that cigarettes represent such an insidiously addicting drug.

Smoking is very rewarding because it produces an optimal mood state, even if the mood lasts for only a few minutes with each cigarette.

Another example of this paradoxical effect involves alcohol. Even though this drug is commonly classified as a depressant, in the early stages of intoxication, increased energy is the unmistakable effect. To recognnize this enhanced energy, we need only observe the initial hours of a party in which alcohol is being consumed. Laughing, gaiety, and a generally heightened mood are common reactions.[13] This apparently paradoxical effect is understandable if we see the alcohol as reducing tension and thus causing energy to rise for a short time. But as will become clear in the next two chapters, tension often acts as an inhibitory or cautionary state, and its reduction can result in increased energy. Caffeine is a drug with a slightly different kind of paradoxical mood effect. Coffee and other caffeine-containing substances are regularly consumed to enhance energy and alertness, not to increase tension. But for many people, ingesting caffeine regularly increases anxiety, tension and nervousness, and they are quite aware of the effect.[14] This suggests that tense-energy is sought even though it has unpleasant aspects. It would seem that calm-energy is preferred but that tense-energy is acceptable because it is at least moderately pleasurable. This is understandable because when faced with required activity, tense-energy certainly is preferable to the fatigue that often motivates coffee consumption. (Some people appear to achieve calm-energy with smaller amounts of coffee. Which mood effect they experience probably is based on the amount of coffee consumed and individual differences in tolerance.[15])

Tranquilizers such as the benzodiazepines (e.g., Valium) often elevate mood, even though these drugs are also classified as depressants.[16] Again, this apparently paradoxical effect is understandable if one sees the drug as reducing tension. Like these examples, with the reduction of tension, energy often increases, and the overall effect can be quite positive.

In all these cases, the apparent paradox can be explained by recognizing that the mood effects from these drugs pertain to two dimensions, energy and tension. To grasp how these effects work, remember that energy and tension have a complex relationship with each other and that they sometimes act together (tense-energy) and sometimes reciprocally (calm-energy or tense-tiredness). The conditions under which these complex moods occur follow certain principles, which will be examined in more detail in the next chapter.

Social Interactions

Social interactions influence mood states. We are social animals, and a process as elemental as mood is likely to reflect this fact. Moreover, there is empirical evidence that social interaction influences our moods, including energy- and tension-related moods. The amount of unambiguous evidence about this isn't great, but it is convincing.

In a study that my colleagues and I conducted, we asked a representative sample of respondents what they do to change a bad mood.[17] We also asked them about how they typically attempt to reduce tension and to raise energy. In each of these cases, the respondents reported that a favorite technique was social interaction. When people are in a bad mood and they want to change it, they often call or talk to someone, or they just try to be with other people.

That social interaction can improve mood is evident from several studies conducted by psychologists David Watson, Lee Anna Clark, and their colleagues. For example, in one study lasting 13 weeks, 85 undergraduates from the University of Texas completed weekly self-assessments of positive and negative affect (measures closely related to self-ratings of energy and tension).[18] They indicated levels of affect for the past week. At the same time, they rated their social activity during the week, including a broad range of interpersonal behaviors. Based on these correlations, it was clear that social activity was a good predictor of positive affect; in fact, it was a better predictor of positive affect than it was of negative affect. This finding was the same as obtained in previous research by these psychologists.

Besides these studies, the scientific literature confirms a significant association between social support and psychological well-being. For example, depression appears to be helped by social support, including interactions with spouses, friends, and organized social groups. This kind of relationship is well documented, and numerous studies confirm it.[19]

Research on the relationship between behavior and genetics calls into question, however, one common assumption that scientists have made concerning the way that this relationship between social support and well-being may work.[20] I comment on it here because this research with identical and fraternal twins is one more indication of a revolution in thinking that is overtaking many reluctant behavioral scientists and it has important implications for understanding mood.

The common assumption has been that social networks facilitate well-being because they enable people to appraise and cope with stress better. That is, on a day-to-day basis our problems are made less debilitating by friendly networks of people who help us see things more realistically and who provide various kinds of support that help us cope.

The most recent research with twins suggests, however, that there are strong genetic influences on this relationship and that these genetic factors may be more important than the direct social interaction. In part, social support and psychological well-being may be related because those belonging to greater social support networks have been genetically predetermined to be this way and these same genetic factors influence well-being. Thus, studies that show a relationship between social interaction and well-being may be missing the real cause of the observed association.

These research results showing strong genetic influences are consistent with current views on personality. From an expanding body of scientific evidence, it is now clear that major variations in personality are not only genetically determined but these genetic influences may also be more important than learning and experience.[21] Findings of this sort are causing a good deal of disquiet among those who were convinced that learning and experience control all aspects of behavior.

This change in viewpoint is important with regard to mood, as the limits and shape of mood variations are undoubtedly influenced by genetic factors, including such matters as how much sleep different people need, how tiredness affects different people, the shape of their circadian energy rhythms (e.g., morning versus evening types), or how strongly various people react to danger. The exact manner in which genes affect people in these ways is still poorly understood, but biopsychological scientists working on mood are confident that we will soon know. When better understanding does come, it is likely that we will see that genetic influences work through many biological mechanisms, some subtle and some not so subtle.

Weather

Biological rhythms are common in the body. Earlier I mentioned that 24-hour circadian rhythms of energy influence many complex moods. In addition, bodily rhythms of less than 24 hours in duration (called *ultradian* rhythms) may be related to mood. Ultradian rhythms, particularly those 90 minutes in duration, have been observed to affect sleepiness, vigilance, EEG readings, daydreaming, and even hypnotizability.[22] Longer cycles also exist. *Infradian rhythms* (those lasting longer than 24 hours) are associated with the female menstrual cycle, and there are other cycles we may be less aware of, for example, those related to the seasons of the year. All this research on cycles indicates that many body processes follow subtle rhythms and that many of these rhythms affect mood.

Seasonal cycles of depression represent a new, potentially valuable area of scientific study. So-called seasonal affective disorder (SAD) has been the subject of much research and theory, with winter depression being the most common seasonal variation observed.[23] Much interest in this phenomenon has been generated, partly because of its obvious relevance to unpleasant weather conditions, particularly the absence of sunlight. But interest may also result from the fact that a form of treatment was discovered that involves daily exposure to bright light. In typical phototherapy sessions, the patient sits in front of a bank of bright lights of about 2,500 lux (approximately equivalent to an open window in sunlight) for 2 or more hours, occasionally glancing at the light. This presumably corrects the light deficit experienced by those persons who are thought to be affected in the brain and other parts of the body by a kind of "light starvation."

SAD is a moderately debilitating form of depression characterized by such symptoms as inactivity, negative affect, weight gain, carbohydrate craving, increased sleep time, decreased libido, and daytime sleepiness. Many researchers believe that it affects 5 percent or more of the population, and females to a much greater degree than males. The onset in a large percentage of these "seasonal pattern" depressions is sometime in the fall or winter, and the depression does not let up until the spring or summer.[24] Apparently, winter depression is not the only seasonal variation, because a similar but less common summer pattern also has been observed.[25] Other patterns may exist as well. Incidentally, the summer depression presents a problem concerning the light starvation hypothesis about seasonal depressions.

Researchers have suggested various theories for winter depression. One is that the distribution of melatonin is abnormal when sunlight is scarce. Melatonin is a hormone secreted by the pineal gland, a small structure in the brain, and it is secreted primarily during darkness. The exact function of melatonin is unknown, but it appears to be important to regulating the sleep–wakefulness cycle, perhaps by influencing sleepiness.[26] A related theory suggests that without sufficient sunlight circadian rhythms are disrupted.[27] Still other theories suggest abnormalities associated with such neurotransmitters as serotonin, dopamine, and norepinephrine.[28]

The melatonin theory is logical in part because of the apparently positive effects of bright light, which is thought to affect the hormone's secretion. The circadian rhythm theory is attractive because some benefits seem to occur when the light is administered for an hour or more in the morning, a procedure that is thought to reset the circadian rhythm. The evidence for these theories is mixed, however. We cannot be sure if there aren't more important causal variables associated with seasonal variations, as well as with the phototherapy. For example, one possibility could be changes in motor activity and its associated dopamine levels in the brain.[29] Or perhaps the effects arise from mere increased stimulation. Another possibility is that the positive benefits may just be the placebo effect, that doing something that is supposed to help does reduce the depression.

Still another problem associated with the basic validity of SAD is that the phenomenon could be thought to exist primarily because of the research procedure that is usually employed in identifying patients. For example, research subjects usually are recruited from media accounts of the disorder, and as one critic suggests, SAD could be nothing more than a statistical artifact having to do with how the subjects were selected.[30] In other words, recurrent depressions could be linked to any season if patients were selectively screened.

Is SAD a real disorder, and if it is, does bright light really cure it? These are questions to which the answers still are not known. Indirect epidemiological evidence from people living in northern latitudes and from observations that depressions are more common in winter months suggests that winter depression is real.[31] Moreover, phototherapy has proved effective in a number of studies. Nevertheless, there are enough unanswered questions about these phenomena for scientists to remain unsure.

In addition to the absence of sunlight, it certainly makes sense that extreme weather conditions could affect mood for a variety of other reasons. As I write this, the newspaper headlines describe frigid arctic temperatures gripping the Midwest, and rains and flooding in Europe. It seems likely that these extremes in geophysical conditions would affect mood. But exactly why would these effects occur? There are a variety of possible reasons, many of which concern only indirect geophysical effects on bodily processes. For example, just the discomfort of inclement conditions and the required adjustments in lifestyle may be sufficient to affect mood. Probably, this would occur primarily through increased tension, but also through the increased requirements of energy, as more effort must be expended to battle arctic blasts and snow. There also could be a conditioning effect that produces negative moods because of past unpleasant experiences with bad weather.[32]

One interesting weather effect that has been the subject of several scientific studies of mood concerns positive and negative ions in the atmosphere. Positive ionic concentrations are associated with smog and often occur with such weather conditions as the warm dry winds of the Santa Anas of Southern California, the chinook of Canada, and the foehn of Switzerland and central Europe. Negative ionic concentrations often are found after rainstorms or around bodies of circulating water (e.g., waterfalls and seashores). They may even be associated with running shower water.[33]

Several studies have been conducted in controlled settings. The ionic concentrations were manipulated, and mood was measured after exposure for a time. These experiments seemed to show that negative ions produce good moods and that positive concentrations produce bad moods.[34] These studies are convincing because it seems possible to change ionic concentration in the atmosphere of a laboratory without the experimental subjects' being aware of what the experimenter is doing. Thus, blind or double-blind experiments can be performed without concern that the results are due to the subjects' expectations.

Why would ionic concentration affect mood? One possibility may have something to do with clean and dirty air. Room purifiers often work by directing a stream of negative ions into the room. Particles of dirt attach to the ions and fall to the floor. Thus, it is conceivable that positive moods are associated with breathing clean air and that dirty air produces negative moods. This kind of elemental biological response makes sense from the biopsychological perspective I have been pursuing.

Still another interesting geophysical effect concerns cycles of the moon. Many people believe that a full moon has a strong effect on mood. For example, during a full moon we always hear about strange behaviors, suicides, disturbances in mental institutions, and violent crimes. Is this just folklore, or is there something to it?

There is a great deal of controversy about these effects, with logical arguments on both sides and a substantial number of published and unpublished studies.[35] Two researchers did a statistical analysis of the combined research findings from 37 of these studies.[36] They concluded that some of the effects were statistically significant, but that generally the effects of lunar phase were small, if they existed at all. They also decided that many of the claims for lunar effects could be attributed to inappropriate analyses and to various statistical artifacts. One specific conclusion emerging from the combined studies was that no more than 1 percent of so-called lunacy behaviors could be predicted by phases of the moon.

Life Events Versus Natural Processes as Causes of Mood

I have left until last a discussion of the causes of daily moods that many people believe are the most important. It is a common assumption that our everyday moods are derived from the pleasant or unpleasant things that happen to us. For example, some years ago the psychologist Peter Lewinsohn and his associates developed a reinforcement theory of emotions and moods that more or less spelled out this idea, and they presented various kinds of supporting evidence.[37] This reinforcement theory was consistent with the behaviorist theory of the 1960s and 1970s and its later cognitive transformations that gradually came to dominate psychology.

Essentially, Lewinsohn theorized that depressed people do not receive enough rewards and have too many punishments in their lives. This theory is consistent with many of the things I have been talking about, particularly when it attributes depression to the absence of pleasant social interactions, surroundings, and experiences of popularity or when it focuses on low reinforcement and punishments associated with poor social interactions and problems on the job. Lewinsohn seems to be saying that outside events control our depression. However, his theory also includes such influences as sleep, food, and sex under the general concepts of reinforcements and punishments.[38] Although such things certainly may be rewarding or punishing, it is not clear whether they represent outside events that affect us or naturally occurring processes. Pursuing this idea further, it soon becomes evident that comparing events and natural processes as causes of mood is artificial because the two are interrelated. Nevertheless, this comparison has some validity, as I shall try to indicate.

Events do influence our moods in just the way that most people think, but the issue is much more complicated than that. First, events that have less immediate biological influence are relatively less important to determining our moods than commonly assumed. For example, having an argument with a coworker can depress our mood, but it probably will not destroy an otherwise good mood. Second, naturally occurring internal processes are likely to be more important than most people think. For example, most people don't realize how much a loss of sleep the night before can damage their mood. Understanding this is important because comparing events and naturally occurring processes helps us understand why moods appear to be so puzzling.

Let us examine these points more carefully. If asked what causes our daily moods, the most common answer is likely to be "This or that happened to me, and after that, my mood was. . . ."[39] Perhaps this is correct. But what is often forgotten, or not realized, is the fatigue or energy state in which the "this or that" happened. What time of day was it, how much sleep did I have, or when did I eat last? How fit am I? Did I exercise recently? (As I argue in the last half of this book, negative moods often can largely be traced to the answers to these questions of physical condition.) These and similar considerations are important to how events and mood are related, as they may color or completely change our perceptions of an event. And because this process is often ongoing and interactive, these naturally occurring internal processes relating to energy and tension levels greatly influence our moods.

I am not saying that events are unimportant causes of our moods, instead, that their importance is not as great as is usually assumed. In the past, many psychologists considered only events. But with the cognitive revolution in psychology of the 1970s and 1980s, we have come to understand that our *interpretations* of events are important determinants of how we react, as opposed to the events themselves. Now it is clear that events happen in the context of biological cycles, health, nutrition, and exercise status, and particularly energy and tension states. These and other natural processes affect us much more dramatically than most people realize.

Another important point is that positive moods are more likely to be influenced by natural processes and that negative moods are more likely to be affected by bad things that happen to us. Good moods usually are related to greater personal resources, or energy, and they often override negative events to produce at least moderately good feelings (e.g., calm-energy or at least tense-energy). From this we can see that positive or neutral moods are likely to be the norm if we are experiencing good health, physical fitness, adequate sleep, and satisfactory nutrition.

On the other hand, an event that we interpret as negative increases our tension level, and this tension interacts with energy to produce a mood that may be the basis of negative thoughts. In times of depleted resources and low energy, the outcome is a bad mood. Thus, when personal resources are high, we feel good. But event-produced tension coupled with low resources leads to bad moods.

Understanding moods in this way allows us to see why they appear to be so mysterious and changeable, seemingly without reason. Moods wouldn't be as puzzling if events were their sole cause. We would think, "Oh yes, I'm in a bad mood because this or that happened to me." But as we try to understand our moods, recent events often do not account for them; rather, most people experience moods as unpredictable elements in their lives. When they consider the causes, most people think of events rather than simple biology, whereas it often is a little of both.

One reason that we are unable to understand our moods is that the underlying natural processes are subtle and shift very slowly. They aren't like events that have definite boundaries and that are often fresh in our memory. Instead, the slowly changing rhythms of our body easily may be missed as causes of our moods unless we become good self-observers or unless we understand the interplay of psychological and biological factors with events.

It is easy to forget that a few hours ago when we felt good it was 11:30 in the morning, the peak of energy for the day. Now it is 4:30 in the afternoon, a low-energy time, and everything looks different. Moreover, these differences may be exacerbated because of forgotten circumstances such as little sleep the previous night or no food since morning.

If we are not aware of these important influences when we consider the reasons for our negative moods, we may just throw up our hands and say, "I don't understand it. It must be biochemical." By this we mean that our moods are beyond our immediate comprehension. Of course, our moods are biochemical. But they also are physiological and cognitive in the sense that they encompass broad bodily processes. Nonetheless, they are predictable, although we must take into account the general rhythms and physical conditions of our body in order to predict them efficiently.

6

How Energy and Tension Interact

Energy and tension form a complex relationship with each other.[1] The two states are sometimes positively related; that is, as one increases so does the other. This is evident in such combinations as tense-energy or calm-tiredness. But sometimes they are negatively related. As one increases the other decreases. This is seen in calm-energy and tense-tiredness. The circumstances in which these positive and negative relationships occur are important theoretical elements of a biopsychological model of mood.

Scientists often create models to understand how something works. The two-dimensional explanation of mood that I have been describing is a model. As in other models, underlying concepts are conceptualized by analogy, allowing us to describe relationships exactly and to make inferences about elements of the model that may remain hidden. Ideally, there is scientific support for all important parts of the model, but often only some parts are supported, and others are assumed if they are logically consistent with the larger conceptualization. Thus, models allow us to make intelligent guesses or hypotheses concerning what to expect under different circumstances.

I have constructed such a model for understanding the relationship between energy and tension, which I will describe in more detail later. Some elements of this model of mood are well supported by scientific evidence, but others await further experimental confirmation. A number of significant implications of these relationships were discussed in previous chapters. For example, I briefly indicated how this kind of an analysis allows us to understand complex moods such as depression (or tense-tiredness) and its underlying biological and psychological causes. I also suggested that optimal moods are associated with calm-energy and, to a lesser extent, calm-tiredness. In addition, I described the way that declines in energy make us more vulnerable to tension, anxiety, or nervousness.

Viewing energy and tension as interrelated in a particular way carries a number of other important implications as well. For example, with this model we can see why reduced tension is associated with energy-increasing activities, such as exercise. The relationship between energy and tension also may clarify the apparently paradoxical effects of various psychoactive drugs that seem to increase and decrease bodily arousal simultaneously. Finally, a part of the model not yet discussed—the condition of exhaustion—enables us to understand the strange sensation of apparent calmness that we feel in very taxing circumstances.

A Serendipitous Finding

My analysis of the complex relationship between energy and tension originated more than two decades ago with an experiment that one of my graduate students and I conducted.[2] We were interested in the effects of stress on mood, and so our experiment involved three different conditions designed to produce varying amounts of stress. We randomly divided the subjects into three groups, all of which completed the same complicated verbal-learning task and made systematic self-ratings of their mood levels on several occasions.

We changed the stress among the three groups by means of instructions and setting, in part, by giving false instructions intended to create stress. (Incidentally, all the subjects were debriefed and given correct information before they left the laboratory.) In the high-stress condition, the participants were told that they would be given an intelligence test that predicted future college performance and also that it was very important to do as well as possible. The experimenter looked quite serious and was dressed in a way that communicated the importance of the experiment. We used the same task and mood measurements in the low-stress condition, but told the subjects that this was only a pilot study and characterized it as less important. The experimenter was dressed much more casually. The middle-stress level used instructions and a setting that were midway between those of the other two conditions.

We expected the tension ratings to rise from low to high in the three graded stress conditions, and that is exactly what happened. We also thought that energy would increase with each level of stress or at least stay the same.[3] But we found that energy did not rise with each increase in stress. Instead, energy level increased only up to moderate levels, and in the high-stress condition, it decreased. We obtained the same result with tiredness, but in reverse. The subjects in the low-stress condition were tired; those in the moderate condition were less tired; and those in the high-stress condition were as tired as those under low stress.

Quite frankly, I was disappointed by the results. Nonetheless, I published the findings but then pushed them out of my mind for a while. Only later did I realize that this was a serendipitous result, an unexpected but valuable finding—not an unusual event in the history of science. That is, these results were unexpected but valuable because they illustrated remarkably well the complex relationship of energy and tension.

A Model of Energy and Tension

My model holds that as tension increases, energy will increase as well (tense-energy), but only up to a certain point. Beyond that, energy will begin to decline, and tense-tiredness will take over. In a similar way, as energy increases from low to moderate levels, tension also increases. But at higher levels of energy, tension decreases, and calm-energy is the result. In technical terms, we can speak of a positive

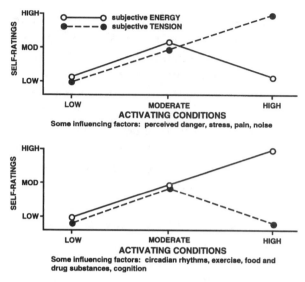

Figure 3 Complex relationship between energy and tension under different conditions

correlation between energy and tension from low to moderate levels and a negative correlation from moderate to high levels. (These relationships are outlined in Figure 3.) Finally, under conditions in which energy declines so much that exhaustion results, tension also declines.

The Parallel Rise of Energy and Tension: The Experience of Tense-Energy and Other Related States

This positive relationship between energy and tension becomes clearer if we look at an example. Sam Smith is sitting at home relaxing when suddenly he remembers an important project that must be completed in two days. The thought produces a sudden increase in anxiety or tension. But because he still has two days to go, the tension is only moderate. Thus Sam changes from a relaxed state to a tense-energetic state, and this motivates him to get the job done.

This scenario is very common. For example, I find that many college students live their lives as Sam Smith does, waiting until the last minute to begin writing term papers or begin studying for a final exam. They appear to rely on the tense-energy they experience as the deadline approaches to motivate them to begin working. But this kind of procrastination, coupled with the motivation that comes with a little anxiety, also is characteristic of people who aren't students. Indeed, many people regularly seem to motivate themselves with a small amount of tension arising from the fear of failure.

Tense-energy as a prevailing mood is characteristic especially of Type A personalities.[4] Such persons never have enough time, and they dislike wasting it. Because they have so much to do, they must continually rush to complete the tasks at hand. In addition, such people often are high achievers, ambitious and competitive. They also may be aggressive and hostile when provoked. Energy and vigor, as well as tension, are characteristic of Type A personalities. For example, consider the views of Ray Rosenman, the cardiologist who originated this concept together with Meyer Friedman. Rosenman describes the Type A as having a "general expression of energy and vigor" and also a "tense, teeth-clenching, jaw-grinding posture."[5]

The average person may feel tense-energy at various times during the normal circadian rhythm. As I indicated earlier, energy rises sharply in the first third of the day after awakening and reaches a peak somewhere between the late morning and early afternoon. In a typical stress-filled day, tension has its own diurnal pattern. When energy is high, tension is relatively low, but when energy drops, tension peaks—for example, in the mid-to late afternoon or in the evening. Of course, this typical pattern may be quite different for some people, but in any event, during each day, there will be several conjunctions of tension and energy. Tense-energy can occur at any time of day, when both energy and tension are high. I think of tense-energy as occurring whenever tension and energy are at the same, or nearly the same, level.

In the next two chapters, I examine some important physiological underpinnings of these mood states, but for now let me comment briefly on what is meant by arousal. Psychophysiologists often have observed underlying physiological changes that can explain the parallel relationship of tension and energy. Imagine a resting person who suddenly hears a loud noise or who gets up and begins to move. The individual exhibits a correlated pattern of many kinds of bodily arousal, with a wide variety of cardiovascular, respiratory, and endocrine arousal processes responding simultaneously, as well as electrophysiological (e.g., EEG) and neurochemical brain activation patterns. This is a well-known process that illustrates a generalized arousal.[6]

We must keep in mind an important qualification concerning the positive correlation between energy and tension. I stated that as tension increases, energy also increases, up to a certain point; alternatively, increases in energy result in increases in tension. But tension increases in parallel with energy only when someone is experiencing conditions that otherwise maintain that tension, anxiety, or nervousness. A person experiencing chronic stress or unremitting personal problems is an example. Without tension-producing conditions—for instance, when on a vacation—tension is absent, and the person experiences only natural variations in energy and tiredness.

High Tension and Low Energy: The Experience of Tense-Tiredness

The way that high tension and low energy occur together may be illustrated by an extension of the earlier example of Sam Smith who was first relaxing at home. If his suddenly remembered deadline is in the somewhat distant future, thereby producing only a moderate amount of tension, he will experience tense-energy. But if his deadline is 1 hour away and it is impossible to meet, the increase in tension is likely to be much greater. In fact, high anxiety might be the result. With this higher tension level, Sam no longer feels energetic; instead, his energy declines, and he feels tense-tired.

The normal circadian rhythm of a person under moderate to high stress produces tense-tiredness, and under lower levels of stress it brings tense-energy. Gradually, as tension increases from morning to late afternoon the individual begins to feel the tension overtaking the energy, and tense-tiredness is the result. This shift from tense-energy to tense-tiredness is likely to be gradual, not abrupt. Although this daily pattern of tension and energy is variable, the common times of day when tense-tiredness occurs are mid- to late afternoon and later in the evening.

Depression is another example of this mixed arousal state in which people experience what seem to be contradictory feelings—tension and tiredness. As we mentioned earlier, the tense-tiredness of some kinds of depression is sometimes felt upon awakening in the morning. But the typical pattern in milder forms of depression shows a peak later in the day when many people experience maximum tension and their energy is low. This pattern was evident in a study by Paul Robbins and Roland Tanck using students at George Washington University.[7] The students kept depression diaries on 10 consecutive days. Most of those reporting depression did not experience high levels but, rather, a little depression, the kind that many people feel frequently. The results indicated gradually changing levels of depression as the day wore on, with the highest depression levels in the afternoon and evening.

Tense-tiredness clearly is a part of mild depression, if not of more serious types.[8] In two studies of women experiencing recurrent mild depression, my students and I analyzed their ratings of energy and tension levels on depressed days compared with days on which they felt no depression. The subjects in these studies had reported feeling depressed several times a week, but they were not medicated or in therapy. The mood pattern associated with depression was both unmistakable and very reliable: elevated tension and tiredness together with low energy.[9]

Serious states of depression also show this pattern of tense-tiredness. The diagnostic manual of the American Psychiatric Association, which is commonly used to identify pathological levels of depression, lists many symptoms suggesting these two arousal states.[10] Among the more obvious ones are insomnia, psychomotor agitation, fatigue, and loss of energy. For a diagnosis of major depressive disorder, these or other symptoms must occur nearly every day.

Another condition in which tense-tiredness occurs is chronic anxiety. Unlike depression, however, an anxious person may or may not experience low energy.[11] Nevertheless, two early large-scale medical studies provide evidence that among patients with prolonged high anxiety, some of the most commonly observed symptoms other than anxiety are "tires easily," "feelings of tiredness not related to physical exertion," and "fatigued all the time."[12] For people experiencing chronic anxiety, low energy depends on time of day (whether a high- or low-energy time) and physical condition.

From these examples of depression and chronic anxiety, it is tempting to assume that prolonged anxiety or tension produces low energy by depleting physical resources. Resources certainly are depleted in these disorders, especially if the bouts of anxiety or depression are lengthy. But when anxiety increases sharply, tense-tiredness can result with hardly any time for physical depletion. This sudden shift is more likely when physical resources already are low. Without going further at this point, I will just say that the inverse relationship between energy and tension probably is at least partially mediated at the level of the brain (Chapter 8), suggesting more rapid shifts rather than gradually increasing tense-tiredness as physical resources decline.

We know that the inverse relationship between tension and energy is not entirely dependent on physical resources because exercise, which uses up resources, can actually give a person more energy. That is, you may be in a tense-tired state and be able to modify your feelings merely by exercising. Therefore, if declining physical resources were the only basis of tense-tiredness, the condition could not be relieved through exercise alone, because this physical activity requires a direct expenditure of energy.

Indeed, there are many everyday examples in which tense-tiredness appears rapidly, with little time for physical resources to become depleted. Perhaps you have had a serious personal problem for a long time, and you feel anxious whenever you think about it. But when you are not thinking about it, you are not anxious. When such thoughts do occur, however, you experience not only a sharp increase in anxiety but also a distinct feeling of fatigue. You may not identify this as tense-tiredness; instead, you may have a sinking feeling when the problem comes to mind or feel deeply resigned. These are signs of tense-tiredness.

A colleague offered another example of tense-tiredness that comes on rapidly. It concerns procrastination about completing unpleasant tasks. She told me about a common occurrence in which she puts off tasks that are somewhat unpleasant while she works energetically on other, unrelated activities. When she finally begins to deal with the aversive tasks, she suddenly feels too tired to complete them. But when she puts them aside, her energy for other activities returns once again.

In these examples, tense-tiredness is present, but without a significant expenditure of energy. I believe that tense-tiredness may occur suddenly and fairly often in daily experience, particularly for a person under stress and in poor physical condition. Merely thinking about psychological conflicts or unpleasant circumstances can produce sudden increases in anxiety and decreases in energy.

Whether it is depression, chronic anxiety, or just thoughts about a problem that produce anxiety and fatigue, tense-tiredness is the pattern that emerges. This negative correlation between energy and tension at high levels is different from the positive correlation we see at low to moderate levels of tension.

When Does Tension Reduce Energy?

I have been somewhat indefinite about the level at which increases in tension can be expected to reduce energy. Instead, I spoke only about a moderate level of tension. The reason for this indefiniteness is that the level of tension at which tense-tiredness begins is not the same for all people, nor is it always the same for any one person. This moderate level depends to some extent on the person's physical resources, and it probably also depends on genetically determined differences in temperament.

For example, an old and frail person might be expected to feel tense-tiredness at a much lower level of tension than would a young and vigorous person. In other words, the same amount of stress that produces an enjoyable level of tense-energy in a young person could produce an unpleasant level of tense-tiredness in an older person. One implication of this is that younger people may enjoy intense and driving occupational demands but older people may avoid them. For this reason, we can understand why older people might avoid the pastimes of the young—fast cars, loud music, and long parties.

The same principle is likely to be true for a person in good physical condition, say an athlete, compared with someone who is out of shape. We know that physical conditioning gives a person more overall energy. A person in good shape would also be less bothered by tension because high energy results in low tension or, at most, only moderate tension. Therefore, people who exercise regularly can be expected to withstand more stress without feeling tense-tired than can those who are less fit.

Because energy and personal resources vary with time of day, the same amount of stress may be expected to produce tense-energy at 11:00 A.M. in the morning but tense-tiredness at 4:00 P.M. in the afternoon. Simple tasks such as calling or meeting a stranger can be relatively easy at late morning but unpleasant in the evening. I think of this example in particular because I was told by one of my middle-aged single students that he often makes enthusiastic plans to attend parties or social affairs during the high energy times of the day, but when evening comes and it is time to go, he begins to feel anxious (tense-tiredness), and so he cancels his plans.

I witnessed a related phenomenon some years ago when I visited Disneyland with my then 5-year old daughter. When we arrived in the afternoon, she immediately wanted to try a fast and scary ride. I was concerned that it might be too much for her, but she insisted and she loved it. She took the ride three more times that day. But the last time, at about 11:00 P.M., was past her usual bedtime, and the ride really frightened her. She said she would never go on it again. Fortunately, on another visit, during the day, she again wanted to take the ride, and she again enjoyed it.

Food probably also influences the level at which tense-tiredness occurs. Immediately after eating a sugar snack, tension may be less aversive, probably as the result of a "sugar high," which we described earlier. Sugar often increases energy immediately after being ingested. But an hour later, the negative effect of stress-produced tension may be increased as the person becomes more tired than before the snack.[13] Perhaps more relevant is the example of not having eaten anything for some time. If you skip breakfast or don't eat all day, stress-producing circumstances can easily result in tense-tiredness. You already have depleted your resources and so feel the added stresses of the day much more. On the other hand, the same stress may have little effect following a nutritious meal.

Earlier we saw that tiredness and low energy produce vulnerability to tension. As an example, I mentioned how an argument late at night can be much more unpleasant than a comparable argument during the day when the participants' energy is high. That is, the same dispute may lead to tense-energy in the day but tense-tiredness at night.

On a practical level, knowing your energy level can be important, and this awareness will become automatic once you learn to discriminate among tense-energy, tense-tiredness, and other complex moods. You can learn to make these discriminations by means of repeated self-observations (see Chapter 17).

Until now, I have focused on increasing amounts of tense-tiredness with changing levels of energy. But there may be stable individual differences in this respect that probably pertain to temperament. For example, stable extraverts, sensation seekers, and thrill seekers may be expected to maintain tense-energy to a much higher tension level than others can.[14] On the other hand, some temperament types, such as shy or highly neurotic people, may feel tense-tired at much lower levels of tension. There is very little scientific research directly applicable to this matter. But there is extensive research on temperament types, and those results are entirely consistent with my theory.

The Mind of the Tense-Tired Person

We have been looking at the complex arousal state of the tense-tired person—the subjective experience of low energy and high tension, which may predispose a person to feelings of depression and many other less serious dysfunctions. But the mental state that accompanies this tense-tired condition is a crucial part of the picture, because the world appears different to a tense-tired person. Perspectives change, problems look more serious, self-esteem is low. The tense-tired person has a pessimistic view of everything.

We should recognize that this mental state is more or less negative, depending on how depleted our resources are. When our resources have not been depleted for a long time, as in the temporary ebbs in energy cycles at 4:00 P.M. or midnight, our thoughts may be only slightly negative. But in the case of a serious depression that may be associated with a lengthy depletion of resources, the mental state can be one of impending doom that signals death, perhaps by suicide, if the condition does not change. All these varying degrees of negative mental outlook are correlated with the tense-tired state.

High Energy and Low Tension: The Experience of Calm-Energy

Let us return to the example of Sam Smith to illustrate the complex mood of calm-energy. Recall that Sam is sitting at home relaxing when he suddenly remembers a future deadline, which makes him anxious. Tense-energy motivates him to get the job done. But suppose that this is 4:00 P.M. and Sam's energy is too low for any effective work. Remembering the effects of moderate exercise, Sam first goes out for a short brisk walk, say 10 or 15 minutes. This increases his energy sharply. The result is calm-energy, a mood that enables him to work effectively for an hour or two.

Just as increasing tension reduces energy and produces tense-tiredness, increasing energy reduces tension. There appears to be a dynamic balance between energy and tension at higher levels: High energy leads to low tension, and high tension leads to low energy. This is an important principle to recognize because it offers a practical way to counteract anxiety, tension, and nervousness: Engage in activities that raise energy (see Chapter 14). I believe that this is exactly what happens much of the time when people seek a means of relieving their anxiety and tiredness, such as eating a sugary snack. Indeed, sugar does raise energy, at least for the short term. Perhaps this is why when we feel anxious, many of us think immediately of good-tasting food. And maybe it is the thousands of "conditioning trials" in the past, starting with the times our mothers gave us a snack if we cried, that make us think of eating. But turning to sugar isn't caused solely by childhood experiences; seeking food to increase energy, and therefore to reduce anxiety, continues into adulthood because it works.

Of course, as I have indicated, it may not work for very long. Within an hour after eating the snack, we may be more tired and less energetic than we were before. Then we may consume another snack, and this produces anxious thoughts. We realize that we cannot control our moods without breaking our previously strong resolve to stay on a diet. This realization reduces our self-esteem and generates more anxiety.

Rather than raising their energy to reduce tension, some people use more direct means of lowering tension, such as alcohol, a tranquilizer, or a drug like Valium. Such drugs are likely to have their primary effect on tension rather than energy. Cigarettes also are commonly used during these times of greater tension, but here the underlying physiological base is more complicated because nicotine appears both to increase energy and simultaneously reduce muscular tension. The principle is the same in all these cases, however. The tense-tiredness is unpleasant, and so it motivates us to do something to change it. We thus seek calm-energy, or at least tense-energy.

Most people recognize the state that I call calm-energy in conjunction with their feelings at a particular time of day. For many, this may occur in the late morning or early afternoon. And as most exercise enthusiasts are aware, physical activity is an excellent way of producing this state. In the earlier example, when Sam Smith feels tired late in the afternoon, he takes a short brisk walk to increase his energy.

In our controlled studies of exercise and mood, we found that as little as 10 minutes of brisk walking led to increases in energy that were almost as great as the peak amount of energy that most of us experience during the day. Moreover, this increased energy, together with reduced tension, lasted for at least 60 minutes. By means of this simple activity, people felt calm-energy.

There is now an increasing and convincing scientific literature that shows that moderate exercise increases energy and often reduces tension.[15] Usually it is the more intense exercise workouts that reduce tension. But these intense workouts probably increase energy after we recover from the immediate fatigue that they generate, about 45 minutes or so later.

In addition to these immediate or slightly delayed calm-energetic effects of exercise, there is an interesting and relevant scientific literature that exercise physiologists have developed in conjunction with studies of elite athletes. William Morgan and his colleagues at the University of Wisconsin coined the term *iceberg profile* to describe the mood of these world-class performers. The term was used because the mood measure that they employed showed high scores on only one aspect of mood—energy—and low scores on several other aspects of negative mood, including tension.[16] Connecting the points on a graph of the various mood states thus makes a pattern that looks like an iceberg. One study of world-class marathon runners, for example, found them to be calm-energetic, compared with other people. This same iceberg profile applied to other star athletes such as wrestlers and rowers.

The concept of an iceberg profile has now been used in several other studies of athletes, ranging from professional tennis players to visually impaired athletes.[17] When Morgan used the term, he suggested that this iceberg profile was characteristic only of top athletes, but any person can have an iceberg profile, at least temporarily, when his or her mood is influenced by exercise.[18] Because exercise often produces calm-energy, it results in an iceberg profile as an immediate effect. It makes sense, of course, that elite athletes would experience calm-energy more often than others do, because they are in such good physical condition.[19]

The iceberg profile is based on the assumption that good training in athletics produces optimal moods, but it probably also works the other way. That is, one could argue that calm-energy is a necessary prerequisite for a skilled athletic performance. An Olympic diver, for example, must be able to execute perfectly coordinated movements that demand a great deal of energy. This exacting performance requires activating certain muscles and also relaxing others. Because optimal athletic performance is inhibited by unnecessary tension, the performer must minimize tension so that it does not impede action. I shall have more to say about the "stop" function of tension in Chapters 7 and 8.

In the martial arts this idea of minimizing tension is well developed, although other terms may be used to describe it. Karate, kung fu, or judo masters do not jump around wasting energy on unnecessary movement. Rather, they wait calmly for the appropriate moment to act. But their body is not totally relaxed; instead, their necessary muscles are primed to be ready for rapid and vigorous movement. Those muscles that are not to be used are relaxed, and unnecessary energy isn't spent on them. For this preparatory state, it is therefore necessary to be calm as well as energized.

Related to martial arts is the Eastern form of meditation in movement called *Tai Chi Chuan*. In this form of meditation, calm-energy is essential, and so a good deal of training goes into producing this mood state during the tai chi exercises. Activating the appropriate muscles and relaxing the reciprocal ones is only one part of this training. In addition, controlling the breathing and mental state both help. For example, a so-called empty mind is a mental state that reduces tension-producing thoughts.

I believe that calm-energy also is the optimal mood for many kinds of skilled mental performance, even though there is not much scientific evidence for this. But my assertion should not be surprising, considering the close association of mind and body. One of my students and I tested this idea in a rather simple way.[20] We used a sample of college undergraduates as subjects. Then over a 3-week period and at many times of day, these students occasionally stopped what they were doing to rate the effectiveness of their recent mental work. Serious students are very good at making these kinds of judgments, as they know when they are concentrating well, when they are understanding and learning the material efficiently, and when they have good recall. At the time that they rated their study habits, the students also rated their energy and tension levels. These various ratings allowed us to determine what mood patterns best predicted good study habits.

Among these undergraduates, calm-energy was the best predictor of study effectiveness. Compared with the efficiency of study in other mood states, heightened energy and reduced tension were by far the best background mood pattern. Tense-energy was the next best mood pattern, and tense-tiredness was the worst. These differences were highly reliable.

Let me briefly repeat some points I made earlier about psychoactive drugs. Their optimal effect often is calm-energy, which undoubtedly is why their use is so attractive. When they work best, tranquilizers reduce anxiety but leave the user feeling normally energetic. Users of illicit drugs hope for a similar pattern. For instance, users of cocaine and amphetamines seek more energy and less or the same amount of anxiety. Likewise, people frequently use recreational drugs such as caffeine and nicotine to enhance alertness (energy), but without a corresponding increment in jitteriness (tension). And although alcohol is a depressant, its initial effects reduce anxiety, which in turn boosts energy for a short time.[21] I believe that an important motivation for using these drugs is to achieve calm-energy.

Time of day, exercise, food, and drugs are only some of the determinants of calm-energy. But whenever this mood state occurs, the biopsychological model I have described is applicable. Energy and tension are inversely related at high levels. Calm-energy is the result of either reduced tension with normal resources (energy) or high resources in relation to moderate or low tension. This inverse relationship between energy and tension is parallel to, but in an opposite way, the high tension and low energy of depression, chronic anxiety, and middle-of-the-night worries about personal problems that are characteristic of tense-tiredness.

In our earlier discussion, my comments about tense-energy, tense-tiredness, and calm-energy may have suggested sudden shifts from one state to another. More commonly, however, the changes between states are not abrupt but are more gradual shifts as relatively more tension or energy are experienced. The changes from calm-energy to tense-energy and then to tense-tiredness, for example, are likely to be incremental, corresponding to gradually declining resources. Or as someone begins to exercise, the shift to calm-energy is gradual as bodily resources are slowly mobilized. The same gradual change can be expected as the morning energy cycle slowly ascends to its peak. Sometimes, however, the shifts are more rapid, as when a mere thought about some problem can switch a person into a state of tense-tiredness. But these changes probably take place when resources are moderately low.

The Mood of Exhaustion.

Using the biopsychological model we have been exploring, let us look at the extreme fatigue that I call *exhaustion*. Remember that the relationship between energy and tension must be understood in conjunction with bodily resources, the wide range of physiological reserves that enable motor activities, thoughts, and feelings of both energy and tension, among other things. As I indicated, abundant bodily resources in the absence of tension produce a calm-energetic mood. But as these resources are depleted and the feelings of energy begin to ebb, stressful circumstances have a much greater impact, and tense feelings increase until tense-tiredness predominates.

At some point in the decline of resources, however, exhaustion sets in, meaning that the previous tense feelings begin to fade together with the decreased energy feelings. In a sense, exhaustion represents a state of calm-tiredness. As I suggest later, exhaustion probably is a biological protective mechanism that imposes temporary calmness and allows the person to get some needed sleep and recuperation.

Most people experience this state at the end of a day when they have been working very hard either mentally or physically. One professional colleague, who works intensely and continuously on mental tasks, told me that at night she is exhausted, but in a good sort of way, especially if she has accomplished a lot. Hard physical labor readily produces exhaustion, of course, but nowadays most people are not sufficiently taxed in this way. Therefore, most of the time exhaustion is the result of intense mental activity, chronic stress, and sleep deprivation. Although the end of the day, just before sleep, is the prime time for exhaustion to prevail, it may also occur in normal waking hours if resources are low, for example, because of prolonged stress and too little sleep.

In the way I am using this term, the mood of exhaustion is characterized by an absence of anxiety or tension, together with very low energy. If exhaustion occurs in the middle of the day, the feeling may seem peculiar and paradoxical. The calmness appears out of place, considering the anxiety that often precedes it. However, since this mood state represents a welcome relief from anxiety, it can be perceived as pleasant and even as a strangely euphoric condition. But when you experience this state, you have a sense that it can't last long. You feel that if you don't get rest and recuperation, your body will give out, which is probably the case.

Let us consider exhaustion from two perspectives: first, resource depletion because of intense physical activity and, second, depletion because of stress. Anyone who has hiked for long distances under difficult conditions, or any marathon runner, probably is familiar with the state of physical depletion.[22] At the end of a long and taxing hike, for example, one feels totally spent. The usual concerns about snakes, bugs, and fastidious eating conditions are absent. If there are unpleasant insects on the food, they are casually brushed aside, and people with mild phobias about snakes react nonchalantly to a nearby reptile. It is as if the physical resources expended on the hike have depleted the resources needed to feel minor fears and anxieties. The result is an absence of tension or anxiety, and the feeling is one of calmness, even in the presence of conditions that otherwise would create anxiety.

The same state may arise from stress, particularly if one has had little or no sleep for some time. Consider a person whose job is in jeopardy. He is desperate to keep his position, but his work demands are great. He spends 12 hours a day at tasks that offer little rest and relaxation. His concentration is continuous, with many opportunities for disastrous errors. His resources gradually diminish, not only because of his immediate job demands but also because he has given up exercise, adequate nutrition, and, especially, sleep.

If such a person isn't exhausted at the end of each night, he probably will find getting to sleep difficult or impossible. When he finally goes to bed, he tosses and turns. The anxiety generated by his job is unremitting, and it clearly inhibits sleep. Finally, as time passes and his resources become sufficiently depleted, he no longer tosses and turns at bedtime; instead he falls into bed and goes to sleep immediately.

For such a person, the exhaustion can extend to the waking hours as well. But in the daytime, the need for sleep is not so great. Instead, an exhausted person may experience a strange mood of equanimity. It feels good in an unusual sort of way, as the anxiety is no longer present. But things aren't quite right. During this waking version of exhaustion, there may be a curious sensation that his body is on autopilot. It is as though his brain is directing each act and movement from a place removed and remote. "Walk to the door." "Open the door and walk out." "Close the door." With each instruction, the body responds.

We usually aren't aware of the way that our brain directs our activities all the time, because under normal conditions, continuous feedback from our body informs us about energy and depletions, and we act accordingly. When we are tired, we rest; and when we feel recuperated, we move on. If the movement is too arduous, we slow down, and so on. In the exhausted state, however, that feedback is absent. There are no variations in energy; we are simply depleted, and this creates something like an altered state of consciousness.

These peculiar mental states and the behaviors that accompany them have been reported in the scientific literature. Studies of sleep deprivation typically produce this state by the second day.[23] Subjects in these experiments take on zombielike characteristics. They move slowly, are unresponsive, and show little emotion. Yet they are not anxious or otherwise troubled. They don't have enough energy for emotion or upset. Reports of concentration camp inmates indicate the same state. Under those exhausting conditions, they often had given up caring what happened to them; even the threat of imminent death failed to move them.[24]

The mood of exhaustion—like tense-energy, tense-tiredness, and calm-energy—is based on the body's resources. In the case of exhaustion, the influence of the body's resources is more obvious than for other moods, but in all these complex moods, resources are vital. When you think of moods in this way, it becomes clear why matters like sleep, nutrition, exercise, and biological cycles are so important.

7

The Evolutionary Biology of Moods

Humans have evolved over millions of years, with virtually every complex system of the body having developed through natural selection. We are resilient because we have retained those characteristics that enabled our ancestors to survive and pass on their genes. This is not an inconsequential fact; indeed, it is quite an optimistic point. Because of the test of survival, we are not weak and vulnerable creatures. In a sense, we are designed to survive under the harshest conditions because we have inherited the bodies of the survivors, not the weak ones.

But it is likely that our body design is not just one of survival. There is evidence that our genetic heritage has enabled us to live with health, happiness, and a variety of positive psychological states. As I argue in this book, we are finely adapted to regularly experience the most optimal moods. But our modern garb and world make it difficult to detect these patterns of evolution in our everyday lives, because most of these changes more likely occurred in the Pleistocene era than in the 5,000 to 10,000 years of recorded history. And certainly the daily activities of people in New York City or Los Angeles are quite different from those of their ancestors who gathered their food from the land, hunted the plains, and huddled in caves against the elements. And yet there are substantial similarities. The same cycles of life that affected our ancestors still affect us. The same needs, the same conditions of danger, and the same moods still hold, although now we understand much better the full psychological and biological significance of these needs, dangers, and moods.

Mood systems have function and utility, or they would not be part of our biopsychology. But what is that function? And what utility would warrant elation, depression, and other moods? The answers to these questions might seem to be unknowable, but I believe that we can make some fairly good guesses. This part of my theory is necessarily speculative, but it makes sense.

Looking at mood systems as part of an evolutionary inheritance, our moods can be seen as vital signs of readiness for action and need for rest and recuperation. Our moods tell us when to be active and to expend our resources and also when to rest and to seek inaction. Feelings of energy and tiredness are among the most important of these subjective signal systems.

Our moods also guide us in regard to when to mobilize our resources, when to be cautious, and when to be completely inconspicuous, to lie low and stay out of trouble, so to speak. Thus, fear, tension, anxiety, and nervousness carry information about danger. They signal mobilization, restraint of normal activity, and wariness. Conversely, calmness signals safety, certainty, and confidence. When we feel calm, we know that we can proceed without concern.

Energetic States

As we look at the body, from its most elemental processes, through all its intermediate anatomy and physiology, and to the awareness of mood, we can see general patterns. One of these patterns, energetic arousal, ties together many of these seemingly diverse processes. That is, our energy levels are related to the most basic elements of life, especially wakefulness, movement, health, and nutrition.

Energetic arousal is apparent throughout the body when we are awake and when we move and exercise. When we are sedentary or asleep, energy levels decline, and different but related physiological patterns emerge—in our brain, our muscles, our blood, and everywhere else in our body. When our health is challenged or food isn't available, our energy decreases. Good health, on the other hand, gives us an abundance of energy. This whole-body pattern that I call *energetic arousal* is wide ranging. The physiology is so complex that it seems to defy analysis, but the pattern readily becomes apparent in our feelings—energy, vigor, fatigue, and tiredness, for example.

Let us consider some of these relationships in the context of their evolutionary significance. The general argument is that those biological functions central to survival are supported by the broadest physiological processes. On a psychological level, they affect numerous aspects of consciousness and motivation. With the many redundancies built in, the ultimate goal can be achieved.

Hardly any function is more central than movement. We must get from one place to another for sustenance, procreation, and defense. Because our survival is dependent on the ability to move, the motor system becomes very important.

Earlier, I spoke of the close association between exercise and energy feelings. Activation of the motor system, from which exercise derives, is absolutely central to life, not only to humans but to other animals as well. Nobel laureate Roger Sperry of the California Institute of Technology said it well when he stated that from humans to fishes, the

> primary business of the brain continues to be the governing directly, or indirectly, of overt behavior. . . . Instead of regarding motor activity as being subsidiary, that is, something to carry out, serve, and satisfy the demands of the higher centers, we reverse the tendency and look upon the mental activity as only a means to an end, where the end is better regulation of overt response.[1]

What he meant is that we take physical action for granted and give mental thought and cognitive processes privileged status. Instead, movement should be regarded as central, as thoughts and other kinds of mental activity help us move from one place to another.

McGill University's Robert Malmo, who might be called the father of psychophysiology, voiced similar views. In his summary analysis of studies involving the electrical activity of muscles (EMG), he observed, "Evidence from the EMG research reviewed . . . provides strong support for the proposition that the motor system is an indispensable part of all activities of the mind."[2] Both Sperry and Malmo, as well as other psychobiologists, regard the motor system as essential to a person's psychic life. Thus it is easy to see why exercise is basic to mood and to mood regulation. Exercise and our energy level maintain an integral association, one that is central to our life and our well-being.

The close interaction of energy and movement also encompasses variations from sleep to wakefulness. A former University of Chicago professor, Nathanial Kleitman, who probably did more for the scientific understanding of sleep than any other researcher, commented on sleep deprivation studies:

> Cortical activity is thus sustained by, and sustains, the wakefulness system and the skeletal musculature. . . . [In regard to keeping his experimental subjects awake,]the subjects could maintain wakefulness as long as they were able and willing to maintain muscular activity. . . . Even a well rested person may have difficulty in remaining awake, if, in addition to the removal of, or decrease in, stimulation through the sense organs, he allows his skeletal musculature to relax. Conversely, tense muscles may be responsible for "insomnia"[3]

It is evident from sleep deprivation studies that movement and wakefulness are linked so closely together that they are virtually inseparable. To stay awake, the sleep-deprived person must move about; if he sits or lies down, he will go to sleep.

Movement, wakefulness, and energy all are interchangeable in one certain respect. Think of energetic arousal as an action system: When we feel energy, we feel a desire to move. Energy impels us to move, either physically or mentally. Conversely, we feel tired when it is time to sleep or when we have expended great amounts of energy. Feelings of energy and tiredness, basic to all our complex moods, are signals of our elemental biological needs.

Tense Arousal

Tense arousal is a feeling of fear, tension, anxiety, or nervousness that informs us that danger or the threat of danger is near. If these feelings are mild, we merely note them and proceed with our work as usual, but we get ready and stay on guard. This awareness continues until calmness returns. When the calm feelings return, the danger has passed, at least as far as we know.

To understand tense arousal and its important bodily manifestations, let us go back in time to prerecorded history. Consider an ancestor coming home to her cave clan during the first glimmers of twilight. She hears a sound that indicates potential danger. Maybe it is a growl, a yelp, or merely a rustling of foliage. Put yourself in her place. How would you act? If this condition represents a potentially catastrophic danger, but it isn't clear where the danger lies, the first thing that you would do is stop and get ready for whatever action may be required. Stopping your activity is useful. You can evaluate the circumstances, listen to and identify the danger, and get ready to react. But in addition, your pausing reduces the predator's ability to detect your presence. Getting ready would take the form of a sharp increase in arousal, in preparation for whatever action might be necessary. If you have ever startled a house cat while walking in the neighborhood during a summer night, you will see this kind of arousal in action. When it first sees you, the animal freezes in a crouched protective stance, ready to act if action is necessary.

This is not, however, the "fight or flight" response so widely described in popular and some scientific circles. Rather, it is the preparation for an emergency action. It is a freeze response that occurs BEFORE fight or flight. In my view, the freeze response is important to understanding many of our deep-seated psychological characteristics, but it has received little attention because people have focused instead on the fight or flight phase of emergency reaction. (Incidentally, Walter Cannon, the originator of the fight-or-flight concept, also described the freeze response, as have other scientists since.[4])

Our ancestor returning to her cave clan does the same thing as the house cat. When she hears a noise, she stops and prepares for action. Momentarily she is frozen. She may crouch slightly, readying herself for immediate protection and for any necessary reaction. The muscles of her shoulders, neck, and back are tense and ready, as are other necessary muscles throughout her body. If we could look inside, we would see a racing heart, providing the necessary nutrients for emergency action. There would also be a sharp increase in blood pressure and respiratory activity. All are necessary to deal with what might ensue.

In addition, the mind of this ancestor would no longer be occupied with the other thoughts of the day. Instead, her attention would be heightened and concentrated on evaluating the danger. Past experiences with these signs of danger would immediately be recalled, and each would be compared with the present circumstances. The thoughts necessary to evaluate the danger would take precedence over everything else.

What is the point of these examples about distant ancestors and house cats? You will see that a person walking through a neighborhood at night in any big city will react to signs of danger just as our ancestor did a hundred thousand years ago. The same bodily arousal in preparation for action, the same freeze tendency, and the same attentional and cognitive pattern are evident in modern counterparts. It is a pattern produced by fear.

But suppose we aren't talking about someone walking in the street at night but, rather, about a woman working at her desk in the late afternoon. She doesn't hear a noise that signals danger, but she still is a little afraid. We call it anxiety when the cause of the fear is not apparent, and it may come from stress. The bodily pattern of this anxious person has many of the same physical and mental characteristics as those of the ancestor traveling to her cave. Although the characteristics aren't as extreme, they are nonetheless similar.

Our modern-day, desk-bound person hunches her shoulders ever so slightly; her neck and jaw are tight; and her back is taut. With heightened anxiety, her blood pressure is up, and her heart rate is greater than necessary for the task at hand. Her attention is not fully directed to her required work, and so she finds it difficult to concentrate. These things are happening because there is danger: Somewhere, somehow, there is an unknown danger.

Is her reaction really different from the cave ancestor? She experiences elements of the freeze reaction, and she is prepared for fight or flight, but now she is in a holding pattern until she can determine the danger. As she tries to work, her thoughts appear scattered, and she cannot concentrate fully. But the thoughts of this anxious person appear to be scattered only because it isn't clear what the danger is. Would there be any question about the focus of her attention if a man with a gun suddenly appeared in the doorway? No. Then her attention would be riveted on the known danger. Rather, her concentration on work is poor because at an unconscious level, her mind is scanning her surroundings to discover the source of the danger.

This is a simple model for understanding feelings of tension, anxiety, or nervousness and the bodily processes that accompany them. These mood states signal danger, telling us to stop and be cautious. Not only do we subjectively experience these states, but our bodies and minds also react consistently to these perceived dangers in our environment. Understanding tension, anxiety, and nervousness in this way has some interesting and practical implications. For example, we can see why concentration on everyday tasks is often difficult for an anxious person. In effect, this is a primitive reaction to danger that prevents us from continuing our work as if all is normal. If the danger in our life is derived from our work and if a fear of failing at that work is of overriding importance, then concentration would be no problem. But if the danger is elsewhere, perhaps registered only at an unconscious level, then our concentration on mundane daily work will not be focused. Therefore, to concentrate better, we must rid ourselves of the unknown danger.

With this understanding, we also can sense the meaning of the muscle tension that accompanies feelings of anxiety, nervousness, and tension. We can understand why our backs and necks hurt when we are under stress (or in danger). These are lesser manifestations of the freeze response. Although we may not be immobile and crouching to avoid detection by a predator, nevertheless, a minimal process of that kind is occurring. Many of the physical problems of a person under stress are directly attributable to this muscle tension and general bodily mobilization. In all kinds of stress, it is not the fight-or-flight response; it is the preparation for fight or flight.

Interestingly, this also may account for why anxious or nervous people tap their fingers, wiggle their foot, or pace. Tense muscles produce a freeze reaction, and finger tapping or nervous leg and foot movements are primitive ways of relieving that tension. They relieve the tension of the freeze reaction slightly but in a satisfying way.[5] (Incidentally, the information about finger tapping and foot wiggling is very useful in determining whether a person is tense, as it is an unerring sign. Later in the book I will show how we can join this idea with the use of exercise in order to relieve tension, or with massage or even with something so minor as worry beads that can be fingered.)

The Interaction of Energy and Tension

Now let us apply this theoretical analysis to the way that energy and tension interact. Imagine our evolutionary ancestors completing their daily work requirements in a predatory environment, probably a common occurrence. Such conditions would demand that they complete their work quickly and efficiently so that they could seek safe surroundings. High-quality work perhaps would not be required, but rapid completion would be necessary.

With these conditions, we ask, What is the most functional background mood? We have seen how danger results in increased tension, thus keeping in our mind the need to be cautious. But to complete the necessary work, energy is also demanded. Thus the mood we have identified as tense-energy is associated with fast and efficient work, as it motivates action in the shortest time. Such a mood prevails when there is danger but when there still are adequate resources available to act. Looking at it in this way, we can understand why tension and energy occur together, influencing each other. It is part of our evolutionary inheritance.

We have also seen instances in which high levels of danger lead to the condition of tense-tiredness. Obviously, it isn't possible to maintain a fast pace indefinitely. Our resources decline, even though the danger may not. Thus there comes a point at which our waning resources require us to rest and recuperate, but at the same time we must remain wary of possible danger that may exist in our environment.

Tense-tiredness is exactly such a state, as it induces a conservation of resources, together with caution because of the possible danger. This is a vulnerable mood: There is danger, but we don't have sufficient resources to deal with it. However, a tense-tired mood is not exhaustion, and we still have some resources available. Yet exhaustion is approaching, and so the conservation of resources with possible replenishment must govern our behavior. Tense-tiredness inclines us to wait, to inhibit our activities and to conserve. However, because we have not yet been overtaken by exhaustion, the tension ensures that we will remain vigilant, on guard, so to speak.

We can apply this thinking to depression, not with certainty, but with analysis that makes sense. As we saw earlier, many, if not all, kinds of depression are states of tense-tiredness. When we are depressed, we don't have enough energy to deal with things effectively, and so we just wait. Our activity is diminished and we do very little. Yet our depression also has a cyclical time course, and eventually it is completed. Perhaps it is finished when an unconscious perception of the danger has diminished, or when our resources are eventually replenished sufficiently so that we are no longer tense-tired. In any event, the depression usually lifts after a time.

To make sense of depression, however, we must understand why a depressed person's thoughts and memories continuously focus on unpleasant past circumstances and thus reinforce the depressed mood. Why is it so difficult for him to think about the good things of life and to forget the negatives? A major part of the unpleasantness of depression often arises from the thoughts and memories that accompany this mood. But from an evolutionary perspective, why would it be adaptive to have congruent moods and thoughts? It is a puzzle that scientists have been trying to tease apart.

A possibility consistent with the model of mood we have been considering is that the depressed person in effect is trying to detect the danger that put him in the depressed mood in the first place. The process is not unlike that of the anxious person who experiences scattered thoughts and is unable to concentrate. Perhaps when depressed, a person attempts to scan his memories for comparable circumstances and thus to understand the bases of the troubled condition. The increased tense arousal of depression signals the individual that there is danger, and so he continuously reviews past negative life circumstances until he locates the danger.

Moreover, this scanning process has a certain urgency because the depleted resources inhibit the person's ability to deal with daily requirements. The reason for the scanning probably lies at an unconscious level, and so the depressed person is unable to say why his thoughts are always negative. Although this explanation may not seem to be complete, in evolutionary contexts we often argue that a distant biological purpose can motivate behavior, even though scientists do not yet understand the immediate psychological mechanisms by which this motivation occurs. (Biologists speak of distal influences and proximal mechanisms of action.)

In this evolutionary analysis of complex moods, let us next consider calm-energy. Since energy is an action, or go, system and since the calmness of this mood indicates no danger, calm-energy predisposes us to continue our activity without hesitation. This is why I said that calm-energy is an optimal mood. The energy predisposes action, and the absence of tension ensures that motor activity and concentration will be sufficient for the task at hand.

But why would high energy be associated with low tension? To answer this question, let us return to the example of our evolutionary ancestor. Suppose that as she stands frozen surveying the environment for the source of danger, she realizes that a saber-toothed tiger is dangerously close. At this point, it is no longer functional to remain frozen. Now she must dash to safety without restraint. To make her escape, she calls on resources from every part of her body. The action system must be fully activated, and the stop system turned off. Energy must replace fear. The mood pattern represented is high energy and low tension; thus calm-energy would be the most functional mood in these circumstances.

A more prosaic but similar analysis of calm-energy focuses on high resources, perhaps brought about by the time of day or exercise or through other ways in which energy is elevated. When energy is at its highest, danger is less of a problem, as one can deal with it more easily. In fact, as I indicated earlier, tension occurs when requirements exceed resources. But calm-energy is a state in which our resources are sufficient to handle any problem. When we experience calm-energy in our daily lives, we are ready to take on a challenge, which may take the form of intense mental concentration or demanding physical activity.

In these various examples, I have spoken of tension and energy in a general sense as stop-and-go systems.[6] Combinations of these states represent varying degrees of action, partial action, caution, or full restraint. In the broadest perspective, these systems are based on resources, depletions, and danger, and moods are signal systems that inform us of these processes.

Exhaustion

To complete this brief analysis of the functional biology of mood interactions, let us now consider exhaustion. I believe that this condition has a definite biological function. To understand it, recall that before exhaustion occurs, declining resources first produce tense-tiredness. Tense-tiredness signals restraint coupled with caution. In such a state, sleep is reduced or eliminated. Thus, a tense-tired person needs rest but cannot get to sleep. A full conservation and replenishment of resources is inhibited. But there comes a point at which the body can no longer tolerate the declining resources. If one goes without sleep long enough, death or serious disability will finally result.[7] Therefore, at some point of declining resources, the tension that has prevented sleep must be eliminated to enable rest. As I have described it earlier, this is the mood pattern of exhaustion: As energy declines, first tension increases but finally it declines as well.

During exhaustion, in the final defense against death or serious disability, tension is relieved. The tense mood that maintained wakefulness lest danger overcome is eliminated. An exhausted person is not fearful, anxious, nervous, or tense; instead, he or she is calm. This may only be temporary, but nonetheless It produces some needed sleep and recouperation.

Conscious Awareness

Throughout this analysis, I have maintained that moods make us aware of some basic states. But from an evolutionary perspective, there is a larger issue here, our very capacity for a conscious awareness of moods. I mention this here because later when we apply these abstract ideas, conscious awareness of moods will become very important.

How does our state of conscious awareness fit into the model of mood that we have been considering? Moods are often judged by behavior, but first and foremost, moods are registered in consciousness. Our evolutionary heritage ensured that we would be able to discriminate and report on our mood states. Like other complex systems of the body, this awareness is not likely to be an accident but evolved because it served an adaptive function.

As we have seen in this chapter, our need to assess bodily conditions and decide on actions makes it useful to know whether we are energized, tired, tense, or calm. These decisions include modifying immediate behavior and planning for the future. This awareness of moods also allows us to communicate with others, and that is important. We are, after all, social animals.

However, conscious awareness and the ability to describe moods clearly is an evolutionarily advanced activity. It is likely to emanate from the activities of the cerebral cortex, the most recently evolved structure of the nervous system. Research on conscious awareness and systematic self-reports of moods demonstrates that under appropriate circumstances people are excellent reporters of these states.[8] This ability to observe one's own mood, report it, and make judgments about it is important in a practical sense. As will become apparent in the last part of this book, it forms the basis of how well we manage our moods. We have within us all the instruments for optimal self-awareness and development, the product of our evolutionary development. But these tools are often left unused. Later we will explain how this natural ability for self-awareness can be developed further for the best management of mood.

8

The Physiology and Anatomy of Mood

So far, we have looked at the physiology and psychology of moods, without carefully examining the complex physiological concepts. Now I will be more explicit.

Some years ago, I set up a psychophysiological laboratory to study how a variety of physiological processes correlate with conscious awareness. The main problem with which my students and I were concerned was the wider relationships among different physiological and psychological systems of the body. We wished to know how closely these systems were related to one another. On a theoretical level, a correlation among systems would indicate that the body is organized in wide-ranging patterns—multilevel arousal systems, for example. On a practical level, if our moods indicate our body's physiology and if we can accurately read those moods, we can learn a lot.

One thing we discovered in this early research was that systematic self-ratings of undifferentiated arousal correlated fairly well with simultaneous measures of various physiological processes that indicate arousal. In other words, given the proper conditions and the best methods of self-rating, people can sense and rate their *degree* of bodily arousal. These kinds of moods can be read with some accuracy, and they indicate something important about the underlying physiology. (Incidentally, the self-ratings were better indications of the change in arousal than were individual physiological measures.[1])

In this research, a common procedure was to study volunteers for about an hour at a time. We continuously monitored a variety of physiological functions and asked our subjects to make systematic self-ratings of how they felt. We made our first assessments when people were calm and relaxed and additional assessments following some activating stimulation. In one often-cited study, the subjects first sat quietly during a baseline period while different measures of physiological arousal were taken.[2] Then they rapidly counted backwards from 100 by sevens. At the same time a loud buzzer was sounded, and the subjects were repeatedly urged to hurry. We simultaneously assessed their heart rate, skin conductance, finger blood volume, and muscle tension (electrical muscle action potentials). The subjects also made systematic self-ratings of arousal. Not surprisingly, we found that the subjects changed from a calm and slightly tired state in the relaxed condition to a state in which they were tense and energized (tense-energy). When activated, the relaxed subjects became aroused in many different ways. Their hearts speeded up, and greater amounts of blood flowed to different parts of their bodies. They began to sweat, and their muscles became tense. This was a general arousal response.[3]

This physiological activation involves many systems of the body that are basic to various moods, particularly to different arousal-related moods. This general arousal response is a whole-body phenomenon, extending from the biochemical level to conscious awareness, and includes the cardiovascular, respiratory, and skeletal–muscular systems. Mood appears to be the conscious component of this activation. In this sense, mood is one part of a larger psychophysiological system.

Most bodily systems are in their lowest state of activation when we are near sleep or sleeping or when we are awake but completely relaxed. Conversely, during periods when we are most alert or intensely emotional or during physical activity, most of the systems of the body are activated.[4] Together with other physiological systems, mood reflects either low arousal (calmness, tiredness, and related states) or high arousal (energy, tension and related states).

Although moods accurately reflect the degree of arousal, there are no commonly accepted physiological markers that differentiate high-tension moods from high-energy moods, especially when a person is physically active. The bodily demands involving motor activities—and particularly the large muscles of the body—result in general patterns of arousal whether the individual feels tension or energy. Energetic and tense arousal are difficult to distinguish physiologically, as are different mood patterns indicating combined high and low arousal. For example, there are no unambiguous physiological markers of conditions such as depression that usually represent the state I call tense-tiredness. Nor is there a good understanding of the exact physiological bases of high energetic arousal and low tense arousal (calm-energy).

A good example of the complexity and misunderstanding of the physiology underlying different moods concerns adrenaline (also known as *epinephrine*). In popular discussions, this substance is usually associated only with stress and anxiety conditions (tense arousal). People commonly speak of an adrenaline response in times of stress, or one hears the phrase "acting on adrenaline" in reference to behavior during periods of exhaustion when heroic activity is demanded. But as we shall see, a good case can be made that adrenaline is more responsible for energetic arousal than for tense arousal, although it is important to both. This multipurpose substance raises glucose levels and speeds up metabolism and heart rate, among its other functions. Thus, an athlete exercising and experiencing calm-energy has high levels of circulating adrenaline.

Having indicated that there is disagreement about the physiological underpinnings of many moods, I next describe some of the physiological systems thought by various scientists to play a part in mood responses. These systems are the best candidates, so to speak, for an understanding of the psychophysiological dynamics of mood. I should remind you that this book is not meant to provide a detailed account of the anatomy and physiology of mood, but I would like at least to touch on the physiological systems about which there is frequent speculation.

Biochemistry of Brain and Mood Relationships

Virtually every knowledgeable scientist studying mood acknowledges the existence of biochemical substrates and also the important role of the brain. But no one is quite certain how this process works or exactly what the biochemical substrates are. When we look at the chemistry of the brain in relation to mood, we see a bewildering array of processes. As a result, the research is so wide ranging and complex that a hundred good hypotheses may be offered for the neurochemical bases of mood.

In my view, at present the only central physiological processes that can be *reliably* described in relation to mood are general arousal responses. More specific neurochemical bases of particular moods may be identified, and in the future it is likely that they will be. But the current state of the science offers reliable identifications only of general arousal patterns.[5]

One major problem concerning mood is that most of the biochemical research on the brain uses animals, usually rats. It should be obvious that this kind of research, while valuable in many respects, presents substantial difficulties in studying human moods, particularly subtle mood variations. In addition, the behavioral researchers who do most of the studies on everyday moods usually do not have access to the complex biochemical procedures necessary for firm conclusions about the physiology of these processes.[6]

Speculations about the biochemistry of mood often arise only indirectly. For instance, certain clinical conditions such as depression respond positively to a class of drugs, which are thought to have particular biochemical pathways of action (usually worked out in animal research). But this process is indirect and uncertain. Instead of discoveries of new drugs arising from a good understanding of the neurophysiology underlying mood, useful drugs frequently are discovered inadvertently or accidentally, but they are used by physicians because they work.

For example, iproniazid, the first antidepressant drug (MAO inhibitor) was originally developed to treat tuberculosis, and imipramine, the first tricyclic antidepressant, was originally developed as an antischizophrenic agent. The value of lithium, a substance commonly used to treat manic states, was developed to test a theory that the urine of manic patients would induce mania. Psychiatrist John Cade

used lithium as a soluble salt for injection of the urine. Only incidentally did he find that the lithium had a calming effect. The discovery
of all these drugs did not arise from a good understanding of the
biochemistry of mood, but this fact does not make the drugs less
useful.[7] Nonetheless, it is an indication of the limitations of our current understanding of mood disorders.

Although a number of drugs may be moderately effective in controlling negative moods, the evidence regarding the causal biochemistry of mood still is imperfect, because there can be many reasons
that a drug works besides the major biochemical pathways that are
thought to exist for particular substances. For example, interactions
of biochemical substrates may be responsible for the drug effect. Another problem with biochemical speculations following help from a
particular class of drugs is that these drugs often work only after
weeks on a maintenance diet, although their physiological effects result within hours of ingestion. Thus, the positive mood effects apparently occur for reasons other than the immediate physiological effects
of the drugs.[8] Finally, even the best of these antidepressant drugs
relieve depression only in a small percentage of cases, compared with
placebos.

In any event, a number of biochemical systems are likely to be important to arousal-related moods. This influence occurs at the level
of the *synapse*, a small space between the *neurons*, which form the
biological "hardwire" necessary for the electrochemical transmission
of information in the brain and elsewhere. Biochemical substances
selectively enhance and reduce synaptic transmission after they are
synthesized and secreted by the transmitting neurons and bind to
specialized receptors of receiving neurons.

Early in the century, scientists assumed that neurons directly influence one another by sending small electrical impulses, almost like the
electrical wiring in a house. We now know, however, that most of the
time minute amounts of chemical substances, called *neurotransmitters* and *neuromodulators*, generally transmit nerve impulses across
the synapse between neurons. After the impulse is transmitted, most
of the substance is reabsorbed to be used again. This is important to
understanding mood, partly because many medical conditions and
drugs can enhance or reduce the neurotransmitters at certain brain
sites, either directly or by preventing their re-uptake.

Three of these neurotransmitters that have been most closely linked to mood are norepinephrine, dopamine, and serotonin. (Based on their composition involving a single amino acid, these substances are called *monoamines*. Because of their chemical makeup, the first two are *catecholamines*, and serotonin is an *indolamine*. They also are called *biogenic amines*.) Although there may well be a relationship between moods and certain neurotransmitters, our knowledge of these biochemical bases of mood still is at an early stage. For example, there have been many studies, mostly with animals, of only a few of the hundreds of the potentially relevant neurotransmitters, not to mention the even greater number of interactions among neurotransmitters and among neural receptors.[9]

Norepinephrine

Norepinephrine appears to be associated with activated states, and thus it probably underlies both energetic and tense arousal. It is likely, for example, that exercise increases the release of norepinephrine in the brain as well as in other areas of the body.[10] Norepinephrine also is associated with the waking state. Furthermore, stressful circumstances result in a greater release of norepinephrine.[11] In addition, activating drugs such as cocaine and amphetamine probably have their major biochemical effect through increased catecholamine activity, especially that of norepinephrine and dopamine.[12]

The greatest amount of research and speculation about brain norepinephrine in relation to mood comes from analyses of depression. The early catecholamine theory of depression maintained that this negative state arises from a relative deficiency of catecholamines, particularly norepinephrine, at important receptor sites in the brain. Conversely, elation presumably results from excess levels of norepinephrine.[13] Some research has indicated that people diagnosed with depression show lower levels of norepinephrine, as evidenced by the breakdown products in their blood.[14] It also has been observed that reserpine, a drug that is used to treat hypertension and that depletes norepinephrine, increases depression. In addition, drugs such as monoamine oxidase inhibitors and tricyclic compounds, which are thought to increase the relative proportion of central norepinephrine at relevant synapses, have a beneficial effect on depression.

The catecholamine theory of depression is theoretically consistent with the model described in this book. For example, depression invariably reduces energetic arousal. Thus, studies showing that low levels of catecholamines are associated with depression suggest that these monoamines are related to arousal. Despite these positive indications, the catecholamine theory of depression has not fared especially well in further study. Part of the problem with this theory is that patients often do not improve from norepinephrine-enhancing antidepressants until they have taken the drug for several weeks. But the physiological effect in the brain is almost immediate. Another problem is that the catecholamine-enhancing drugs such as cocaine and amphetamines do not improve clinical depression.[15] In addition, newer antidepressants such as fluoxetine (e.g., Prozac) improve depression, even though they do not primarily affect norepinephrine.

Dopamine

Most of these mood-related characteristics in regard to norepinephrine also apply to dopamine, a closely related catecholamine, though they do differ. Dopamine once was thought to be only a precursor of norepinephrine, that is, a substance from which norepinephrine is formed. But dopamine is now known to be found in anatomically distinct neurons, and in certain ways it appears to have a functional role separate from that of norepinephrine.[16] For a number of reasons this neurotransmitter is likely to be especially important to arousal-related moods.

As only one indication of the significance of dopamine to mood, neurons activated by this monoamine appear to be among the most important parts of the brain stem's reticular formation, a complex network in the center of the brain.[17] This anatomical structure is believed to play a central part in general bodily arousal, including sleep–wakefulness and motor activity.[18] Through its influence in different parts of the brain, dopamine appears to be crucial to various kinds of motor behavior and to circadian rhythmicity.[19] As I indicated, these processes are at the heart of energetic arousal.

In other mood-related respects, dopaminergic (dopamine) systems are likely to be important bases of the pleasurable aspects of cocaine ingestion and of the kind of pleasurable self-stimulation in the brain that has been demonstrated with implanted electrodes in animals.[20] In general, dopamine could be at the base of many positive emotional states.[21] But this neurotransmitter may also be central to brain responses associated with anxiety and stress.[22] Because of these various characteristics, dopamine seems to be related to both energetic and tense arousal.[23]

Serotonin

Serotonin is a likely biochemical underpinning of mood and particularly of energetic arousal, as well as a likely modulator of general arousal states involving wakefulness compared with sleep. During wakefulness, serotonergic (serotonin) neurons in the brain are most active with general motor activity and other kinds of behavioral arousal.[24] Drugs that activate serotonergic systems in the brain also result in decreased depression. These characteristics suggest an underpinning for energetic arousal. In other respects, behaviors that are associated with serotonin also are associated with energetic arousal. For example, increased central serotonin apparently suppresses eating.[25] This association with energetic arousal is particularly relevant if we assume that increasing energy levels, or the related diminished tension levels, signal a reduced need for food.

The reciprocal interaction between energetic and tense arousal also suggests an important function for serotonin. For example, the pattern of high tense arousal and low energetic arousal that is part of the mood model featured in this book has a possible neurochemical parallel with that of serotonin. Although serotonergic neural activity is unchanged during many stressful circumstances, unlike the activation of neural systems associated with norepinephrine and dopamine, serotonin does appear to play a role in curtailing the sort of violent and impulsive behavior that could be mediated by tense arousal. [26]In a way, serotonin seems to act as a "stop system" for certain negative emotional behaviors. These relationships involving serotonin are similar to the reciprocal relationships of energetic and tense arousal.

Another association of serotonin with energetic arousal comes from drug-related findings concerning this neurotransmitter. Serotonin was a part of many news reports about Prozac, the so-called wonder drug (the competing drugs Zoloft and Paxil are now also available). Prozac was prominently featured in a 1994 issue of *Newsweek* and numerous other media outlets.[27] This drug is thought to work in part because it selectively reduces the re-uptake of serotonin at the level of brain synapses.[28] In effect, this results in greater concentrations of serotonin in certain synaptic areas of the brain. Prozac has proved particularly valuable because it has few undesirable side effects.

The positive therapeutic results of Prozac seem to suggest that serotonin plays an important role in mood, or at least in depression. But the importance of Prozac, and thus of serotonin as a basis of mood, is by no means clear. For example, careful scientific studies in which the subjects do not know whether they are taking Prozac or a placebo indicate that Prozac provides about the same relief from depression as other, older antidepressants do, and these other antidepressants appear not to have the primary effect of increased serotonin concentrations.[29]

As a case in point, clinical trials comparing Prozac and the older antidepressant imipramine showed similar beneficial effects on depression.[30] In fact, imipramine was actually slightly more effective in combating depression, although it had more negative side effects. This finding is relevant to our discussion because imipramine appears to work primarily by blocking the re-uptake of norepinephrine while also affecting the neurotransmitter serotonin.[31] So the neurochemistry is more complicated than it may appear.

Because Prozac has received so much public attention, let us consider it a bit further. Some people suffering from major depression are able to get relief from this drug (in one typical study, a little over 60 percent benefited from Prozac, compared with a little less than 40 percent with a placebo[32]). This suggests that energy is raised by greater serotonin activation. However, the known side effects of Prozac mean that it also may increase tension in some people. In fact, the side effects of Prozac include nervousness, insomnia, and other indications of tension.[33] Looking at the drug in this way, Prozac seems to result in either calm-energy or tense-energy. In any event, either state is likely to relieve depression, at least temporarily.[34]

But why do some people experience such dramatic effects from Prozac? In an influential best-selling book, *Listening to Prozac*, psychiatrist Peter Kramer indicated that in many of his patients the drug resulted in basic personality changes.[35] This kind of change may be possible if a person taking the drug begins to experience different reactions of energy and tension in a variety of situations in which those reactions were previously absent or muted. It is as though these emotional reactions, which provide efficient feedback for normal people, are activated in the formerly depressed person once the drug takes effect. Such activation would result in different learned adaptations over time. In this way of thinking, the drug does not affect personality traits directly. Instead, the healthy reactions of energy and tension gradually make changes in personality traits.

Endorphins

I want to mention one other class of neurotransmitter, not because it is important to mood, but because of the common perception that it is important. The chemical structure of opiates (including heroin, morphine, and codeine) is similar to that of certain naturally occurring peptide neurotransmitters—in particular, the endorphins (short for endogenous morphines and including enkephalins). Researchers have discovered that these opioids seem to counteract the effects of extreme stress and pain.[36]

Scientists have theorized that these endorphins produce feelings of pleasure in extreme situations. This, in turn, has led to popular beliefs that endorphins are behind all kinds of positive moods. However, the evidence for such mood effects is quite limited. (In a humorous example of how widespread this belief is, a character in the movie *Postcards from the Edge* tells Meryl Streep about her sexual escapades, and says that she is "in it for the ENDOLPHIN rush.")

In many sections of this book, I talk about the mood-enhancing effects of exercise, particularly moderate exercise. Because of the popular beliefs about endorphins, many people assume that moderate exercise has a pleasurable effect because of the release of these substances. But there is little evidence that the pleasurable effects of moderate exercise come from endorphins. Although intense exercise may be associated with endorphins, even here the evidence is mixed.[37] Other explanations for the pleasurable effects of exercise are more likely, although the role of endorphins cannot be ruled out on the basis of current research.

In this part of the chapter, we have briefly considered only the most widely discussed elements of the neurochemistry of mood, including norepinephrine, dopamine, serotonin, and endorphins, but there is a great deal more that we did not mention. In sum, we are left with much speculation and lots of questions. In the future these matters will be understood.[38] But at present I can only repeat a statement made at the beginning of this section: Knowledgeable scientists assume mood is linked to the biochemistry of our brain—the chemical soup of neurotransmitters we have looked at briefly in this chapter. Unfortunately, no one is quite sure how these transmittters in our brain combine to create what we experience as mood.

Hormones as a Basis for Mood

Adrenaline and Cortisol

Although most arousal states are associated with high levels of catecholamines (e.g., norepinephrine) in certain parts of the brain, the various moods that I have described may be differentiated by hormones in other parts of the body. For example, Richard Dienstbier of the University of Nebraska identified two systems of arousal that he believes are similar to energetic and tense arousal.[39] He sees these two arousal systems as having different functions and different effects on behavior.

In his intriguing theory, Dienstbier describes one arousal system that involves the hypothalamus, a small structure in the central part of the brain, and the sympathetic nervous system, a peripheral network of nerves that influence internal organs that prepare the body for vigorous activity.[40] The sympathetic nervous system affects the adrenal medulla, a gland that lies just above the kidneys and is responsible for the release of adrenaline. This adrenaline response results in "desirable forms of energy at minimal psychological cost."[41]

In many respects this arousal system appears to parallel energetic arousal. For example, adrenaline levels are closely associated with the intensity and effort of exercise, and in a wide variety of ways adrenaline is known to enhance the exercise response.[42] Moreover, as Dienstbier maintains, this adrenaline response to demand tends to become more efficient with activities such as regular exercise that "toughen" the exerciser.[43] These are exactly the characteristics of energetic arousal.

The second arousal system that Dienstbier identified may be basic to the experience of tension, in that it is activated in stress and emergency circumstances.[44] This system is associated with hypothalamic stimulation of the pituitary, a kind of master gland about the size of a pea that lies at the base of the brain. Among other hormones, the pituitary influences the release of adrenocorticotropin (ACTH), which in turn affects the adrenal cortex, a part of the pituitary gland. In this way, cortisol is released.

A large cortisol response has special implications for understanding mood because abnormal cortisol levels have been found in people with certain kinds of depression. Excessive cortisol secretions occur in 40 to 60 percent of depressed patients.[45] Many researchers believe that dysregulation of the hypothalamic–pituitary–adrenal system is a biological indicator of affective disorder.[46]

One physiological test that has been used to diagnose depression is the dexamethasone suppression test (DST). About half the patients with major depressive disorders show a lack of cortisol suppression by normal inhibitory processes in the body following an earlier injection of the synthetic steroid dexamethasone.[47] This indicates that the body does not adequately control cortisol levels. On the other hand, nondepressed persons show normal suppression. There has been some hope that the DST would be the long-sought physiological test of depression, but unfortunately, it has not proved to be a conclusive indicator because many people diagnosed with depression have a negative DST result.

Insulin and Blood Glucose

Research has demonstrated correlations between increased blood glucose levels and feelings of energy with reduced tension.[48] This strongly suggests that central moods are related to blood-sugar levels.

An especially convincing demonstration of this relationship was offered by Ian Deary, Ann Gold, David Hepburn, and their colleagues at the University of Edinburgh.[49] They were studying hypoglycemia, an abnormal condition in which the body is unable to maintain enough glucose in the blood to sustain the brain and other vital organ functions. Under blind conditions, this group manipulated blood glucose over several hours by means of infusions of insulin. The subjects began with a normal state and then shifted to a hypoglycemic state before returning to a normal state. Insulin and placebo infusions were randomly employed so subjects could not know what they had been given. The effects were quite dramatic. The investigators were able to drive tension up and energy down during the hypoglycemic states, which were maintained for an hour. Following the reintroduction of normal glucose levels, energy and tension converged as they had before the introduction of insulin.

Besides demonstrating an important physiological basis for energy and tension feelings, these findings suggest a reason for the tendency of people to seek sugar snacks when their energy is low and their tension is high (tense-tiredness). In other words, as people sense low energy levels and increased tension, they seek an immediate remedy in sugar snacking. We already have behavioral evidence for this—we know what people do—but the physiological basis has been more difficult to demonstrate.

Arousal-Related Anatomical Structures

It is clear that there are neurochemical bases for one or more generalized arousal systems. Subject to some interpretation, these systems appear to be parallel, and possibly to underlie, the mood systems that I named *energetic* and *tense arousal*. Various parts of the brain and peripheral systems of the body contain anatomical structures that are largely associated with the neurochemical systems just described and that undoubtedly are part of those arousal responses.

Reticular Activating System

One structure that probably mediates both kinds of arousal, but especially energetic arousal, is the reticular activating system. This was so named by neuroanatomists because of the netlike appearance of the tiny nuclei that occupy the central core of the brain stem. In evolutionary terms, this is an old and very basic neural structure, as it influences the elemental functions of sleep, wakefulness, motor activity, and general bodily arousal. (The raphe nuclei, which produce serotonin, and the neurochemical systems associated with norepinephrine and dopamine are major elements of this part of the brain.[50] These multiple neurochemical systems indicate that more than one kind of arousal is mediated by this part of the brain.)

Limbic System

If the reticular formation has a particular influence on energetic arousal, a case can be made that the limbic system plays a primary role in tense arousal. This system of interconnected structures (e.g., the hypothalamus, amygdala) lies in the center of the brain below the cerebral cortex. It influences many vital functions in the body (e.g., the autonomic and somatic areas) and also the cerebral cortex, the outermost portion of the brain that is most evolved in humans.[51] It is sometimes joked that the limbic system regulates the four Fs of motivated behavior: fleeing, feeding, fighting, and sexual behavior.

For purposes of this discussion, I should point out that a great deal of research underscores the importance of this brain system in emotional behavior, especially in regard to the fear responses that are so much a part of tense arousal. Fear and anxiety are mediated by various parts of the brain, including the prefrontal cortex and the endocrine connections of the hypothalamus, though the limbic system plays an integral part.[52]

Given the likelihood that many parts of the brain contribute to both arousal systems, it is too simple to assert that the reticular activating system mediates energetic arousal and that the limbic system mediates tense arousal. However, because the types of behavior that these systems influence are so central to the two kinds of arousal, I would say that the reticular activating system must be involved in a major way with energetic arousal, as is the limbic system with tense arousal. If that is the case, there is ample evidence of excitatory and inhibitory influences between the two brain structures to account for the positive and negative relationships between energy and tension.[53]

Cerebral Cortex

Two hemispheres of the cerebral cortex may mediate different kinds of arousal-related moods. This is evident from observations of stroke victims who suffer damage to the left cerebral cortex near the frontal pole.[54] Such people are especially likely to be depressed.

Evidence consistent with this phenomenon can be found in studies of electrical impulses (EEGs) emanating from the cortex that indicate that right frontal asymmetry is associated with negative emotions. (Strokes in the left frontal area may reduce activation in that portion of the brain and result in unopposed activity in the right.) Conversely, left-hemisphere asymmetry is associated with positive emotions.[55] Nathan Fox and Richard Davidson have proposed an interesting model of cerebral differentiation in which approach tendencies occur with left asymmetry and avoidance tendencies with right asymmetry.[56] The behaviors that Fox and Davidson classify with these two tendencies suggest close parallels with energetic and tense arousal.

An additional point related to cerebral asymmetry is that there are complex interactions between the lower brain structures and cerebral cortical processes.[57] Thus, mediation of energetic and tense arousal at the level of reticular and limbic systems may interact with cerebral mediation. In these complex interactions, it is possible to see why thoughts are closely associated with moods.

Autonomic Nervous System

An important mediator of arousal—but in this case both energetic and tense arousal—is the autonomic nervous system. One of two reciprocal branches of this peripheral nervous system (sympathetic) is responsible for organizing, mobilizing, and expending energy, and the other branch (parasympathetic) is associated with conserving energy.[58]

Many different parts of the body are influenced by sympathetic nervous system activation, including respiration, heart rate, vasomotor tone, blood pressure, carbohydrate and fatty acid metabolism, and sweat gland activity. As can be seen from these examples among the many elements of sympathetic activation, this part of the nervous system is an important part of the response to any kind of bodily demand, including exercise, stress, and strong negative and positive emotional prompts.

Parasympathetic activation, on the other hand, generally balances sympathetic activation. Usually, both systems are usually active at the same time, but their relative balance sets the tone of bodily arousal. Parasympathetic effects are quite varied, including such processes as decreased heart rate, constriction of the bronchi of the lungs, and increased digestive activity. These and other bodily functions that occur with parasympathetic dominance are present during periods of low tense and energetic arousal, periods associated with energy conservation and recuperation.

Although a great deal of psychological research has employed indexes of sympathetic activation in relation to studies of negative emotions (e.g., anxiety), it would be a mistake to accept these physiological measures as unique indicants of tense arousal. Instead, they indicate general bodily arousal. The sympathetic nervous system is activated during exercise and the associated energetic arousal, as well as during stress, anxiety, and many other kinds of bodily demand. This system dominates when there is bodily mobilization in a wide variety of circumstances.

Skeletal-Muscular System

I stated earlier that skeletal–muscular tension is likely to be involved in tense arousal. In particular, the freeze response is a characteristic pattern that can be observed in lesser form in an anxious person through tight muscles in the back, neck, face, and other parts of the body. For this and other reasons I have argued that one primary difference between tense arousal and energetic arousal is skeletal–muscular tension of the sort that contributes to an inhibitory pattern.

Tense-tiredness could be based on a mechanism associated with skeletal–muscular tension. Moreover, this physiological mechanism may explain why moderate exercise reduces tension and increases energy. Fear, anxiety, or nervousness are characterized by muscle tension with an absence of directed motor activity and also by shallow and uneven respiration. This pattern of muscle strain and inadequate oxygen consumption points to a process that exercise physiologists call *anaerobic energy metabolism*.[59]

Anaerobic metabolic processes occur when a person engages in rapid, emergencylike actions, such as running up two flights of stairs as fast as possible or making a 50-yard dash at top speed. It is also involved in isometric tension exercises, which hold muscles tightly for a minute or so. The latter example suggests a kind of muscle tension, particularly for certain muscle groups in the shoulders, neck, and back, that may be similar to what occurs at high levels of tense arousal.

At the physiological level, anaerobic metabolism—which breaks down energy stored in tissue as quickly as possible to supply the muscles—results in a rapid increase in the production of lactic acid and some reduction in energy supplies (e.g., creatine phosphate and glycogen). It results in subjective fatigue fairly quickly but not immediately. The exact physiological basis for fatigue is not clear, but it probably occurs because this type of metabolism operates without oxygen and is a very inefficient energy supply system. The increases in lactic acid are particularly noteworthy due to the possible association of blood lactate with symptoms of anxiety.[60]

Thus the anaerobic processes that may be associated with skeletal–muscular tension (uneven breathing that produces an oxygen deficiency, rapidly occurring fatigue, and increased lactic acid formation) suggest tense arousal. Using this metabolic process to explain fatigue and tension is attractive because it also could account for the effect of exercise in reducing tension. The mechanism for this is a second kind of energy metabolism, *aerobic metabolism*.

Unlike the anaerobic supply system, the aerobic metabolism is much more efficient. It utilizes oxygen and can draw on a wide base of carbohydrate, fat, and protein sources. Although anaerobic metabolism can produce a large amount of energy rapidly, as might be necessary in an emergency, the energy supply cannot be sustained, possibly because of the excessive accumulation of lactic acid in the muscles. Aerobic metabolism, on the other hand, is a slower supply system, but it can efficiently break down the acidic by-products of the anaerobic activities as well as utilize wider sources of energy. This may account for the increased feelings of energy that result from moderate exercise.

Using these two metabolic processes to explain the reciprocal relationship between energetic and tense arousal seems valid intuitively, but this explanation still has problems. Anaerobic metabolism is usually related to short-term maximal exercise. This metabolic process has not been investigated very much in relation to muscle tension of the sort that characterizes anxiety. Nevertheless, the metabolic process explanation remains promising.

Other Bases of General Bodily Arousal

Because of the limited scope of this book, it is not possible to review many other systems of the body associated with arousal and thus with mood. For instance, basic metabolic processes are involved in all arousal responses. The cardiovascular and respiratory systems are absolutely basic to arousal states. Many unmentioned elements of the endocrine system also interact. Consider all the arousal-related processes associated with sleep, wakefulness, physical activity, emotional response, and, in general, health and illness. These biological processes are intrinsic to mood, and most of the complex mechanisms of the body contribute to these processes.

This brief review of selected portions of the physiology and anatomy of arousal should have made clear that there are many unanswered questions. The two major arousal systems posited in this book as basic to mood undoubtedly are mediated by many parts of the body. There are promising possibilities for identifying physiological differentiators of energetic and tense arousal and, furthermore, for identifying complex states such as tense-tiredness and calm-energy. But certainty about these remains in the future. At the present time, the only reliable statements that we can make about the physiological causes of mood must focus on patterns of general bodily arousal. But aside from these general patterns, the psychological dynamics of mood are clearer at present than the physiological bases.

PART TWO

The Self-Regulation of Mood

9

Self-Regulation: Why, How, and How Effective?

Moods intrude into our consciousness, and bad moods often motivate us to take action.[1] But neutral moods may also result in action—usually, behaviors that will make us feel even better. This is an elemental process that underlies much of our behavior, which is actually nothing less than the principle that people seek pleasure and avoid pain. Variations of this motivational view have been apparent for thousands of years, and most human behavior follows this pattern.

Whether we are conscious of it or not, moods motivate us. We regularly notice our feelings and attempt to regulate or change them. If our mood is bad, we may try to control our thoughts, seek out a friend, find something good to eat, have a cup of coffee, drink some wine, or any of a wide range of other behaviors. The possibilities are numerous and largely unique to a person's own experience and personality.

This mood-regulation process probably occurs at a low level of awareness while it is happening. We often act impulsively, on the spur of the moment, with little awareness of why we are raiding the refrigerator or taking a walk. But it is possible to recognize these relationships. The research that I describe in this and the following chapters makes clear that once a pattern develops, thoughtful people can identify behaviors or strategies that they regularly use to control their moods.

Let me be more specific. Obviously, there are many reasons that we eat, drink, socialize, and watch TV, but at least some of the motivation for these and many other acts is to regulate our moods. Slowly, over time, we associate various things that we do with feeling good, which prompts us to continue or expand that activity. We also learn to avoid doing things that lead to negative feelings. In this way, we develop habits that help us feel better.

With mood in mind, we can understand many undesirable behaviors—actions that may seem automatic and uncontrollable but that really follow a predictable pattern. That is, the undesirable behaviors persist because they help us regulate our moods. Once we accept this principle, many of our behaviors become more intelligible. For example, instead attributing our desire for sugar snacking to good taste or hunger satisfaction, we should focus on how we feel when the urge for the forbidden food is greatest. We should also notice that the snack causes us to feel good right after we eat it. The immediacy of these feelings is important.

Decades of psychological research on learning have shown that certain conditions stimulate a behavior and that a positive reinforcement which occurs immediately after the behavior teaches us, in a sense, to repeat the same sequence another time. In a way, we come to associate this behavior with emotional prompts and with good feelings afterward. Moreover, it may not be just an increase in good feelings that perpetuates a behavior; it may also be a reduction of bad feelings. Thus, certain mood states stimulate a behavior, and the behavior is continued if it produces less tension or good feelings (e.g., more energy).

When behaviors are reinforced by certain feelings over a long period of time, the habits they create become extremely resistant to change. Each time that doing something is reinforced, the habit is strengthened, especially if the reinforcement is consistent and immediate. During a lifetime, these habits can become so strong that changing them is very difficult, but it isn't impossible. The first step is to understand the dynamics of the process.

Consider this analysis in relation to illicit drugs. The use of these substances is viewed as a major social problem today, and vast amounts of money are devoted to curtailing this activity. Nonusers think of those who use drugs as driven by some kind of mysterious and irrational craving. Often lost in this thinking is the realization that people use drugs because they make them feel good. In other words, drugs are mood regulators, and this is a primary motivation for their use.[2]

Think of this idea in relation to cigarettes. Most addicted smokers want to stop, but they can't, because the mood regulation that cigarettes produce is too powerful. The problem is complicated. Smokers sometimes use cigarettes as a pick-me-up and at other times as a calm-me-down, so to speak. But in either case, feelings stimulate the craving, and the mood consequences of the nicotine control the behavior. Addicted smokers who try to stop thus encounter negative mood effects almost immediately. Their feelings tell them that they must have a smoke, and once they have a few drags, their feelings tell them that this is what they needed.

Mood effects can be used to understand alcohol use as well. I will illustrate this case in a slightly different way to make another point. Most people dislike the taste of alcohol when they first experience it. And yet with learning, it can become a sought-after substance. Slowly but surely, these positive mood effects influence the attractiveness of the alcohol. It is all part of the learning process. To understand the short-term motivation for drinking and especially problem drinking, think about the mood that is present when a decision is made to have a drink. Now consider the immediate effect of the alcohol on the mood of the drinker, as well as the effect some time later. Following this line of thinking, we can see how feelings often predispose a person to have a drink, and how the mood changes from the drink may encourage the continuation of the drinking behavior. Drinking takes place in an emotional context.

But it isn't only substance use that follows principles of mood regulation. Many habitual behaviors yield to the same analysis. For example, watching too much TV is another behavior that many people believe is a problem. The average American family watches more than six hours of TV a day.³ Why is this medium such a draw? Again, consider this activity in light of the relationship between TV watching and mood. Aside from interest in a particular program, think about the feelings that motivate us to turn on the TV and to continue watching it even if our interest lags. Instead of, say, picking up a book, we continue watching. To understand this behavior, we must notice our feelings when we turn on the TV and how the TV watching affects our moods, both immediately and over time. In each of these cases—smoking, alcohol use, and TV viewing—the motivation is complicated but understandable in the context of mood. Moods prompt us to act in a certain way or to eat or drink something. The immediate mood effects of the substance or behavior contribute to its habitual nature and sustain it.

From a wider perspective, it is clear that we allow many kinds of substances and activities to have the same control over us. In a sense, we are not just regulating behavior but also trying to maintain order in and control over our lives. Through mood-regulating habits, we structure our day in fundamental ways. This may include waking ourselves up in the morning with a cup of coffee and putting ourselves to sleep at night with some light TV watching, and many of the behaviors in between. In each case, the antecedents and consequences of the habits—the feelings that stimulate them and that they produce—keep the habits in place.

Management of Momentary Moods

In addition to mood-regulating behaviors that occur over time—such as sugar snacking, coffee drinking, socializing, and TV watching—mood also is regulated on a moment-to-moment basis. Recall my description in Chapter 7 of instantaneous assessments of mood levels and how they affect our most basic behaviors. We do this all the time, continuously sensing the energy we will need to complete a task, including very simple ones like getting up from a chair or walking fast or slow. We then adjust our effort level accordingly.

Similarly, we may judge ourselves to be too nervous for comfort or to complete some task. In response, we do something to get control. It might be a simple matter like telling ourselves to relax, or it might be more complex behaviors like stretching or taking a walk, things that have worked in the past to relax us. In any case, our moods are basic to the behaviors. This is an interactive process because not only do our energy and tension levels affect behavior but the behavior also affects these feelings.[4] This momentary assessment of and reaction to energy and tension are continuous activities that take place at a very basic level, but they operate in the same way as do more general strategies to control depression and other kinds of moods. Momentary assessments and reactions allow us to manage our behavior and most of our moods. This is the basis of mood regulation.

Mood Management and Awareness

At the most fundamental level, regulating mood is, first, noticing a mood and then taking corrective action to change it. Often this entails sensing the mood and at the same time, thinking about the behavior that could correct it. However, sensing a mood and thinking of a behavior to correct it may not be obvious, as we may be only dimly aware of some vague discomfort and react almost automatically. It is these low-awareness reactions that often are the most difficult to control.

Let us look at an example of low awareness with the moods that we have been discussing. In the case of low-level tension, for example, you may notice that you are tapping your fingers or wiggling your foot. Perhaps you become aware that your neck hurts or that you are especially impatient. Pains in your stomach or a tight jaw are other signs. Once you notice these signs of tension and recognize them for what they are, the feelings of tension should become obvious. You become aware of muscular tension throughout your body, your cognitive distraction, anxious thoughts, and, in general, your bad mood.

Such awareness is so complex that sometimes it is the behavior or substance that corrects the mood that is the clue to your negative feelings. For example, one of my students who is a particularly good self-observer indicated that she knows when she is tense because she thinks of ice cream. Before making this connection, she wasn't aware of her low-level tension. Instead, when she was tense, she simply started thinking about good-tasting food, and the thought often led her to eat some ice cream. In this example and others like it, even the lowest level of awareness can lead to self-regulating behaviors.

The same process applies to awareness of energy level. You may notice a feeling of weakness, especially after missing a meal, or you are too tired to do something that otherwise would be fun. Secondary signs of low energy such as sadness, bad feelings about yourself, and pessimistic viewpoints about the future also can be a clue.

There is a practical side to this discussion of awareness. If you can detect these connections in your own life, you can get to the bottom of some of your daily habits—ones that you may have vowed to break, like snacking, smoking, or drinking. This awareness gives us a certain amount of self-control. By recognizing this process, we can exercise what I call *cognitive override*. We can choose to change the conditions that produce a negative mood or to find a better way of correcting the negative mood than our customary undesirable habit.

The behavior we engage in to regulate our moods we probably learned from past experiences of what worked and what did not. But this is complicated because sometimes behaviors such as sugar snacking work only temporarily and not for very long. Accordingly, the temporary lift in mood we experience from sugar encourages us to continue snacking, even though it is counterproductive in the long run. On the other hand, better strategies for lifting mood, such as going for a walk, may appear to require too much effort at the moment, but they can be the most effective in the long run. This is when an awareness of delayed mood effects is particularly important and cognitive override is especially valuable.

The Basics of Mood Regulation

At its most basic, mood regulation really means raising and lowering your energy level and reducing your tension. Two practical implications follow from this. First, mood will become relatively easy to regulate if you learn to identify your energy and tension feelings. Without knowing what to notice, you can be overwhelmed by the vast amount of information your brain and body process at any one time. Second, once you realize that the important motivators for a particular habit are the moods that predispose it and the mood effects that the behavior produces, you can choose an alternative means of affecting these moods. For example, more healthy means of raising energy and reducing tension can be substituted for the bad habit you want to eliminate.

How Do People Regulate Their Moods?

Research Findings

Exactly how do people self-regulate their moods? Moreover, what works, and what does not? Finally, do some people regulate their moods in different ways than others do; for example, is there a difference between men and women? These are some of the subjects we shall turn to now. Over the past several years, my colleagues and I have carried out four major studies to answer these questions. The results of this research, together with the results of studies by others, give us a good picture of how people self-regulate their moods.

What Behaviors Are Used for Mood Regulation?

First, let us consider three earlier studies that addressed this topic, which focused on all the ways that people try to change bad moods. In 1976, Vicky Rippere, a psychologist from the University of London, asked 50 people, "What's the thing to do when you're feeling depressed?"[5] She received hundreds of answers. They frequently included responses such as "See people, a friend," "Think of a reason for it," and "Go for a walk." Less common responses were "Avoid social events, avoid people" and "Avoid thinking of possible sources of failure." Although this study was useful for demonstrating what people do, it used only a small sample.

In 1981, two researchers at the University of New South Wales in Australia asked 103 routine medical patients at four clinics to complete questionnaires about mood regulation.[6] They asked their subjects which of their behaviors were increased or decreased if they faced the breakup of an important relationship or if someone close had become increasingly critical of them. The behaviors that increased were "Think through the problem," "Busy yourself in work," "Try to discuss the problem with that person," and "Do something to take your thoughts off the problem."

These two studies involved relatively small numbers of people, and their subjects were not chosen to be especially representative of the general population. With respect to representativeness, the best study comes from a 1986 Gallup poll of 1,007 Americans.[7] When asked what they did to relieve depression, 77 percent of respondents reported "Spend more time alone with a hobby," "TV," "Reading," or "Listening to music." The next most frequent responses were "Seek out friends to talk with" (68 percent), "Seek out family members to talk with" (66 percent), and "Eat more or eat less" (64 percent).[8]

Although these three studies took place in different parts of the world, the results were similar. For example, seeking social interaction and attempts to control thoughts about the matter were frequently mentioned. Many people also mentioned distracting themselves by means of various behaviors.

With these studies as background, my university colleagues and I set out to make a systematic study of the most common behaviors that people employ to regulate their moods. We wanted to know what people do when they are in a bad mood and wish to change it. We also wanted to know how people attempt to raise their energy and how they reduce nervousness, tension, or anxiety. These questions were related to my theory that common moods are based on variations in energy and tension and on associated thoughts.

We began by asking people to complete questionnaires anonymously and with the request that they be absolutely honest. We wished to find out all the behaviors that they used, including socially undesirable ones (e.g., sugar snacking or drinking alcohol) and even illegal ones (illicit drugs). Because we asked for written answers to questions, with no limitation on what could be written, we hoped to obtain the broadest array of responses possible. We gave these questionnaires to 102 males and females who ranged in age from 18 to 88 years. Many of them were college students, but a large number were professionals and nonprofessionals from the general population, and about 20 percent were members of a local Leisure World retirement community.

The many answers that we received were read carefully by two of my students, Mary Ann Cejka and Bonnie Shrewsbury, and by myself. We then did what is called a *content analysis* of the results, which involves determining a relatively small number of meaningful categories within which each answer could be placed. My two students then made independent judgments of some of the questionnaires, sorting the answers into our predetermined categories. Because these independent judgments of the two readers agreed quite well, we were more confident that we could correctly classify the many different kinds of answers that we received.

What we found were 32 different categories of behavior that people commonly use to change a bad mood, raise energy, or reduce tension (see Tables 1, 2, and 3 for a modified listing). The relatively small number of categories is interesting, considering all the possible behaviors a person might use.[9] One result of this phase of the study was that the subjects reported essentially the same behaviors when they tried to raise their energy level or reduce their tension and when they attempted to change a bad mood. Of the 32, only 3 categories differed for behaviors that changed energy or tension than for behaviors that change a bad mood, and this is to be expected if bad moods represent a combination of low energy and increased tension.[10]

After this phase of the research, we used these categories of behavior to study a more representative cross section of the population. In addition to myself, this part of the study involved one of my colleagues, J. Robert Newman, an expert on decision making and mathematical statistics, and several of my students, Tracy McClain, Bonnie Shrewsbury, and Janice Metz. In addition to learning what people commonly do, we wanted to determine how well the various behaviors worked in regulating mood. We also wanted to know which people regulate their mood differently; in other words, were there demographic or personality differences with respect to regulating mood?

To do this, we constructed a three-part questionnaire using the 32 behavioral categories already obtained. The subjects could check off behaviors on this Mood Regulation Questionnaire that they commonly used to change a bad mood, to raise their energy, or to reduce their tension, anxiety, or nervousness. Besides checking off behaviors, the respondents also indicated their preferred way of regulating their moods and rated its success on a 9-point scale. Because we wanted to sample a wide and representative cross section of the population, we obtained anonymous responses from 308 males and females, ranging in age from 16-year-old high school students to 89-year-old retirees. This group also represented all educational and occupational levels. Finally, we obtained self-ratings on weight and on an introversion–extraversion scale.

Behaviors Used to Change a Bad Mood

The behaviors that the respondents reported using to change a bad mood are presented in order of frequency in Table 1. As in the other studies I mentioned, the most common responses were social interaction and cognitive (thought) control. Somewhat unexpectedly for us, music was often mentioned as a way of changing a bad mood, and as will become apparent later in this chapter, this technique turned out to be effective.

This questionnaire also included a section in which the respondents were asked to indicate any behaviors that they commonly used but were not listed among the items. A relatively small number of other behaviors were described in this section, and they generally were variations of the listed behaviors. From this we concluded that our list was quite complete.

About one-third of the behaviors generally used to change a bad mood are related directly to activities that affect energy and tension, such as exercise, relaxation techniques, rest, sleep, caffeine, and other drugs. About 20 percent involve using various distractions, such as seeking pleasant activities, doing chores, reading, and watching TV. About 15 percent of these behaviors are related to cognitive activities such as controlling thoughts, evaluating the situation, and seeking a new perspective. Another 10 to 15 percent of behaviors pertain to seeking social interaction, including calling or talking to someone, or, conversely, avoiding social interactions. Several other behaviors do not readily fall into one of these categories.

What can we conclude about the various behaviors that people use to regulate moods? First, even though we may distinguish among categories such as these, they actually are interrelated, particularly in respect to energy and tension states. Of the categories described, the largest percentage is behaviors that either increase energy or decrease tension in rather direct ways. The most obvious examples of this direct relationship can be found with exercise and relaxation techniques. Depending on the level of exercise, energy is either increased immediately or decreased and then followed by an increase in energy

Table 1.   Behaviors Used to Change a Bad Mood, Ranked According
to Percentage-Endorsing Item

- Call, talk to, or be with someone (54%).
- Control thoughts (e.g., think positively, concentrate on something else, don't let things bother me, give myself a "pep talk") (51%).
- Listen to music (47%).
- Avoid the thing (person) causing the bad mood (47%).
- Try to be alone (47%).
- Evaluate or analyze the situation to determine mood cause (47%).
- Try to put feelings in perspective (44%).
- Change location (e.g., go for a drive, go outside) (44%).
- Rest, take a nap, close eyes, or sleep (42%).
- Exercise (This may include taking a walk) (37%).
- Engage in pleasant (fun) activities (35%).
- Use humor (e.g., laugh, make light of situation) (34%).
- Eat something (34%).
- Watch TV (movie) (32%).
- Tend to chores (e.g., housework, schoolwork, gardening) (31%).
- Engage in emotional activity (e.g., cry, scream) (29%).
- Go shopping (25%).
- Take shower or bath or splash water on face (25%).
- Read or write (24%).
- Engage in stress management activities (e.g., get organized, plan ahead, make lists) (22%).
- Use relaxation techniques (e.g., deep breathing, stretching and bending, muscle relaxation, massage, visualization) (21%).
- Engage in self-gratification (e.g., pamper oneself) (19%).
- Engage in hobby (18%).
- Engage in religious or spiritual activity (16%).
- Drink alcohol (15%).
- Drink coffee or other caffeinated beverage (12%).
- Have sex (9%).
- Smoke cigarettes (8%).
- Use drugs (other than alcohol, cigarettes, or coffee) (5%).

some time later. In addition, exercise often reduces tension, but not always.

Relaxation techniques, on the other hand, reduce tension, probably because of the close association between skeletal–muscular tightness and negative moods. Moreover, when tension is reduced, energy often is enhanced. The model outlined in the first part of this book predicted that these two kinds of behaviors would be among the most successful ways of regulating mood because of their direct influence on energy and tension. Other behaviors such as eating, drinking coffee, or taking drugs also have direct effects on energy and tension states, but as I indicated earlier, these behaviors may not be as good at regulating mood because the effects of these substances are temporary and often result in the opposite effect a short while later.

Although only 15 percent of mood-regulating behaviors can be categorized as directly involving cognitive activities, this figure is somewhat misleading. A number of other behaviors, such as those associated with various forms of distraction, also have a cognitive component, and because cognition is so much a part of behavior, all the mood-regulating behaviors reflect this influence to some extent. Clearly, mind and body cannot be separated.

Our thoughts influence our moods in many respects, especially in regard to tension. For example, thoughts are much like other stimuli that elicit a conditioned response—in this case, one of anxiety.[11] When we are not thinking about a problem, we have little anxiety, except perhaps through unconscious mechanisms. But when we think about it, our tension rises. It's no surprise that our respondents reported trying to control their thoughts in order to change a bad mood. In fact, this was one of the most common behaviors we found. People might deliberately stop a negative thought, which is equivalent to eliminating the stimulus that elicits a conditioned anxiety response. Or people might evaluate the problem, put it into perspective, and reevaluate it as less important.

The 20 percent of behaviors included in the distraction category may also regulate mood by cognitive means. That is, when we engage in a distracting activity, it often stops our thoughts about personal problems. This short-circuiting of tension-producing thoughts is a practice central to many of these mood-regulating behaviors. Reading, writing, engaging in a hobby, or tending to chores, for example have the effect of focusing our mind on some task and not on problematic life issues. In this way, we reduce tension and enhance energy.

These distracting activities can also be pleasant, and in that respect they are similar to the category Engage in pleasant (fun) activities. Therefore, people who choose a pleasant activity to regulate their mood are also in a sense distracting themselves, especially if the activity takes their mind off a personal problem. But pleasant activities also enhance energy and reduce tension more directly than that. Pleasant activities increase energy through cognitive stimulation—a positive thought stimulates energy—and physical activity often enhances energy as well. In addition, the positive feelings that derive from doing something fun tend to be incompatible with tension and thus mitigate negative moods. As I indicated earlier, there is a good deal of research data demonstrating the value of pleasant activities as a way of reducing depression.[12]

Another behavioral category commonly used to change a bad mood is Call, talk to, or be with someone. Energy and tension probably are involved in a number of ways in these kinds of behaviors, though some are not obvious. Most researchers assume that the main benefits of social interaction have to do with social support, which is thought to relieve tension. We feel better when we talk to someone who reassures us, telling us not to worry or when a friend points out that we have misinterpreted a troubling situation. After talking, we feel less tense. Social interactions also are cognitively distracting and thus can act like the other distractions already mentioned: They take our mind off troubling thoughts. Social interactions can also be pleasant activities, and they enhance energy and reduce tension for this reason as well.

Another less obvious way that social interactions change a bad mood is that they require a certain amount of energy. Being attentive, smiling, and saying appropriate things all demand energy. It takes energy to monitor our conversation and activity so it is reasonable and appropriate to the occasion. (This is often why we avoid social gatherings when we are tired.) But because energy is necessary for social interactions, these occasions tap unused reserves. This is especially true for mild depression when reserves are adequate, but the person is reluctant to raise and expend any energy. Once we put ourselves into a social interaction, however, we must mobilize our energy because of the requirements of the interaction, and once mobilized, this energy improves our mood. Often we don't want to go to a party—or whatever—but once there we have a good time. We can see this kind of behavior–energy interaction in various situations. Although we feel tired and quiet, if we begin talking to someone, we may go on talking for some time—not just because of cognitive stimulation, but also because our energy reserves, once tapped, sustain our activity.

General Strategies for Altering Mood

The next thing that our research team did was to try to find any general patterns or common strategies among the various individual behaviors that people use. For this, we employed what is called *factor analysis*, a mathematical–statistical technique that determines common groupings of behaviors (variables), or behaviors that tend to cluster together. From the factor analysis, we found that the behaviors fell into six categories, representing the six main strategies that people use to change a bad mood.

We called the first mood-regulating strategy Active Mood Management, and it included a number of the behaviors from the original 32 categories. With this strategy, when people find themselves in a bad mood, they use a combination of "relaxation techniques," "stress management activities," "control thoughts," and "exercise."

By means of this strategy, people actively try to change their mood, dealing with it directly. It is not a passive response or one in which a person waits for the mood to change on its own. This strategy includes behaviors that increase energy (through exercise and possibly through cognitive means), as well as other behaviors that simultaneously decrease tension (relaxation, stress management, and cognitive means). This is a further indication that moods—in this case bad moods—contain central energy and tension components.

The second strategy we identified, Seeking Pleasurable Activities and Distraction, included engaging in pleasant activities such as humor or a hobby, listening to music, and changing location. This strategy might also be thought of as active, although it does not engage the mood as actively as the first strategy does. Instead, it consists of distracting oneself with pleasant things.

The third strategy is much less active. Accordingly, we called it Passive Mood Management and viewed it as the most passive of all. Watching TV or movie, eating something, or resting, napping, or sleeping—all are part of this strategy, as they engage the mood indirectly and in a minimal way. Also part of this strategy is to go shopping. Although this may not seem at first to be passive, its grouping with the other more passive behaviors is important, as shopping shares something with the other more passive behaviors. One possibility is that for many people, shopping is distracting, like watching TV.

The fourth strategy we called Social Support, Ventilation, and Gratification because it groups the items Call, talk to, or be with someone with Engage in emotional activity, Smoke cigarettes, and Eat something. In our view, this strategy requires less active management of the mood than the first strategy does. Once again, the grouping of the various items provided by the factor analysis gives us some insight into the aspects of various behaviors that may contribute to the regulation of moods. For example, Call, talk to, or be with someone seems to involve social support and all that this implies. But it is closely grouped with Engage in emotional activity (e.g., cry, scream), which suggests that people regulating their mood by means of social interaction may be seeking someone to whom they can express their emotions, as opposed to seeking social support only. Nevertheless, both motivations probably are involved to some extent.

The fifth strategy is called Withdrawal-Avoidance, because it primarily includes Try to be alone and Avoid the thing (person) causing the bad mood. People using this strategy do not confront the causes of the bad mood; instead, they simply withdraw.

The sixth strategy, Direct Tension Reduction, includes using drugs, drinking alcohol and having sex. All, but especially alcohol, are direct measures to reduce tension, and the results are rather immediate. This strategy is more active than the preceding two.

Effectiveness of Behaviors and Strategies

How successful are people at regulating their moods with these strategies? Are some specific behaviors better than others? These are difficult questions to answer definitively, but we have some evidence based on our subjects' self-ratings and on independent experts' judgments. For the self-ratings, the participants in our study systematically gauged the successfulness of each behavior when they used it as their preferred way of changing their mood.

The comparative results were quite instructive. The most successful behavior was exercise. Based on the rating scale, our participants indicated that this behavior was successful most of the time. The next most successful behaviors were listening to music; calling, talking to, or being with someone; and tending to chores. On the other hand, behaviors such as avoiding the person or thing causing the bad mood and being alone were rated as only sometimes successful.

These behaviors are clustered together to form strategies, and the various strategies are especially interesting in regard to rated successfulness. The average successfulness of the behaviors making up a strategy was calculated using the ratings of individual behaviors, thus providing a kind of effectiveness score for each general strategy. The six strategies are ranked here according to their successfulness:

1. Active Mood Management
   Relaxation, stress management, engage in cognitive activity, exercise

2. Seeking Pleasurable Activities and Distraction
   Engage in pleasant activities such as humor or a hobby

3. Withdrawal-Avoidance
   Be alone, avoid person or thing causing bad mood

4. Social Support, Ventilation, and Gratification
   Call or talk to someone, engage in emotional activity, smoke, eat

5. Passive Mood Management
   Watch TV, drink coffee, eat, rest

6. Direct Tension Reduction
   Take drugs, drink alcohol, have sex

Our participants rated the first strategy, Active Mood Management, as the most effective at changing a bad mood. This ranking is not surprising if you think about mood in terms of its bodily manifestations. However, in our culture it is not clear that most people would rank it first on the basis of common knowledge. That is, it is quite possible that people would rank the second strategy highest, at least if asked about the two. This second strategy, Seeking Pleasurable Activities and Distraction, was in fact also rated as mostly successful at changing a bad mood. Although the rated success of this strategy was lower than for the first one, by a significant amount, these first two strategies were rated to be considerably more successful than the remaining four.

The third strategy, Withdrawal-Avoidance, was rated the next most successful. Because it involves withdrawing from and avoiding the problem, it is curious that this strategy would be rated so highly. Although this strategy was rated third, it was judged as only slightly better than "sometimes successful," only one point on our rating scale.

The fourth strategy, Social Support, Ventilation, and Gratification, would appear at first glance to be a successful strategy because the element of social support generally is valued in our culture. We are often told to "talk it over with a friend." The ventilation or expressing of emotion (crying, screaming) that is part of the same strategy may not be seen as quite so valuable, but on the other hand, many people believe that not bottling up emotion is healthy. Smoking and eating are likely to be less valued. However effective some of these behaviors may appear, the combined set of behaviors that make up this strategy was rated as only sometimes successful. Again, this strategy was not rated to be as successful as the first two, although it was rated close in success to Withdrawal-Avoidance.

The fifth strategy, Passive Mood Management, was rated close in success to the third and fourth strategies. But this strategy was rated as less successful than the two just described (only sometimes successful). Television viewing, drinking coffee, and eating were not rated as particularly successful, even though they are commonly used as ways of regulating mood.

According to our participants' ratings, Direct Tension Reduction was the least successful strategy. This behavior pattern, involving drugs, alcohol, and sex, was rated as seldom successful and significantly less successful than the first three strategies. In summary, the success of the six strategies may be regarded in three general groups. The first two strategies are the most successful. The next three strategies are close to one another in successfulness, but less so than the first grouping. Finally, this last strategy, Direct Tension Reduction, is considerably less successful than the other five.

Psychotherapists' Ratings of the Strategies

To obtain an independent assessment of our subjects' ratings, we decided to conduct another study of the likely successfulness of the various strategies, one in which self-ratings were not used as the main basis of judgment. Using expert ratings is a way that psychologists often determine the value of a test or set of measurements. In other words, what do experts in the field think about the behavior? One problem with this approach in a study such as ours, however, is that there are no clear experts. Until now, the scientific evidence regarding mood has been minimal and widely scattered. For example, systematic successfulness ratings of a comprehensive set of behaviors such as those listed here have never been published in scientific form. Even though there may be lots of opinions, nobody knows for sure how to change a bad mood.

Aside from researchers working on the subject of mood, psychotherapists appear to come as close to expert status as any professional group could. In their work, psychotherapists probably are confronted daily with questions from their clients about mood. And whether or not they always know the answers to these questions, at least they have thought about the questions quite a bit. Moreover, psychotherapists are trained to spot pathological moods, such as depression. Accordingly, we decided to ask the help of a panel of professional therapists.

To obtain these judgments, we were fortunate enough to gain the cooperation of a local mental health association. We sent questionnaires to these professionals, and we had a very good return rate. In my experience, psychotherapists are quite cooperative in furthering scientific research, and this group was no exception.

The questionnaires included the six strategies that our subjects used, and we asked our panel of therapists to rate the probable success of each strategy in changing a bad mood. The sets of individual behaviors that made up each strategy were provided in random order to our panel but were not named. Each set was judged with the same rating scales that our subjects had used. The therapists were highly experienced, and many of them were well-known professionals: The 26 Ph.D. or M.D. panelists included 15 males and 11 females with an average of 17.2 years of professional experience.

The results were very useful in confirming our earlier findings. With only one exception, the experts' ratings were the same as our subjects' self-ratings. The professional therapists ranked the strategies that would be most successful as follows:

1. Active Mood Management
   Relaxation, stress management, engage in cognitive activity, exercise

2. Seeking Pleasurable Activities and Distraction
   Engage in pleasant activities such as humor or a hobby

3. Social Support, Ventilation, and Gratification
   Call or talk to someone, engage in emotional activity, smoke, eat

4. Passive Mood Management
   Watch TV, drink coffee, eat, rest

5. Withdrawal-Avoidance
   Be alone, avoid person or thing causing bad mood

6. Direct Tension Reduction
   Take drugs, drink alcohol, have sex

Although Withdrawal-Avoidance fell from third ranking to fifth, the rest of the strategies remained the same. Thus, both the therapists and respondents making self-ratings agreed on the best two strategies, the middle strategies, and the poorest strategy. This similarity between the two sets of ratings gave us great confidence about the relative effectiveness of the various strategies.[13]

It is not clear why Withdrawal-Avoidance would be perceived differently by therapists and persons who rate their own behavior. Perhaps the difference occurred because therapists know that social withdrawal can be an indication of more serious psychopathology. Moreover, therapists may see this strategy as a denial of the problem, in which case it would appear dysfunctional. In this study, however, we were considering bad moods of the sort we all have, not serious psychopathologies. Perhaps withdrawing from the apparent cause of the bad mood allows our natural rhythms of energy and tension to stabilize, thus eliminating the mood. Or this might be a strategy to avoid confrontation, walk away from the problem, and blow off steam. Another possibility is that among normal, well-adjusted people it is a suitable temporary strategy. But among people with serious problems, it could be a habitual, dysfunctional strategy.

As a last point, one of our therapists offered an insight into the Direct Tension Reduction strategy, that drugs and alcohol may have

Table 2.   Behaviors Used to Raise Alertness or Energy, Ranked
According to Percentage-Endorsing Item

- Rest, take a nap, close eyes, or sleep (68%).
- Take a shower or bath or splash water on face (55%).
- Go outside and get some fresh air (45%).
- Do something to keep busy (43%).
- Drink coffee or other caffeinated beverage (41%).
- Listen to music (41%).
- Eat something (37%).
- Exercise (This may include taking a walk) (28%).
- Call, talk to, or be with someone (28%).
- Control thoughts (e.g., give oneself a "pep talk.") (27%).
- Change location (e.g., go for a drive or go outside) (25%).
- Use relaxation techniques (e.g., deep breathing, stretching and bending, muscle relaxation, massage) (20%).
- Watch TV or a movie (18%).
- Evaluate or analyze the situation to determine the cause of the fatigue (13%).
- Smoke a cigarette (6%).
- Use drugs (other than cigarettes or coffee) (2%).
- Drink alcohol (2%).

---

one effect immediately but another effect that is delayed. Drugs and alcohol, for example, probably are used when a person is in a bad mood because they work and work quickly. We have already seen that behaviors are continued because of their immediate effects and that delayed effects have little influence unless the person has observed these effects through systematic self-observation. In this respect, tension reducers such as alcohol and drugs are likely to work only temporarily but not over time.

Behaviors Used to Raise Energy

Effective mood regulation involves raising energy, and so it is important to learn how people do this. The behaviors that our study participants used to increase energy were somewhat different from those they used to change a bad mood, although they employed similar categories of behavior (with appropriate wording changes).[14] These behaviors are listed in Table 2. As might be expected, resting and sleeping and coffee and food are frequently mentioned. Exercise, social interaction, and cognitive techniques are often used—not unlike the strategies we found people using to change a bad mood.

Our study participants rated Control thoughts (e.g., give oneself a pep talk) as the most successful behavior to raise energy in the short term. Close to this in rated effectiveness were Listen to music, Take a shower or bath or splash water on face, Exercise, Rest, take a nap, close eyes or sleep, Do something to keep busy, Eat something, and Drink coffee or other caffeinated beverage. The last behavior was rated somewhere between mostly and sometimes successful.

The question of effectiveness is important, and so we tried to gauge it in another way. We decided to use the people from our sample who employed the best strategy for changing a bad mood as judged by our psychotherapists (Active Mood Management). In other words, we considered the people who used the best strategy to change their bad moods to be experts, so to speak, and we identified what behaviors these "experts" used to raise their energy levels.

In completing that analysis, we found that these experts used Exercise first, followed by Use relaxation techniques, and then Evaluate or analyze the situation to determine the cause of the fatigue. That these experts were most likely to use exercise was particularly interesting, since our previous research found exercise to be very effective in enhancing energy. With the use of relaxation techniques, they appear to have discovered that reducing tension has the effect of increasing energy as well. We saw this as excellent evidence for the validity of the mood theory described in the first part of this book (i.e., the reciprocal relationship between tension and energy).

Behaviors Used to Reduce Tension, Nervousness, or Anxiety

The behaviors employed to reduce nervousness, tension, or anxiety also are important to regulating mood. Therefore, we were interested in these results from our study. The behaviors used for this purpose are listed in Table 3. The behavior most frequently used was seeking social interaction, followed by using cognitive control techniques and then listening to music.

These behaviors are more like the methods people use to change a bad mood than like the techniques used to raise energy. This could

Table 3. Behaviors Used to Reduce Nervousness, Tension, or Anxiety,
Ranked According to Percentage-Endorsing Item

- Call, talk to, or be with someone (59%).
- Control thoughts (e.g., think calming thoughts, tell oneself to calm down, try not to think about problem or situation) (58%).
- Listen to music (53%).
- Exercise (This may include taking a walk) (44%).
- Use relaxation techniques (e.g., deep breathing, stretching and bending, muscle relaxation, massage, visualization) (44%).
- Rest, take a nap, close eyes, or sleep (37%).
- Engage in nervous behavior (e.g., pacing, biting nails, biting pencil) (31%).
- Engage in stress management activities (e.g., get organized, plan ahead, make lists) (31%).
- Tend to chores (e.g., housework, schoolwork, gardening) (27%).
- Watch TV or a movie (27%).
- Eat something (26%).
- Take shower, bath, or jacuzzi, or splash water on face (26%).
- Read or write (24%).
- Do not drink coffee or other caffeinated beverage (17%).
- Engage in emotional activity (e.g., cry, scream) (15%).
- Engage in religious or spiritual activity (15%).
- Engage in hobby (14%).
- Go shopping (12%).
- Drink alcohol (11%).
- Smoke cigarettes (9%).
- Have sex (9%).
- Use drugs (other than alcohol, cigarettes or coffee) (5%).

indicate that bad moods are caused more often by tension than by low energy. If that is the case, it could be important theoretically, but some other results of these studies are not consistent with this idea. Therefore, at this point I am uncertain.

In judging the effectiveness of the behaviors used for reducing tension, nervousness, or anxiety, our participants indicated that Engage in religious or spiritual activity was the most effective. Their average rating indicated that this behavior was mostly successful. The behaviors judged as the next most successful were Listen to music, Tend to chores, Exercise, Call, talk to, or be with someone, Use relaxation techniques, Control thoughts, Engage in stress management activities, and Rest, nap, or sleep.

The high rating for religious or spiritual activity is interesting for a number of reasons. The first is that this finding is consistent with results of the previously mentioned Gallup poll that looked at the ways Americans deal with depression. Those polled reported religious techniques to be the best way to deal with depression. Although Gallup found that this behavior was the most effective, it was close to exercise in judged effectiveness. Because that poll was commissioned by the Christian Broadcasting Network, I have some uncertainty about how to regard these very high percentages for religious practices: Forty-eight percent listed using prayer, meditation, and Bible reading to reduce depression.

Psychologists tend to be a nonreligious lot, and being no exception to this tendency, I must admit some surprise about our result indicating that religious or spiritual activities received the highest rating. However, it called to mind a study conducted by Sheena Sethi and Martin Seligman in which they found that fundamentalists in various religions appear to be more optimistic than people in other religions, and this may be a variation of being in the best mood.[15] Some skeptics may think that such optimism really represents denial of feelings, but I'm not so sure that these positive mood effects aren't valid. If there are such positive mood effects associated with religiousness, we might understand the motivation for religious activity in relation to the good moods that it produces. This would be another aspect of mood regulation.

We used an additional way of judging the success of the various behaviors, determining the effectiveness of the various behaviors on the basis of the so-called experts—those that used the best method of changing a bad mood. When we analyzed the way that this group deals with tension, we found that they are most likely to use stress management activities, followed by exercise and relaxation techniques. Once again, we see the emergence of exercise and relaxation techniques, the behaviors predicted to have the greatest effect on mood regulation.

What Works Best to Regulate Moods?

Considering all three parts of this study, we can make a number of observations. First, the data suggest that exercise is the best overall mood regulator. This behavior was judged to be the most successful at changing a bad mood and quite successful at raising energy and reducing tension. In addition, exercise was the preferred mode of raising energy as judged by those who used the best methods of changing a bad mood. Moreover, these "experts" used exercise second only to stress management techniques as a way of reducing tension. Clearly, exercise appears to be a highly effective mood regulator.

In recent years, exercise has been widely advocated. The popular advice generally cites benefits related to health and longevity, particularly cardiovascular fitness, which is probably the primary motivation for many who begin an exercise program.[16] Responsible weight control programs also require regular exercise, which is as important as not overeating. But considering the responses of our subjects and experts, an important benefit of exercise is mood control. In some respects, mood control may be the most important benefit of regular exercise because good feelings are likely to continue over time in a way that abstract health values may not. Although mood control is an obvious benefit of exercise, health benefits also accompany the positive moods.

If exercise enhances mood so effectively, why isn't everyone exercising regularly? The first answer to this question is that many people already know about the mood benefits of exercise. They are the ones who faithfully go to the gym or who work out regularly in other ways.[17] Ask anyone who exercises regularly, and you will get positive comments about mood. Although people may start exercising for some other reason, soon it is likely to be the mood regulation that prompts them to continue.

A related point is that a kind of formal knowledge of exercise is needed for optimal mood regulation. Mood regulation is dependent on the type and intensity of exercise, and you can easily learn how to get the best mood benefits from your exercise routine. In the last section of this book, I indicate what is necessary to know about the psychology of exercise so that it is maximally valuable as a mood regulator: how much you should exercise, how intense a regimen you should follow, what mood effects you will notice, how best to motivate yourself, and when you will notice the positive effects.

A surprising result of these mood-regulation studies was the value of listening to music. Listening to music was judged to be highly effective in the three parts of our study: changing a bad mood, increasing energy, and reducing tension. When I reviewed the scientific literature on music and mood, I found only a small number of studies that were consistent with this finding.[18] Without question, however, a vast industry is associated with music recording sales, and many people regularly attend various sorts of concerts. Moreover, music therapy is a program of study offered at a number of universities. Our results thus would certainly warrant considering these music-related activities as effective mood regulators, and thoughtful observers may recognize from these results that mood regulation can be an important motivator for listening to music.

But why is listening to music such a good mood regulator? There are a number of possible reasons. First, familiar music is often associated with positive memories of pleasant experiences. This is actually a conditioned emotional reaction. Second, the lyrics of musical pieces may have positive associations. I suspect, however, that the mood enhancement properties go beyond these reasons, that the music reduces skeletal–muscular tension and that this is a major part of the positive mood benefits. Certainly, rhythmic musical pieces that induce a movement or dance mode, so to speak, could relax muscular tension. This is most evident with "toe-tapping" music, but all kinds of music can have this effect. In any event, to move—or to imagine moving—in rhythm with music is inconsistent with muscular tension.

Another general observation from these studies, the rated success of Call, talk to, or be with someone as a means of regulating mood is consistent with a substantial literature confirming that there is value in seeking social support for dealing with stress.[19] Just being with someone is a behavior that we can readily employ when we are in a bad mood. This may be a particularly good lesson for men to learn (see Chapter 10 for differences between men and women).

In addition, the rated value of various cognitive techniques matches the cognitive psychotherapies often used with depression.[20] Even though we were not considering serious depressions in our studies, it appears that cognitive techniques are effective in regulating everyday moods as well as serious depressions. The idea that our thoughts help control our feelings and mood is supported by our respondents and the panel of experts.

Before concluding this chapter, let us look at the strategy most effective in changing a bad mood—Active Mood Management. People using this strategy combine relaxation, stress management, cognitive, and exercise techniques. It is a strategy that supports the mood theory described in the first part of this book, partly because it includes a wide range of cardiovascular, endocrine, and cognitive activities. In other words, it involves the whole body.

Our bodies do not operate as a series of independent systems; instead, moods follow general patterns and affect the entire body. A practical implication of this interrelationship is that if one element in the system is modified, we should see other elements change as well. For example, reducing muscular tension also alters tension-related thoughts, and vice versa.

If relaxation, stress management, cognitive, and exercise techniques are employed together, it follows that the mood effects will be both increased energy and reduced tension. This is calm-energy, the mood we have recognized as the optimal mood.

In closing, it is worth considering the noted lack of effectiveness of Direct Tension Reduction, particularly the use of drugs and alcohol. The ineffectiveness of this strategy isn't especially surprising; many people regularly use alcohol and drugs to feel better because they work right away. The immediate effects of this strategy is enhanced mood; yet our data show that overall they do not work well in the long run.

10

Individual Differences in Mood-Regulating Strategies

It is now evident that people self-regulate their moods in a variety of ways, using many behaviors, sugars and other foods, as well as drugs such as caffeine, nicotine, and alcohol. But people aren't all the same. In our research, we found pronounced differences in ways of self-regulating, depending on the type of person. For example, men and women have quite different ways of reacting to a bad mood. Significant differences also can be found between young and old, professionals and nonprofessionals, better or less educated, and even different weight types and levels of introversion and extraversion.

The greatest differences that we found were between men and women. This isn't surprising given the decades of scientific research indicating the many ways in which they differ psychologically as well as physically. Gender is probably the best documented individual difference, with thousands of studies showing variations. It also is the subject of numerous best-selling books.[1]

Our findings also have important implications for mutual understanding between the sexes. For example, a 30-year old returning student listened to one of my lectures on our research about male and female differences in mood regulation, and for the first time she understood why she became so upset with her husband after an argument. I had indicated that women react to their bad moods more often by seeking social interaction than men do. On the other hand, men turn to their hobbies or try to use humor.

My student described to the class the way an argument between her and her husband would put both of them into a bad mood. She usually wanted to continue talking about the problem, as her mood was a stimulus for further social interaction, not separation. But typically her husband would bolt out the door and into the garage to work on his car after making a halfhearted attempt at humor concerning their differences. She said that until she heard my lecture, she had never understood him; she thought he was just a jerk. But now she realized that many men would react in the same way: "It's the way men and women deal differently with their moods." She also mentioned that her husband didn't understand why their telephone bills were so high. But she knew the answer. When they had an argument, she would call a friend or a family member, just to talk, because she felt better when she did. We now recognize this as a form of mood regulation. Her husband, on the other hand, hardly ever called a friend when he was in a bad mood.

Another male student in the lecture admitted that he now realized why his girlfriend liked shopping so much. As a way of changing a bad mood, this behavior also differentiates women from men. Some women use shopping as their main method of changing their bad moods, and those that do rate this form of behavior as a highly successful mood regulator.[2] Conversely, my male student observed that far from helping him feel better, shopping puts him into a worse mood.

These findings about women's shopping for mood regulation are supported by cultural patterns. The degree to which women shop more than men is evident at any mall in the United States. Count the stores devoted to women compared with men, and you will find a ratio of perhaps ten to one. Interestingly, in the department stores, the men's section is often located right next to the entrance so men can run in, grab what they want, and leave immediately. From our findings we can readily understand these differences. Shopping helps many women, but not most men, to change their bad moods.

Exactly why shopping relieves a bad mood isn't clear. But one possibility is that it can be distracting, and therefore troubling thoughts are temporarily forgotten. The distraction strategy described in Chapter 9 is one of the best mood-change strategies. Shopping may also require moderate exercise. Walking around the mall is invigorating if the exercise isn't overdone, and then there are the pleasant feelings that come from having new things.

If shopping is such a good mood regulator for some women, why isn't it also good for men? One reason may be that men never really learn to shop; perhaps it is a practice that mothers teach their daughters but not their sons. More important, men find shopping uncomfortable because they don't like to ask a shop clerk for help or to inquire about how something looks.

In regard to another mood-regulating behavior, a 26-year-old male student, after listening to a lecture on gender differences, noted that this made him understand why his girlfriend was so emotional. Our findings show that more women than men engage in emotional activities such as crying and screaming as a means of dealing with a bad mood. Women are not necessarily more emotional than men, although this may be the case.[3] But our results indicate that women find emotional expression to be a way of regulating their bad moods. (Incidentally, our data show that this is not a very successful way of changing a bad mood.) On the other hand, men turn to sex as a way of changing a bad mood significantly more than women do. (Again, this was not rated as particularly effective, but because of the small number of ratings of this behavior by itself, we can't be sure about this.[4])

These differences in individual behaviors are interesting, but in some respects, more general patterns of behaviors are even more enlightening. Of the six strategies previously described for changing a bad mood, four of them have big gender differences, which may explain why some women are very good at changing their moods and some men are very poor at it. On the negative side, they also may account for distinct differences in the rates of depression between men and women—on average, women are twice as likely as men to be depressed.

Recall that the best strategy for changing a bad mood, Active Mood Management, is a combination of relaxation, stress management, cognitive and exercise techniques. Although there are no significant sex differences in this strategy, subgroups differ in their patterns of use. Professional women are more likely to use this strategy than professional men are. Probably there is something about professional women's experience and education that leads them to be more sophisticated about these ways of dealing effectively with their moods. Or once the behaviors that work become evident, professional women may be better at consistently using them.[5]

Despite this use of the best strategy by professional women, men as a whole are slightly more likely to use this strategy than women as a whole are. This greater tendency of use by men also is consistent with their employment of active strategies, compared with women's use of more passive mood-regulating strategies. As I shall show, this active–passive difference could be a key to understanding differential rates of depression.

Let us next consider the worst strategy for changing a bad mood. Men are much more likely to use alcohol, drugs, and sex than women are. This can be a way of dealing directly with the mood: A shot of alcohol may immediately reduce tension and enhance energy. But the positive effects usually are only temporary. This strategy is thus ineffective a short while later and as a regular activity. The tendency of men to use this mood-regulating strategy more often than women is borne out by the ratio of male to female alcoholics, probably three to one. Greater male than female drug use of all kinds is also evident in research statistics.[6]

Although some of our results indicate that males are less efficient than females in regulating their negative moods, other ways in which men use behaviors are better. Men are much more likely than women to turn to the strategy that we named Pleasant Activities and Distraction. As I stated in Chapter 9, this strategy is very effective and a close second to the best one.

Support, Ventilation, and Gratification, a strategy often used by women, is much less effective than the distraction strategy used by many men. We know that this strategy is used more by women than by men from our sample of more than 300, and we also have a second kind of judgment concerning this from our panel of psychotherapists. This group made predictions about whether men or women would be more successful in using this strategy. Almost all of them believed that women would be more successful with this strategy than men. If true, it is not surprising that women use this strategy more often; it is more successful for them.

The second strategy that is used much more by women as a whole than by men is Passive Mood Management. As a means of changing a bad mood, this strategy uses such behaviors as watching TV, drinking coffee, eating, and resting. It was rated as slightly less successful than the other one used by women. In addition, it was rated as only sometimes successful by our participants, as the fifth most successful strategy of the six by our study participants, and as the fourth most successful by the therapists.

Women and Depression

These differences between men and women are interesting, and knowing about them can improve communication between the sexes. But they may be important for another reason, having to do with the unexplained phenomenon that women are much more likely than men to suffer depression.

In 1990 an American Psychological Association task force of women psychologists published the results of an analysis documenting a differential depression rate for the two sexes. These differences in rates of depression varied, but on average women were about twice as likely as men to be depressed.

> Women are at higher risk for most types of depression, whether one looks at case records or community surveys. This is one of the most consistent findings in the literature. The difference holds for White, Black, and Hispanic women and persists when income level, education, and occupation are controlled. In addition to the United States, gender differences in depression have been reported in Denmark, Scotland, England, Wales, Canada, Nigeria, Kenya, Iceland, Israel, Australia, and New Zealand. Gender differences in help seeking or in willingness to report symptoms do not adequately explain women's excess in depression.[7]

These gender variations in depression are especially interesting to mental health scientists, but currently no one is certain about why they exist.[8] Possible explanations include hormonal differences or differences in brain neurotransmitters. Particular genetic predispositions and female personality tendencies such as passivity, dependency, and less ability to express anger also have been suggested. Another possibility is that these differential rates simply represent the greater tendency of women to seek out help for depression and thus to be counted in surveys of differential rates. Or they might represent the greater tendency of women, compared with men, to admit depression. Still another possibility is that men disguise their depression by means of alcohol and other drug use.[9] The earlier-cited three-to-one statistic of greater alcoholism among men than women makes sense in this regard. However, scientists working in this field have provided fairly convincing evidence that the much greater rate of depression among females is real and is not due to different reporting rates.

If these explanations cannot account for the sizable differences in depression between men and women, then what can? One of the most promising explanations has been offered by Susan Nolen-Hoeksema of Stanford University. She proposed what she calls a *response styles theory of depression*, in which she suggests that the increased depression among women has to do with differences between the sexes in how they respond to symptoms of depression.[10] She believes that women tend to ruminate about their problems and their negative condition, whereas men are more likely to seek distractions when they are depressed. Women's strategies of continuously thinking about their condition may be counterproductive, but men's strategies appear to be much more effective. She also indicated that women's styles tend to be passive and that men use more active methods, with, again, differing degrees of effectiveness. This is consistent with gender differences observed elsewhere.

From an early age, women are socialized to be more passive, and men to be more active. A National Public Radio segment discussed this point. Attending a giant toy fair designed to exhibit the complete wares of the toy industry, Margot Adler repeatedly encountered action toys designed for boys and style toys designed for girls. Searching in vain for any exceptions to these stereotypes, she finally concluded, "In 1992, boys' toys still teach them how to do things, and girls' toys teach them to be pretty."[11] In our society, women have been subtly—

and not so subtly—conditioned to be passive, in many different ways. Although this is changing with the larger numbers of professional women, two-occupation families, and single-parent households, it is still true for many women. Given this training from the earliest years and continuing into adulthood, is it any wonder that woman use more passive mood regulation techniques than men do?

With these ideas in mind, it seemed to us that our research on how people change a bad mood could provide important new evidence about the response styles theory of depression as well as about alternative ideas. Even though our research does not apply directly to depression, it certainly has indirect implications, and it is clear from our research that men and women regulate their moods in different ways.

What support did we find for the response theory? First, it showed that when many men are in a bad mood, they use various pleasant activities, and in general, they try to distract themselves. Just as Nolen-Hoeksema suggested, our male subjects were more likely to turn to a hobby or some other pleasant activity, or they might listen to music or try to use humor. Consistent with the response theory, men who use this strategy are employing one of the best ways of alleviating their bad mood.

On the other hand, as we have seen, women as a whole use less effective strategies to regulate their moods. Their use of Social Support, Ventilation, and Gratification is a good example of a less effective strategy, and it may confirm Nolen-Hoeksema's notion that women brood excessively about their depression symptoms. The combination of social support and ventilation is consistent with the idea that when these potentially depressed women interact with others they do so to discuss their psychological problems, perhaps endlessly and in a kind of ruminative manner.

The use of Passive Mood Management is another good example. Women are more likely to watch TV, eat, or drink coffee or caffeinated beverages when they are in a bad mood. Again, this is a less effective strategy than the distraction strategy that men use, and again it supports Nolen-Hoeksema's idea that the ways that men and women deal with their depression symptoms are differentially effective.

But what about the Direct Tension Reduction strategy, including the alcohol and drugs that men use more often? It is the least effective strategy as determined in our research. This finding still may be consistent with the Nolen-Hoeksema theory in that it is a more active strategy than those used by women. And although it is clearly dysfunctional in many respects, including increased alcoholism and aggression, it may not result in greater levels of depression.[12]

One other difference between the way that men and women regulate their moods should be mentioned because of its great interest to so many people and because it may be related to depression. This concerns eating to regulate mood. In our research, we found that women had a significantly greater tendency to eat something as a way of changing a bad mood than men did. This finding is curious considering that women are more concerned with their weight than men are and spend more time on diets.

Although our finding seems to contradict the greater concern of women with their weight, we feel fairly confident about it because of other evidence of gender differences in eating behavior. For example, medical researchers Neil Grunberg and Richard Straub conducted an experiment in which they manipulated stress by means of films.[13] They also provided snack food for the subjects to munch on and kept track of what and how much was eaten. The women ate nearly twice as much sweet food under stress than in the control condition, whereas males ate less under stress. The Grunberg and Straub study makes sense in relation to the literature on eating disorders, for example, anorexia and bulimia, as women are many times more likely than men to be diagnosed with these psychological problems.[14]

Still, the question remains why women would be more concerned about their weight than men and, at the same time, eat more to regulate their bad moods. An obvious reason for the greater female concern about weight is the substantial emphasis in our culture on women's looks as a primary means of validation. But it seems that this would reduce their use of food as a mood regulator owing to its negative implications for weight.

The explanation of this curious phenomenon is by no means clear, but these findings show that women should be particularly vigilant about how they regulate their moods. Given their greater tendency to eat when they are feeling bad, they should seek other means of mood regulation instead.

Other Individual Differences in Mood Regulation.

Many other individual differences in mood regulation emerged in our research. For example, introverts are significantly more likely to try to be alone when they want to change a bad mood, whereas extraverts are more likely to seek out people. This difference is not surprising considering the well-known variations in behavior between these two types. For example, Hans Eysenck, the leading scientific interpreter of this aspect of personality, described introverts as quiet and retiring, introspective, fond of books rather than people, and distant except with close friends.[15]

Our findings extends the common view of introversion. In addition to behaviors usually associated with this characteristic, introverts also have their own preferred way of self-regulating their mood. This difference in mood regulation tendency may play a causal role in the larger pattern of introverted behavior. Although a single finding is not sufficient to draw such conclusions, it does reveal some interesting theoretical possibilities. In any event, this finding emphasizes the point that introversion is correlated with a wide variety of behaviors.

This association brings up another issue as well. Because introversion and extraversion are known to have significant genetic bases, the genetic influences on mood regulating behaviors may be similar as well. Many scientists estimate that genetic determinants account for two-thirds of the variations observed between introverts and extraverts compared with only one-third coming from learning and experience.[16] We must bear in mind these genetic influences when considering the underlying causes of mood regulation strategies. It is highly likely that at least some of the reason that people prefer one behavior to another reflects a genetic origin.

We found another difference in the people who chose to be alone. This behavior was the choice of people who were underweight, compared with normal or overweight people. Why this would be the case is by no means clear, but I suspect that it has something to do with body type. Many years ago, William Sheldon described differences in the three body types that he called *ectomorphs*, *mesomorphs*, and *endomorphs*.[17] Underweight people are more likely to be ectomorphs, and overweight people, endomorphs. The differences in aloneness that we observed are similar to temperament differences that Sheldon described.

According to Sheldon, a common genotype accounts for both body type and behavioral tendency. Although many critics discredit Sheldon's work, his ideas still have force among biologically oriented personality scientists, who increasingly view body differences as related to behavior in very basic ways. In the next decade we may see a resurgence of Sheldon's ideas, perhaps in a more sophisticated form.

Although the tendency to want to be alone may have a genetic origin, another finding suggests the importance of learning and experience as the basis of this behavior. In our sample, this behavior is more likely to be found among younger than older people. Thus, increasing age apparently reduces a person's desire to be alone when dealing with a bad mood. Perhaps younger people, with greater physical resources, are more able to tolerate a bad mood on their own. But it is also plausible that young people haven't yet learned the best way of changing a bad mood.

Age plays a large role in determining the types of behaviors that a person will choose to regulate mood. Young people are much more likely to vent their emotions (e.g., cry or scream) when trying to change a bad mood. Young people also are more likely to listen to music or engage in pleasant activities to change their mood. Therefore, it is possible that the greater frequency of these behaviors among younger people may be based on mood regulation.

On the other hand, older people are more likely to tend to chores or engage in religious or spiritual activities to change their negative moods. Aging is often a learning experience, and tending to chores makes sense—it has the advantage of taking a person's mind off the troubling circumstances that could be the immediate stimulus for the bad mood, and it has the added advantage of accomplishing some necessary tasks, thus providing some personal satisfaction. Even though this satisfaction might be slight, in the scheme of things it can help lift a bad mood.

Older people also turn to religious or spiritual activities, so it is possible that they have learned the value of this behavior in modifying mood. On the other hand, this finding may reflect the general cultural patterns of the older generation. Moreover, the closer to death that one comes, the more interest that one has in religious interpretations of life and afterlife. If older people spend more time on religious and spiritual activities, they might associate these activities with mood regulation.

Although some of these differences may be puzzling, others make sense. An example is that overweight people reported a greater likelihood of eating something when they are in a bad mood. The implications of this are obvious. If someone uses food to regulate mood, then overweight is the inevitable outcome. If weight control is important to a person, this self-observation would seem particularly meaningful. And of course, this tendency is consistent with other research showing that negative moods stimulate eating behavior, especially among dieters.[18]

Related to this issue of weight and mood regulation, we also found that overweight people report a greater tendency to watch TV as a way of changing a bad mood. This sedentary method of dealing with negative moods, combined with eating, seems especially likely to result in overweight. Once again, awareness of these mood dynamics is important to weight control.

Finally, we discovered that when dealing with a bad mood, professionals are significantly more likely to use humor, to try to change their location, or to have sex, compared with nonprofessionals. In reducing tension, anxiety, or nervousness, professionals also were significantly more likely to use stress management techniques or exercise. Furthermore, people with more education reported using exercise to reduce tension significantly more often than people with less education did. Still another finding was that professionals were significantly more likely to choose a simple means such as going outside for some fresh air in order to increase their energy.

11

Mood Substitution: Different Ways of Achieving the Same Mood

In the movie *Clean and Sober*, Michael Keaton plays a hotshot Philadelphia real estate agent who uses cocaine. Although at first he denies it, he really is an addict. Because of some legal problems, he enters a drug rehabilitation program to hide out for a while. In part, the movie is about his experiences of coming to grips with his addiction and detoxifying from the drug. In one scene Keaton is meeting in a restaurant with his "sponsor" M. Emmit Walsh. Walsh is a veteran Alcoholics Anonymous member whose role is to help and advise Keaton, particularly during times when his urge to use cocaine is overwhelming. In this scene, Walsh is eating chocolate ice cream and chocolate cake. As they talk, the two of them drink several chocolate milkshakes. It is somewhat incongruous to see adults eating such large amounts of sugar, but this is actually quite an accurate representation of what might happen in similar circumstances. That is, the effects of sugar are being used as a substitute for the cocaine-induced mood.

Recovering alcoholics use a similar process. Visit any AA meeting and you will see large amounts of coffee and sweets. Cigarette smoke is everywhere as the alcoholics seem to be seeking a fix in some way other than with alcohol. While people are trying to ward off the urge to have a drink, they are essentially using a substitute way of achieving a similar mood. These anecdotal examples are supported by systematic studies. For example, Ohio State nursing professors Sharon Rosenfield and Joanne Stevenson studied oral behaviors among recovering (first-year) alcoholic women.[1] Over a 4-month period, they found that these women ate significantly more sweet foods than comparison groups did. The women also smoked significantly more cigarettes. These findings are consistent with those of other research. In one study, psychologist Scott Verinis discovered that recovering alcoholics at a Chicago medical center drank significantly more coffee and also ate more chocolate. Recovering alcoholics also seek a wide variety of other means of achieving mood relief when they are in the throes of withdrawal.[2]

Research shows that alcoholism is only one of the dysfunctions in which people substitute other substances for the one that they crave. For example, those attempting to stop smoking usually eat more good-tasting foods. Sharon Hall and her associates from the University of California at San Francisco studied people enrolled in a program to stop smoking.[3] These people received training concerning smoking-reduction skills, monitored their food intake during the smoking-reduction program, and were randomly assigned to different quit dates. Hall and her associates found a clear relationship between the time that the subjects stopped smoking and their increased ingestion of sucrose and fats. In other words, when these people could no longer smoke, they began eating more good-tasting foods, and this is likely to be the basis of the well-known phenomenon of people's gaining weight when they stop smoking.[4]

Although not so well documented, abstinence following addiction to other drugs tends to produce similar effects.[5] I am reminded of an anecdote told to me by a former student who traveled with a particular rock group that was notorious for its drug use, including a good deal of cocaine. In his words, these musicians used one substance to wake up in the morning, another to get up for the concert, and still another to come down when it was time to go to sleep. But when they traveled to foreign countries, they didn't dare risk bringing their drugs with them. When deprived of their usual drugs, according to my informant, they ate lots of sugar, as the sugar effect helped them deal with the absence of the desired drug effects.[6]

I believe that mood effects are the key factors in all these examples of people who attempt to substitute one substance for another. It is not the particular physiological effects of the substance that is used, although this probably accounts for some of it. In other words, those who are trying to break an addiction are reacting to the dysphoric mood created when the needed substance is not available. They are attempting to correct the mood imbalance, to reestablish their good mood.

The importance of dysphoric mood states in various kinds of substance use and withdrawal is further exemplified in an examination of the conditions of relapse among different kinds of addicts. In most cases of relapse among smokers who are trying to quit, for example, the physiological withdrawal effects do not create the relapse, especially after the first few days.[7] Instead, the negative mood brought on by day-to-day stress and general life circumstances causes the relapse, a discovery consistent with studies of relapse among other kinds of drug users.[8]

It is important to recognize one of the most significant motivations of substance use: mood regulation. Alcohol, cigarettes, and even sugar are drugs in this sense. Once this principle of mood regulation is understood, the use of drugs is no longer so mysterious. It is a behavior that people use to "self-medicate." When we look at it in this way, we see many more examples in which a substance, usually food, is used to compensate for a dysphoric mood. For example, people suffering from seasonal affective disorders find sugar to be one means of relieving their immediate symptoms.[9] Similarly, PMS sufferers often crave carbohydrates.[10] Indeed, as stress levels increase generally, so does the use of substances and foods to regulate mood, particularly for certain groups of people.[11]

We can see the role of mood in various eating disorders. Binge eaters can rapidly consume a large amount of good-tasting foods when they are in a bad mood. A quart of ice cream or a whole chocolate cake is not unusual. The importance of mood in this phenomenon was apparent in a study of outpatients at a Chicago medical center conducted by Craig Johnson and Reed Larson.[12] In this study, bulimics and control subjects maintained their normal daily routines but were paged at different times of day. After being paged, the study participants quickly completed questionnaires indicating where they were, what they were doing, and how they were feeling. Over a week-long period, hundreds of reports were gathered.

These findings fit the mood principles presented in the early chapters of this book. For example, the binging and purging tended to occur in the afternoon and evening, times when people's energy is low and they are predisposed to greater tension. The mood that immediately preceded the binging was what I call tense-tiredness. Just before the binging, the study's participants recorded significant increases in feelings of irritability, weakness, and constraint.

A *Theory of Self-Regulation: From Tense-Tiredness to Calm-Energy*

The self-regulation of mood extends to a wide variety of behaviors, some we would not ordinarily consider.[13] These behaviors include everything from telephoning a friend when we are feeling down, to working on a hobby, to watching TV. Mood regulation includes not only general behaviors like these but also moment-to-moment adjustments. We continually sense our energy (and tension) levels and make finely tuned adjustments in our behavior. Our moods gently push us toward activity, rest and recuperation, or caution. The behavior takes many forms but essentially enables us to regulate our moods. The self-assessments that lead to these acts of mood regulation provide continuous information about our general bodily state, and the motivation for these acts comes from good or bad feelings generated by the various mood-regulating behaviors. Ultimately, this means that we are hedonic creatures who do things that feel good and avoid things that feel bad. Although we may temporarily overcome these hedonic prompts, in the long run, they control our behavior.

Habits are built up through continual experience with relationships involving behaviors and subsequent feelings. Mood-regulating behaviors are habitual, and we often are not aware why we prefer a particular activity or substance. We may see this behavior as inexplicably driven in a way that seems to defy all self-control. People do many things to feel better, and they use over and over those things that work. Sometimes they know why they do what they do, and other times they haven't a clue. In any event, with these behaviors, people are essentially regulating their moods.

Usually people avoid negative moods and seek positive moods. Tense-tiredness is the basis of most negative moods; calm-energy is the basis of most positive moods; and therefore these moods are central to self-regulation. There are variations within this continuum, of course. For example, tense-energy is a moderately positive mood, and so many people seek this state. Calm-tiredness, a variation of calm-energy, is positive (usually at bedtime), but not to the same degree that calm-energy is. Most of us avoid tense-tiredness, the stimulus that pushes us to take corrective action. Because the feeling of fatigue, tiredness, or a lack of energy combined with tension, anxiety, or nervousness is unpleasant, we try to avoid it. In addition, tense-tiredness often prompts action because it reminds us of a much more unpleasant state to come. In this sense, it may act as a signal, what psychologists often call it a *conditioned stimulus*. Substance users frequently have this reaction; that is, tense-tiredness is the warning to seek out the substance before their feelings worsen.

Although you can sense tense-tiredness in bodily sensations, it may be apparent only in your thoughts. For example, depression-related thoughts of hopelessness can be a signal of tense-tiredness. And sometimes tense-tiredness is not an identifiable bodily sensation or a thought but just a vague unpleasant feeling, what we have when we are down, so to speak, or in a bad mood. In one way or another, however, a wide variety of moods, thoughts, feelings, or bodily sensations prompt self-regulation and involve tense-tiredness.

If the tense-tiredness is intense, the motivation to self-regulate will be much stronger, and the self-correcting behavior may take on a certain desperate quality. The drug addict who must have a fix immediately is an example. A more common example is the two-pack-a-day smoker who has been without a nicotine fix for a couple of hours and has a certain desperate need when out of cigarettes. Physiological withdrawal symptoms probably interact with mood to amplify the urgency in the case of highly addictive substances. But always the mood is there and demands change.

On the other hand, mild states of tense-tiredness may simply incline a person to act in a particular way, but with no special urgency. We may be feeling just a little down, and so the thought of a friend comes to mind. We pick up the telephone. When we sense mild tense-tiredness, we think that a candy bar or some pastry would taste good. Perhaps the thought of a good cup of coffee comes to mind. This sensing system that leads to self-regulation is so finely tuned that we often take actions in anticipation of an impending negative mood. In these cases, we may be feeling moderately good, in a tense-energetic state or even a calm-energetic state. But we have a sense that our energy is declining ever so slightly and that soon the good feelings will be gone. This may account for the drinker who already is feeling good but, sensing a small diminution of positive feeling, drinks more.

We self-regulate for another reason as well. Aside from avoiding the unpleasant tense-tired mood, we also seek calm-energy when our mood isn't bad at all. This motivation is not based on correcting a deficit; instead, we wish to enhance an existing mood or induce a highly pleasurable mood. While trying to enhance calm-energy, people engage in behaviors and substances similar to those used in avoiding tense-tiredness. A cup of coffee, some good-tasting food, social interaction—all of these and many more behaviors contribute to this kind of enhancement. One of the best example of this in today's society can be found in the activities of exercise enthusiasts. These people are not the ones who do the obligatory 20 minutes a day, three times a week; these are the persons who are regularly at the gym or on the playing fields because they want to feel good while they are doing it.

Some recreational drug users provide another example of this search for calm-energy. They are not driven by a need, and they are not feeling especially tense. Rather, they turn to their substances of choice when they are seeking good feelings, not avoiding bad ones. These substances may be illicit drugs, or perhaps a small amount of alcohol or a cigarette. Having a glass of wine at the end of the day when you come home from work is another example of this kind of self-regulation. You don't necessarily drink the wine to reduce tension and relax but, instead, to increase pleasure.[14] As is well known, however, some people can't use drugs and alcohol in moderation, because it is too easy for them to become addicted psychologically, if not physiologically.

We see a number of variations of the general principle of avoiding tense-tiredness and moving toward calm-energy. Tense-energy

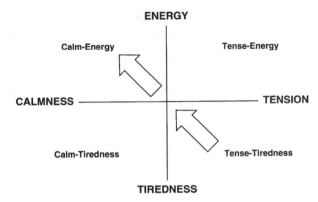

Figure 4   Predominant changes in self-regulation of mood

is very pleasurable to some people, and so they may desire this state rather than calm-energy. Type A personalities may crave the urgent, driving activity of a time-demanding schedule. Or a person feeling calm-energy late at night, near bedtime, may do things to feel even less energetic and prepare for sleep—perhaps take a warm bath or eat a snack that enhances tiredness. This may be a routine that this person often follows without being aware that calm-tiredness is the aim. Or people feeling calm-tiredness may try to energize themselves to complete some task. Even though they are tired and calm, they must temporarily increase their energy to get the task done, and they have their favorite ways of doing it. (The general principle of avoiding tense-tiredness and seeking calm-energy, together with these variations, is portrayed in Figure 4.)

Avoiding Tense-Tiredness in Eating, Smoking, and Substance Use

If tense-tiredness is the mood that often prompts self-regulation, then the many studies of eating and using different substances should have revealed some evidence of it. Unfortunately, no study yet done is perfect in this regard, but the reasons for the study defects are quite informative. The problem is that the information comes mainly from retrospective reports by the people being studied, and this reduces our ability to determine exactly what feelings they had and when they had them. Because moods are so variable, feelings that were present an hour earlier may have little effect on the mood-regulating behavior. To be most sure of what mood motivates the behavior, we must know what feelings were present in the moments before the behavior occurred. And since behavior is often generated by thoughts, we must consider, when possible, the moments before the thoughts about the behavior occur.[15]

From studies of eating undesirable or excessive amounts of food, we can get a picture of how regulating mood contributes to eating habits. A study already described of binging by bulimics, conducted by Craig Johnson and Reed Larson, is a good example for our purposes because the subjects were paged at random times of day and were given an opportunity to report their feelings. But as good as this study was, it did not indicate the subjects' feelings in the moments right before they binged or right before they thought about binging. Recall that in this study the bingers reported feeling irritable, weak, and constrained before their binging episodes. Tension is clearly indicated in irritability. It is a combination of reduced energy and heightened tension. Constraint, or a feeling of being closed in, is a variation of this tense feeling, and weakness is a sign of low energy or tiredness. Thus tense-tiredness appears to have been the stimulus for those eating binges.

Other studies of relapse among dieters showed similar results. For example, Carlos Grilo, Saul Shiffman, and Rena Wing at the University of Pittsburgh studied dieters to determine the differences between the times that they lapsed and ate the forbidden foods and the times that they withstood the temptation.[16] The average time at which relapse occurred was late afternoon (4:34 P.M.), about 4 hours after their last meal, and when they were moderately hungry. These times and conditions are exactly those in which low energy and moderately increased tension would be predicted—again, tense-tiredness. Reports by the study participants indicated that the majority of cases for temptation and relapse were characterized by upset, including anger, and by depression or tiredness. Here we have clear indications of tense-tiredness as well. Depression, as we have seen, represents a mixed arousal pattern of low energy and moderately high tension. Studies showing that depression stimulates eating provide some of the best evidence that tense-tiredness is an important stimulus.

The tiredness that the subjects reported in the Grilo and associates' study is another indication of tense-tiredness. Being tired and also under stress produces this state, and it frequently is a circular process. Dieters often are hungry, tired, and in need of energy. And low energy leaves them vulnerable to any negative thoughts and to the many stressors of the day. We can assume that because they are dieting, dieters are more affected by stress and more prone to tense-tiredness.

But what are we to make of the reports in this research of anger preceding the eating? When we are angry, we are most likely tense, but we must also have some energy. This presence of increased energy during anger episodes is an evolutionary necessity because in order to attack (the biological consequence of anger), energy is required.[17] But since anger readily drains energy, reports of anger some time before eating relapses may represent the aftereffects of the anger episode and probably tense-tiredness. In other words, people don't seek food during the active phase of their anger but rather, after it is over, when they are feeling drained. Reports of anger really represent the condition of being upset, a state in which one is vulnerable. The energy reserves of upset people are stretched thin, and so they become irritable and often are about to lose control.[18] They do not have sufficient resources to deal with the demands made on them.

A possible qualification concerning tense-tiredness and eating is that the research on dieters (often called *restrained eaters* by scientists) suggests that these people may react differently to unpleasant mood states than nondieters do. In her review of the literature, Audrey Ruderman, a psychologist at the University of Illinois, concluded that negative moods, and especially depression, increase eating mainly among dieters.[19] Nondieters may not eat more when they are in a negative mood, although the evidence here isn't as clear. If Ruderman's interpretation is correct, then tense-tiredness may lead to eating as a way of self-regulating mood only among some people (restrained eaters). Nondieters use different means of self-regulating mood when they are in a tense-tired state. But nonetheless they all use some kind of self-regulation.

The influence of tense-tiredness was evident in an interesting way in a study of dieters by David LaPorte, a psychologist at the University of Minnesota.[20] In his research, LaPorte studied people who were at least 30 percent overweight and who ate only a fasting supplement that supplied 420 calories per day. He followed them over a 10-week period, in part to determine what emotions they-felt when they occasionally broke their diets. LaPorte found that negative emotions preceded violations of the diet only in the second month, a time when this partial fast would begin to have what he called a *fatiguing effect*. For example, in the beginning of the diet there was no relationship between anxiety and noncompliance. People did not break their diets when they were more anxious. But in the second month, with increasing fatigue, the higher anxiety levels led them to cheat on their diets.

This study illustrates well the process by which anxiety joins declining resources to lead to tense-tiredness. Anxiety states per se are not necessarily the same as tense-tiredness, however. In the case of moderate anxiety, tense-tiredness results when the anxious person experiences decreases in energy of the sort that occur periodically as energy goes up and down. The declines might be at low times of the day, following an expenditure of energy that depletes the person temporarily, or over longer periods.[21]

LaPorte discovered another interesting finding in the same study. By the ninth week, increases in depression resulted in broken diets, whereas earlier they did not. This study revealed that increasing levels of tense-tiredness produce greater and greater difficulty withstanding the temptation of eating. In other words, as people lower their calorie intake below normal levels, they become more fatigued, and daily emotional occurrences affect them more and more strongly. At the beginning of the diet, their resolve is firm. But as the food restriction takes its toll on their energy, their resolve finally crumbles, and they eventually begin eating more than they should.

Obesity is another condition in which overeating is commonly associated with negative emotions. In his review of the available research, psychologist Richard Ganley cites many studies that show this.[22] The conditions most closely associated with emotional eating, he points out, are anger, depression, loneliness, boredom, and anxiety. As we have already seen, depression and anxiety often imply tense-tiredness, and anger, particularly being upset, may also imply this condition.

But what about loneliness and boredom? Although boredom is often thought to be nothing more than a low arousal state, a better interpretation is that a bored person is both slightly tense and tired. Observe yourself sometime when you are bored, and you will detect the unmistakable signs of tension: fidgetiness, distracted attention, and unpleasant feelings.[23] Loneliness is a similar state. The lonely person is not calm and filled with energy. Instead he or she is slightly sad and a bit agitated as well. Tense-tiredness is the underlying mood in both boredom and loneliness.

Other substances also are used to regulate mood in the same way as food is. Psychologist Saul Shiffman and his associates conducted a number of studies of smoking in relation to emotional states.[24] In one study of addicted smokers who had stopped but were tempted to smoke again, the most common precipitating emotions they reported were anxiety (41 percent), depression (25 percent), and anger (25 percent). Indeed, in several studies the emotions commonly associated with the inability to abstain from smoking read exactly like those of dieting relapse—depression, anxiety, anger, and boredom.[25]

Alcohol use is similar as well. For some time, scientists have been quite sure that reducing tension or anxiety is a primary motive of drinkers.[26] Even though experts sometimes disagree on this, studies that show a relationship between stress and alcohol support this assumption.[27] An indication of the importance of alcohol to the mood states I have been discussing can be found in the acronym HALT, coined by Alcoholics Anonymous; that is, alcoholics are warned to recognize the danger signals of Hunger, Anger, Loneliness, and Tiredness.

Alcohol and food are not unique in their relationship to mood. Studies of other mood-regulating substances yield very similar results: People who use opiates and other drugs report many of the same emotions that precede their use of the substances. These emotions are like those found in studies of eating, smoking, and alcohol.[28]

Self-Regulating During Normal Moods: Seeking Calm-Energy

We regulate our moods not only because we are tense and tired. When we are in a normal state, we often seek a more positive mood, essentially, some variation of calm-energy or perhaps tense-energy or calm-tiredness. Unfortunately, the evidence for this kind of self-regulation is not nearly so strong as it is for avoiding bad moods; the research simply has not adequately addressed this flip side of self-regulating behavior.

There is some evidence relevant to self-regulating during positive moods, however. For example, in the Grilo and associates study of dieters, a substantial percentage of the subjects reported that their relapse crises were preceded by happy feelings, and not what I would call tense-tiredness. These feelings often occurred in social settings with family and friends, probably times in which these people were relaxed and enjoying pleasant social interactions. In such conditions, eating can be almost like a drug that is used to perpetuate and enhance good feelings.

Smoking and alcohol frequently are used when a positive mood is already present.[29] Particularly in the case of these two substances, seeking pleasurable moods may motivate use in up to half the cases or even more. Having a cigarette right after a good meal or a satisfying sexual experience are examples of this. Another is having a drink with a friend when we aren't feeling bad but just want to feel better.

This kind of self-regulation often involves conditioning arising from past experiences. In the same way as avoidance of tense-tiredness probably includes the influence of conditioned stimuli, seeking calm-energy often occurs when someone encounters cues that stimulate that desire. For example, smokers report that they especially want a cigarette at certain times—at the end of a meal, with a drink or coffee, or when others are smoking. These associations become entrenched over years of conditioning. In many ways, we are like Pavlov's dogs, but instead of salivating to a bell, we experience an urge for a cigarette or a drink, or we want to call a friend. They all are the same kind of conditioned response.

Viewed in this way, it should be clear that our motivation often is to feel really good when we otherwise feel fine. Recreational drug use probably is an example of this, although scientists have not studied it extensively. Some of my students have described candidly why they use cocaine or marijuana on social occasions. Contrary to popular opinion, it isn't some crazed behavior over which they have little control. Instead, they are already having a good time, but they want to feel even better.

We all can identify with this behavior if we associate it with the more innocuous experience of eating chocolate or some other sweet treat. We may feel fine, not hungry at all and in no particular need. But we want the sugar snack nonetheless. It may not be evident that this is a kind of self-regulation, but a good mood is definitely the goal, even if it is only a few minutes of good feelings.

Still another example of this phenomenon, of which many people may not be aware, is exercise. Frequent exercisers probably know this quite well, but couch potatoes haven't discovered it. It feels good to work out, and not just for cardiovascular fitness or to lose a few pounds. One of my students described the experience in this way: "Sometimes when I don't have a lot of other things to do, I just put on my workout clothes and head for the gym. I look forward to it. I know that within minutes of beginning I will feel a surge that is very pleasurable. I anticipate the surge, and it is usually there."

In all these examples, self-regulating behaviors are used, not just to correct a deficit, but also to seek a positive state, a state of pleasure that exceeds the otherwise normal state that we are in. In one way or another this pleasure is connected with calm-energy, the optimal mood.

Once we understand that our motivation to avoid tense-tiredness and to seek calm-energy drives a lot of our behavior, controlling it becomes easier. In the first part of this chapter, I described the many ways that people substitute one substance for another in order to achieve a desired mood. But can we substitute more desirable ways of achieving the mood and avoid the undesirable ways?

12

Rational Mood Substitution: Exercise More and Indulge Less

People do a variety of things to regulate their mood, and a common method is to eat. This activity is quite evident at my university at around 4:00 P.M., the time that many people experience an afternoon slump in energy but when their demanding schedules are still stressful. The local snack area is filled with students eating muffins, cookies, ice cream, or any other foods they feel will give them a lift. I suspect that if we could observe these same people for the rest of the day, this snacking pattern would hold at other low-energy times as well. A few hours after dinner, when students begin to get tired but still have to study, we would see trips to the refrigerator or wherever else snacks are kept. Diets are very difficult to maintain on these occasions, as the motive to avoid tense-tiredness is powerful.

Dieters who observe themselves carefully will realize that they experience stronger urges to snack when they are in a certain mood than at other times. As I stated in Chapter 11, negative emotions are especially powerful inducements to eat. They are powerful because they often are associated with a loss of energy. Tense-tiredness is the mood that most threatens diets.

My students and I started thinking about this and wondering whether it might be possible to provide a healthier way of achieving the same mood effect as a sugar snack offers. If the mood were the underlying motivation, this would make the snack less tempting. In other words, if we could obtain similar effects, we should be able to substitute a healthy mood-enhancing activity for eating. Based on our past research, exercise seemed like a good candidate. In our scientific experiments, we found that moderate exercise—something as simple as a short brisk walk—increased energy and reduced tension. These walks, lasting no more than 5 or 10 minutes, result at least temporarily in calm-energy. These aren't dramatic changes, of course, but the effects of a snack also are only subtle and fleeting.

Would it be possible, we wondered, to substitute short brisk walks for sugar snacks? In other words, if people who crave a sugar snack because they are tense and tired, took a brisk walk instead, would their urge for a snack decline because the walk reduced their tense-tiredness? That is, we would substitute another behavior (the walk) for the desired mood-regulating behavior (the snack). We reasoned that it should work because the mood obtained from the walk would be similar to the mood obtained from the sugar snack.

In addition to the logic of this idea of substitution, it makes sense because substance users make a similar kind of substitution to self-regulate their mood. People trying to avoid alcohol often eat sugar, smoke cigarettes, or drink lots of coffee, essentially trying to achieve a similar mood or the same sense of relief as the forbidden substance provides. They are using an alternative substance in place of the one to be avoided. The same kind of mood substitution should occur in the case of a short brisk walk rather than a sugar snack.

Several of my graduate students—Don Peters, Paula Takahashi, and Angela Birkhead-Flight—joined me to study this matter. First, we reviewed the scientific literature to determine whether any other evidence supported the notion that exercise-produced moods could cause people to eat less. We found that no research had been done in such a way as to demonstrate that exercise influences mood, in turn reducing the urge to eat. But although they didn't measure mood states directly, the relationship between exercise and eating was the subject of a number of experiments. Based on the results of these studies, the idea seemed promising.

We quickly realized that the matter was not as straightforward as it first appeared. For instance, studies of lifestyle that consider changes in energy expenditure and food intake are difficult to control in human subjects, as they depend on potentially unreliable measurements (e.g., food diaries and extended exercise reports). One problem is that if energy expenditure temporarily increases with regular trips to the gym, it is difficult to know whether other physical activity is subsequently reduced.

Studies of animals are much more easy to control, of course, and they do provide a certain amount of valuable information. But such studies do not ensure that comparisons from these animals to people will be valid. Human experiments in which people first exercise and then measure their appetite offer some of the best kinds of evidence regarding this relationship. But to my knowledge only a few inconclusive experiments of that sort have been done, and I'll discuss them shortly. For our study, we first reviewed a number of different kinds of research, which provided both questions and encouragement for our line of thinking.

Some of the first scientific studies that we reviewed seemed to argue against using exercise to reduce eating, and we mention these ideas here because it allows us to understand food intake much better. Researchers in this area make a fundamental assumption about the underlying biology—that an equation exists between energy intake and output. Biologists assume that if people exercise more, they will eat more, and if they exercise less, they will eat less. In this way, the body stabilizes its energy demands and requirements, presumably because appetite is the homeostatic mechanism that controls this equation.

Nonetheless, appetite and related influences may lead to other outcomes. We have already seen that many people develop an appetite in response to negative emotions and that these feelings are often associated with low levels of exercise. Eating allows these people to feel better temporarily. But since the negative emotions do not expend much energy, this kind of motivation results in a positive energy balance over time. In other words, such people create more food energy than they expend. Ultimately, such people gain weight.[1]

This positive energy balance makes sense from an evolutionary point of view. In our evolutionary past, a negative emotion often signaled that we would need more energy. This demand in turn required adequate nutrients to deal with the potential emergency. Even a weight gain has meaning in this way of thinking: The extra reserves in the form of adipose tissue (fat) that can be easily converted to energy will stand a person in good stead for extended emergencies. As much sense as this makes, however, someone with an ideal of thinness will not be pacified by an explanation from evolutionary biology. But the message is clear that successful dieting should take into account a person's emotional state. That is, successful diets appear to depend in large measure on a relatively positive emotional life. At the very least, successful diets probably depend on reducing the bad mood of tense-tiredness as the prevailing state that follows from extended periods of low energy intake, particularly in conjunction with day-to-day life stress.

In addition to the research on negative emotions and eating, we found a few studies that examined food intake following different amounts of exercise. One of them, a set of now classic experiments with animals that are often cited by scientists, was conducted decades ago by Jean Mayer and associates at the Harvard Medical School.[2] Mayer concluded that food intake first decreases with moderate exercise and then increases with more intense exercise. If applied to humans, this would suggest that one could increase one's physical activity by a certain amount—say 20 percent—without subsequent increases in appetite. Some qualifications are necessary, of course, as is true of most scientific findings. Several later research studies indicated that the relationship between energy intake and output depends to some extent on athletic condition and weight. For example, athletes increase their food intake with more exercise, but untrained and overweight people do not.[3] This is consistent with the ideas proposed in this book because athletes would have much more practice in sensing signals that the body provides. Moreover, the increased energy that athletes experience counteract the negative emotions that otherwise influence eating. An alternative explanation is that athletes are leaner than less active people, and consequently they have a much closer match of bodily needs to nutrient intake.[4]

William Reger and Thomas Allison at Wheeling Hospital in West Virginia studied exercise and appetite directly. They employed nine women in three experimental conditions. After not eating for some time, the subjects were either placed on treadmills for up to 30 minutes under two different workloads or put into in a no-exercise control condition. The researchers found that the appetite ratings of the subjects in the exercise conditions fell for up to 2 hours.[5]

Similarly, Deborah Thompson and her associates at Queen's University in Canada studied 17 male subjects following a 12-hour fast. They were placed on an exercise cycle early in the morning in one of three conditions: 68 percent of maximum workload, 35 percent of maximum workload, or sedentary control. The 68 percent workload condition resulted in a lower appetite for the full 50 minutes of the study, but only the first 5 minutes significantly differed from the comparison groups. The 35 percent workload showed some lessening of appetite, but these differences were not reliable.

From these different kinds of research, we found some support for the idea that moderate levels of exercise might reduce appetite. But other lines of evidence also gave us support: Scientists are well aware that cocaine, amphetamines, and other such activating substances not only increase euphoria and excitement but also suppress appetite. This is the principle behind the widely prescribed diet pills.[6] These substances probably affect the norepinephrine and dopamine systems in the brain, the same systems that are likely to be activated by exercise (see Chapter 8).[7]

More relevant to our research is the fact that diet pills and other substances that suppress eating also increase energy, and since energy level is enhanced by moderate exercise, it follows that this kind of exercise should reduce the urge to eat. In other words, moderate exercise has some of the same mood effects as diet pills do.

An Experiment with Exercise and Snacking

These various lines of evidence suggested that our idea of using moderate exercise to suppress food intake made some sense, and so we decided to conduct an experiment to study sugar snacking directly.[8]

We planned to measure mood as it changed following exercise, and also to measure appetite, and to study their relationship. Also, to make this experiment as similar as possible to people's daily routines, we planned to study sugar intake and exercise on many occasions over several weeks.

The experiment involved asking subjects either to take a brisk 5-minute walk or to sit quietly before eating a sugar snack on 10 separate occasions and to self-rate their mood both before and after walking or sitting.[9] We recruited 18 trustworthy volunteers who normally snacked on sugary foods at certain times of day. These men and women ranged in age from 18 to 52 years and habitually ate candy, doughnuts or some other sugary snack. As part of the carefully controlled procedure, each day they carried around the necessary snacks and mood measures to complete the study, together with hidden instructions that told them at the agreed-upon times whether or not they were to snack. They measured their mood and urge to snack before and after they either walked or sat quietly doing something else for the same period of time.[10] In the last part of the experiment, the participants ate the sugar snack if they wished, and we measured the time until they ate it. We followed this procedure with the same subjects for 3 weeks.[11]

The results of the experiment supported our theory exactly as we had expected. The walking reduced both the subjects' urge to snack and the time that they waited to eat it. After walking, their urge to eat the candy bar decreased significantly, but after sitting the subjects felt an even greater urge to eat the candy. Although these differences were small, they were reliable. Not only did their urge subside following the walk, but on average, the subjects also waited almost twice as long to eat the candy after walking as they waited after sitting. Clearly, walking dampened their urge to eat and caused our subjects to wait longer to eat.

Walking also increased energy and decreased tension, compared with sitting. Even though the energy increases were much greater than the tension decreases, both were statistically significant. These mood effects were similar to those found in previous research, even though the subjects had walked for only 5 minutes in this experiment. Once again, this research showed that the primary mood effect of moderate exercise is increased energy and that the secondary effect is decreased tension.

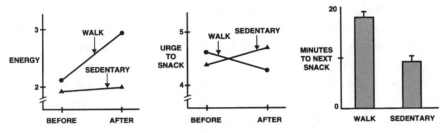

Figure 5 Sugar snacking experiment

Walking changed energy much more than it did the urge to eat a sugar snack or the time a person ate the snack, though these also were clearly affected. The differences in tension were small but statistically significant. Comparing these effects suggests that the energy boosts caused the urge to snack to decrease and to increase the time until the next snack was eaten. Unfortunately, in this kind of research such a causal relationship cannot be firmly established, but the results did strongly suggest that mood is an important basis of the urge to eat. Finally, since the walking influenced energy much more than it did tension, these results imply that energy increases are more important causes of reduced urges than tension decreases are. (See Figure 5 for graphs of energy, urge, and waiting time.)

This experiment indicated that moderate exercise can temporarily reduce the appetite for a sugar snack, but maybe there is something unique about sugar urges and exercise. What about other kinds of mood regulation? Would the mood produced by exercise influence these other mood-regulating behaviors as well? To test this idea further we decided to experiment with another common way of regulating mood, so we chose smoking.

Smoking and Self-Regulation Theory

Just like sugar snacking, smoking is often used to regulate mood. The two substances are somewhat different, however, because nicotine is highly addictive, and habitual smokers suffer a range of unpleasant physiological withdrawal symptoms if they are deprived of a cigarette for a while. Tension is especially evident. You can see telltale signs of it by watching people who smoke two or more packs a day but haven't had their needed fix for an hour or two. They appear agitated and often pace, bounce their leg, wiggle their foot, or tap their fingers with nervous movements. If they have been in a movie or at a theater where they couldn't smoke, during the intermission they walk rapidly toward the door. There is no doubt that nicotine is a drug and that these are addicts.

We have already seen that tiredness amplifies the negative effects of tension. Thus, tense-tiredness is often a signal to the smoker that a cigarette is needed. And if that is the case, it should be possible to reduce temporarily the urge to smoke with moderate exercise, an activity that counteracts tense-tiredness. Research on exercise and smoking offers some confirmation of this idea. For example, medical researcher Ovide Pomerleau and his colleagues at the University of Michigan found that sustained high exercise had an immediate effect on the urge to smoke.[12] Using exercise bicycles, they studied 10 male smokers in two conditions: 20+ minutes at 80 percent of maximum workload capacity or the same amount of time cycling slowly to simulate normal daytime activity.

The subjects in the strenuous-exercise condition had less desire to smoke. Although this experimental effect was not sufficient to achieve statistical significance, given the small number of subjects, it was definitely noteworthy. In fact, the researchers indicated that, after vigorous exercise, 3 of the 10 habitual smokers asked whether they were required to smoke. (The requirement to smoke a cigarette was part of the experiment.)

Other studies have also shown that exercise reduces the urge to smoke. For example, exercise researcher Robert Grove and his associates at the University of Western Australia followed 13 female smokers during a week when they had stopped smoking.[13] Each day, half the smokers used an exercise bicycle for 15-minute workouts at 75 percent of their maximum heart rate. The other half remained in the laboratory but did not exercise. Before exercising or sitting quietly, the subjects rated their craving for cigarettes. Those in the exercise condition craved cigarettes significantly less than did those scheduled for no exercise. Apparently, just exercising for this amount of time each day was sufficient to reduce their urge.

Some studies have demonstrated that exercise helps smokers stop. For example, medical researchers at Stanford University studied 42 smokers who had had heart attacks and 3 weeks later were given treadmill exercise training. They were compared with 26 patients who did not exercise. At 28 weeks, those in the exercise group reported smoking significantly fewer cigarettes each day than did those in the no-exercise group.

Indirect support for our idea also comes from studies showing that exercisers are less likely to smoke than are those who do not exercise. A good example is a large-scale study of almost 10,000 Canadians who were questioned about their exercise and smoking habits.[14] For older and younger men and younger women, increasing levels of physical activity was correlated with less smoking. Older women showed a trend in the same direction, but these differences were not statistically significant.

An Experiment with Exercise as a Substitute for Smoking

Given our results from the sugar-snacking experiment, we decided to use the same approach to study smokers and exercise. If our self-regulation theory were correct, moderate exercise should reduce the urge to smoke. My graduate students and I tested the idea in the same way that we tested sugar snacking and exercise. We recruited 5 male and 11 female smokers for this experiment, ranging in age from 18 to 44 years, smoking between one and two packs of cigarettes a day.[15]

These smokers followed the same procedure as the snackers did. They completed self-ratings of mood and urge to smoke before and after either walking briskly for 5 minutes or sitting for the same length of time. They were then free to smoke whenever they wished, but they had to record how much time elapsed before the next cigarette. They repeated this procedure 10 times for 3 weeks. As with the snacking experiment, each smoking trial followed 45 minutes of sedentary activity, during which the subjects didn't smoke, eat, or drink.

For the most part, the results of this study paralleled those of the snacking experiment. The walks caused small but significant decreases in urge to smoke, and the smokers waited twice as long to smoke their next cigarette after they had walked than they waited after sitting for a comparable time. The walks also produced significant increases in energy. Again, the energy changes were greater than the changes in urge (see Figure 6).

We found one difference in the results of this experiment compared with those of the previous one: Tension was not reduced as much by the walks in the case of the smokers as it was for the snackers. This

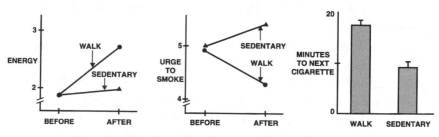

Figure 6   Cigarette smoking experiment

is an interesting finding that illustrates the mood effects of walks and that may tell us something about the motive to self-regulate. The smokers probably were more tense than the snackers to begin with because they had to wait 45 minutes or more since their last smoke, and a two-pack a day smoker becomes tense after an hour or so without a cigarette. A similar wait by the snackers would create less tension. If this is the case, the walk may not have been sufficiently long and physically demanding to lower this higher level of tension. Once again, we know that moderate exercise primarily affects energy levels and has secondary, but weaker, effects on tension.

The smoking urge was changed by the walk, and energy was changed to an even greater degree, but tension was changed much less than either urge or energy. We obtained similar results in the sugar-snacking experiment, and they indicate that the motivation for substituting self-regulating behaviors involves greater energy even if tension isn't changed. If this is true, the tiredness part of tense-tiredness may be the most important influence in the motivation to self-regulate. In the case of our tense smokers, this level of exercise wasn't enough to reduce their tension, but the energy derived probably enabled them to manage their tension better. Unfortunately, we can't be certain about this from the results of a single experiment.

Regulating Moods and Breaking Bad Habits

With both smoking and snacking, we found that people could use moderate exercise to reduce these urges. Mood and the change in mood that exercise created seem to be the clearest explanations for the delay in smoking and snacking we observed. What is particularly important here is that it is possible to substitute one behavior for another as long as it elevates mood. In other words, we can substitute a healthy activity, such as exercise, for one we would like to reduce, such as smoking or snacking.

The statistics regarding the success of programs that help people diet and stop smoking are not promising, as most attempts end in failure. The principles we have discussed here do not offer instant solutions and success for people wishing to indulge less, but they do offer a means of understanding the kinds of problems that such people will encounter. And I hope they offer some general strategies that will be helpful in controlling some of these urges.

We know that mood is central to smoking, alcohol, and other drug use. Much of the time, negative moods, especially tense-tiredness, motivate us to use these substances. So if they are to be successful, programs aimed at abstinence must take into account the participants' mood. A strong resolve will work only for a while. To be successful in abstaining, we need to understand when weakness is greatest and how it can be counteracted.

Most important, the situation is not hopeless; we can change bad habits. An understanding of energy and tension in our lives offers valuable ammunition for those wishing to indulge less. It is possible to predict with some certainty when one will become tense-tired, and such information is extremely useful, especially if there are ways of changing the tense-tiredness without using the undesirable substances.

Certain times of day leave people especially vulnerable to substance use, and often these correspond to the circadian rhythms of energetic arousal. Most people feel their energy wane in the late afternoon and later in the evening. These people's low-energy times require special attention. Sleep, general health, a nutritious diet, physical conditioning, stress, negative thoughts all interact to produce periods of tense-tiredness. What can intelligent people do to counteract this dangerous state? Exercise is one solution that clearly affects the moods that control behavior.

Would you be able to diet successfully or stop smoking only by using short brisk walks to curb your most demanding urges? Probably not. For real success, you must employ well-known principles of diet and abstinence programs. But the short brisk walks can be useful. If you can just get over that occasional bad time, you will often succeed with the abstinence program. The fact that a brisk 5-minute walk before smoking or snacking caused our regular users to wait longer until indulging is important information. But more than using exercise as a tool, this success emphasizes the importance of the underlying mood states in substance use. Increased energy and reduced tension are the keys to avoidance, and the reason that the walks work is that they affect mood. All of us, consciously or not, avoid tense-tiredness and seek calm-energy—this is the basis of many behaviors that we use to self-regulate our moods.

PART THREE

Optimal Mood Management

13

The Practical Psychology of
Self-Regulation

So far, I have not offered practical applications for the concepts about mood that I have described. Yet many of these concepts can be helpful in understanding everyday moods and behaviors. When I teach courses on mood, my students repeatedly request practical information. So each semester in my Psychology of Mood class I devote a small portion of time to this[1].

The Many Faces of Tense-Tiredness

I stated earlier that we avoid the mood of tense-tiredness and that this motivates us to regulate our behaviors in some way, whether by smoking, snacking, or drinking a glass of wine or just by simple behaviors like telling ourselves to think differently or calling a friend. In addition, this mood pattern underlies depression and a number of other unpleasant feelings associated with a wide variety of negative thoughts and behaviors.

Generally, when we are in a bad mood, some variation of tense-tiredness is at the base of it. Recognizing this state can help us regulate our moods because it can tell us why we indulge in certain behaviors and help us substitute healthy behaviors. Let us examine a few of the immediate reactions to tense-tiredness in real-life situations. The vignettes in this and the next chapters are from my students, past and present.

> Rhonda, a 23-year-old elementary teacher, described to me her reactions in a tense-tired mood state. She had become familiar with this concept from one of my classes and continued to notice the effects of tense-tiredness, although she no longer is a student. In the following example she speaks about being at work during a demanding day: "When I am in a tense-tired state, it is hard to remain pleasant and polite. I want to snap at people. My forehead perspires and my tongue is dry in my mouth."

When not in a tense-tired state, Rhonda is quite pleasant and polite. But when in this mood she finds it difficult to maintain that behavior. It is as though the effort is too great, which is probably the case. Although pleasant social interactions seem effortless, it is clear that at least a moderate amount of energy must be expended in these everyday interactions. Think of the complexity of a simple social interaction. Someone says something to us, and we respond. But on another level, we not only hear what they say but also think about what it means. In addition, at some level of awareness, we monitor how our words sound and how our facial expressions appear. If the other person isn't responding appropriately, we may change our words in mid-sentence and say something else, and our nonverbal communication extends this expenditure of energy even further.

Moreover, we often try to present ourselves in a particular way, to create an appropriate image.[2] This may sound absurd to someone who hasn't thought about it, but almost all of us do it, at least in some ways, for example, in the way we comb our hair or the particular clothes we choose. These are ways of presenting ourselves, and they require a certain amount of energy.

When our personal resources start to become depleted, perhaps late in the afternoon, or later in the evening, we may be so tired that even polite social interaction demands too much. One student told me about walking out of his way to avoid meeting someone that he saw coming in the distance. The interaction would not have demanded much; just a smile and a few perfunctory remarks were necessary. But even that was too much in his tired state.

In Rhonda's case, however, she speaks of snapping at people, which represents more than simple fatigue. Tiredness plus tension is the basis of this kind of behavior. Tiredness leaves us particularly vulnerable to even mild stress, and the tense-tired state that emerges from this tiredness and stress has many and varied effects. Social interactions require effort, and tense-tiredness may stretch our resources beyond a pleasant level. Thus we can easily become irritable, which leads to sharp and even angry responses.

A second point that Rhonda makes is that her forehead perspires and her tongue is dry, classic physical symptoms of anxiety or tension. The sympathetic branch of the autonomic nervous system (see Chapter 8), in particular, is activated under these conditions. After millions of years of evolution, humans have developed these reactions as part of an emergency reaction. Although Rhonda is hardly in a life-threatening emergency, at some level it is as though she thinks she is.

Let us turn next to a somewhat different reaction to tense-tiredness.

Christina is 25 years old and works as a rehabilitation aide at an adolescent center. It is a very emotionally demanding job because it requires working with mentally disturbed adolescents. She supervises groups to enhance self-esteem and she teaches anger management, social skills, ceramics, and sports. Having learned about tense-tiredness in my class, she is well aware of this negative state. She observed, "The children and my coworkers can really sense my energy level as well as my tension. If I have not gotten enough sleep or food, I tend to have less patience with the kids. Also, I may get lethargic and end up not participating in their games during the sports group. Sometimes when I get tense, I tend to isolate myself during my break time. My coworkers (who are my friends) don't understand why I'm so quiet. In this tense-tired state, I feel like I'm being pulled in a hundred different directions."

Like Rhonda in the previous example, Christina focuses on the difficulties of engaging in smooth social interactions. But in this, more is required than just polite talk. Christina has responsibilities with children who are not easy to deal with. She must pay attention to discipline as well as what she is teaching. This is hard work that demands real effort, and so diminished energy levels have an immediate effect.

Christina speaks about withdrawing and not participating, but notice that this withdrawal is different from Rhonda's, who stated that she snaps at people. Both reactions might be expected, however, probably depending on the individual's temperament. But in both cases, it is the tense-tired mood state that precipitates the negative reactions. In the following chapters, I will indicate how each woman might better react to this tense-tiredness, but for now I will just say that personal awareness of the state is the first step before change is possible.

Both these examples highlight social reactions to tense-tiredness. Undoubtedly, these disruptions in social interactions are related to the women's negative thoughts, and often the thoughts themselves indicate the tense-tired state. They can be either moderately or extremely distressing. The following vignette illustrates a mildly negative mental state that develops from tense-tiredness. It may just represent some unpleasantness that passes with no effect, or over time, it may progress to depression and even to major life changes.

Mark is 45 years old and has a family and a job with many responsibilities. These and other matters create a certain amount of tension. In addition, Mark probably is undergoing a midlife crisis that many men of this age suffer. From time to time he pauses in his busy life to take stock. He asks himself how things are going and whether he is doing what he wants to do. "I sometimes awaken at 3:00 A.M. in the morning, at least 3 hours before I have gotten my needed sleep for the night. I think about my life and how things are going. During this tense-tired time the prospects usually look grim. It seems as though my life is bad and nothing can salvage it. When I pause to think about why things look this way, together with the mood theory that I now know, I try to stop my thoughts. This isn't the right time to think about this, I tell myself."

Mark is experiencing a tense-tired period that may occur at several times during the day as the cycle of energetic arousal ebbs and flows. Three in the morning is only one of those low points. Any troubling matter in Mark's life is likely to appear more serious when his energy is low. He might have had a similar negative perception just after awakening, in the late afternoon, or just before bed at night. That is, the time of day can be extremely important to how we look at our problems. They can appear hopeless at one time but at another time may seem to be of little concern.

As I stated earlier, there are many individual differences in circadian rhythms of energetic arousal. Thus, one time may be quite bad for some people, whereas others find that this same time is not so bad. What is important is not the exact hour of the day but the gradually shifting cycle of energy and tiredness. This natural circadian rhythm is easy to recognize when you start paying attention to it.

Mark's problems give him discomfort when he thinks about them in those moments when his mood is low. If these negative perceptions frequently crop up and persist, he may be suffering from depression. Or on the other hand, in these moments he may decide to make a radical change in his life, one that he later will regret. Although for most of us, such moments come and go, leaving us with mild feelings of dissatisfaction, some people conclude from such times that they are unhappy and must make major changes.

As we have already seen, because negative thoughts are associated with tense-tiredness, it should be no surprise that if you take stock of your life only when your energy is low, you are likely to conclude that you are unhappy. If we can understand the close tie between feelings or moods and our thoughts, we can begin to see how biological rhythms and cognitive processes are enmeshed. This awareness is the first part of change.

Worry is another common reaction to the tense-tired mood, as the next example illustrates.

Dina is a 36-year-old graduate student. "Since I am older and a first-time mother, I was completely exhausted when my year-old daughter was still not sleeping through the night. Then the evening arrived when she finally slept the night through. Unfortunately, I couldn't sleep because of the fatigue that I had been experiencing continuously from my extended tense-tired state. That night my sleep was interrupted by all of her little breathing noises, which I could hear (thanks to the modern science of baby monitors). I kept worrying about whether she was breathing all right. Then I worried that there might be an earthquake, and so on."

The mood of tense-tiredness continually influences the mental life of the person experiencing it. Worry about both big and little things is a common reaction. When in this mood, one becomes preoccupied with the troublesome parts of one's life, and events and circumstances that might otherwise be seen as benign can loom large.

Reactions to tense-tiredness aren't always minor, however. Sometimes events coincide with an energy-reducing physical condition that leads to more serious results. Things may be going reasonably well, but in even a short while, a major stressful event occurs. And if it is coupled with protracted tense-tiredness, such as can happen with a debilitating medical condition or, for a few women, with intense PMS, the result can be quite dramatic. The following example shows why:

> Ann is a 31-year-old photographer. She is successful and capable and manages her personal relationships quite well. But in this example we see a troubling episode in her life that occurred because of an unusually influential set of events and personal circumstances. "I recently experienced the death of my mother, and the resulting sadness is normal. But her death occurred about 5 days prior to my period, and I think my feelings of depression were exacerbated by this timing. Throughout the following month the sadness continued, but just prior to my period, I began feeling especially unattractive and irritable. I was in a time of extended tense-tiredness. These feelings were so strong that I told my boyfriend that our relationship was not working, and that we should no longer see each other. I said it was because I realized he didn't like me any longer. The pressure of my work, together with the relationship, seemed unbearable. We broke up, but later I was sorry.

Ann experienced a protracted period of tense-tiredness because of several influences that coincided. It was not just the time of day or immediate work pressures that were important, although they contributed significantly to Ann's tense-tired mood. In this case, her mother's death put her into an extended period of mourning, during which time she probably ate poorly and did not get enough sleep. Each time she thought about her mother, she probably felt anxious. In most months, her menstrual period may not have been a problem for her, but this month, the conjunction of stressful events plus the menstrual tension arising from cramps, bloating, and other unpleasant bodily sensations pushed her into behavior that she later regretted.

Ann's behavior also was influenced by feelings of low self-esteem. She speaks of feeling unattractive, and apparently she saw herself as unintelligent while in this tense-tired mood. Reduced self-esteem is one of many effects we have seen with tense-tiredness, and it can have a major effect on behavior, as evidenced by Ann's willingness to terminate her relationship with her boyfriend, only to regret it when her mood changed. Clearly, decisions—and especially far-reaching actions—taken in such a mood are risky.

A Test of Tense-Tiredness

Let me offer an idea that may sound extreme: Most of our negative thoughts, particularly worrisome ones, arise from a tense-tired mood. When this bad mood lifts, the unpleasant thoughts seem to vanish also. There is no question that events and circumstances do result in negative thoughts at times when we are neither tense nor tired, but the most worrisome thoughts usually come during tense-tired moods.

Awareness of this phenomenon is useful. Although it often is difficult to control negative thoughts consciously, it is easier to control energy-related moods. A small amount of exercise, some needed sleep, or even a nutritious meal can do the trick.

In Chapter 4 I introduced the concept of the congruence of mood and cognition. Essentially, this well-established principle holds that our thoughts tend to have the same valance as our moods; that is, negative thoughts are associated with negative moods, and positive thoughts with positive moods. Thus, one of the most negative moods, tense-tiredness, is usually associated with a wide variety of negative self-perceptions (e.g., low self-esteem), together with pessimistic outlooks on the present and future.

You may recall a series of studies we discussed in Chapter 2, which examined the relationship between the time of day and the perception of the seriousness of personal problems. This research revealed evidence that personal problems appear more serious at certain times of day. For example, all other things being equal, in the late afternoon the same personal problem seems slightly more serious than it does late in the morning. From this research, we concluded that the energy and tension levels underlying natural circadian rhythms were the probable causes of these changes in perception.

These findings make it important to monitor our moods. I use a practical aid with my students to test the presence of a tense-tired mood. It really is an index of tense-tiredness in that its answers indicate the likely degree of this negative condition. This test is useful when you are mired in an unpleasant mood state and everything looks bad. For it to be most effective, you should take the test whenever negative thoughts arise. At first, you may find it necessary to look at the test each time you take it, but after a short time you will be able to use it as a quick mental survey.

INDEX OF TENSE-TIREDNESS

1. What is the time of day?
2. How much sleep have I had recently?
3. When did I eat last (and what kind of food did I consume)?
4. Have I been sedentary for a long period (when did I exercise last)?
5. How good is my general health?
6. What is my general stress level?
7. (For women) What time of the month is it?
8. Have I recently taken any psychoactive drugs (including alcohol), or am I avoiding psychoactive drugs (including nicotine and caffeine) on which I have become dependent?
9. What is my current energy level?
10. What is my current tension level?

How should we interpret these answers? Remember that not all of us exhibit the same patterns and habits we use throughout the day to control our moods. The first item, time of day, can be interpreted in various ways depending on one's own characteristic circadian rhythm. As noted earlier, mid-to late afternoon and late evening are the times when most people are tense-tired. Just after waking in the morning also can be a time of tense-tiredness, particularly if one's thoughts aren't fully occupied with preparations for the day.

Tense-tiredness may regularly appear at other times of day as well, according to individual differences. Only systematic self-observation (see Chapter 17) can provide a true indication of one's critical times of day. Nonetheless, most people are at least vaguely aware of their low-energy periods, usually late afternoon and late evening.

The second item, sleep, is a good predictor of mood. Sleep researchers agree that most adults and adolescents do not get enough sleep (see Chapter 3). Indeed, sleep is often given a low priority in a fast-paced lifestyle, the first thing sacrificed when one is busy. However, lack of adequate sleep leads to frequent periods of tense-tiredness, usually at certain times of the day.

Most people tend to overlook sleep as the reason for their bad mood, especially if they have gradually cut back their hours of sleep. But it is highly likely that this deprivation has a continuing mood effect. And even if you usually get enough sleep, a 1- or 2-hour-loss the previous night or for the past couple of nights is likely to result in periods of tense-tiredness and often in uncharacteristic bad moods.

The third item, the last time you ate, is not always easy to interpret. As with the first item, a good appraisal of the relationship between food and mood requires systematic self-observation. You must spend a moderate amount of time watching your mood reactions to food. But your observations will clarify the food–mood connection.

The most likely reason you are experiencing tense-tiredness is a skipped meal. Going without food probably will result in decreased energy and at least some increase in tension, especially if you are used to eating at a specific time and you skip the meal. It is not surprising that research on dieters showed that their fatigue may be an effect of long-term diets.[3] From this, tense-tiredness naturally follows, and the desire to regulate this bad mood with a variety of behaviors.

Sugar can also be a culprit. Our research found that people initially felt an increase in energy as a result of a sugar snack. But within an hour, their energy actually decreased below what it had been before they had the snack. And an hour after eating the snack, the subjects felt significantly more tense.[4]

These findings allow us to understand the research by Christensen and his colleagues at Texas A&M University who found that diets eliminating sugar and caffeine apparently reduce the feelings of depression that many people experience.[5] According to Christensen's research, not everyone had this positive effect, but a significant number of people did. One implication of this is that sugar and caffeine first increase energy but later result in tense-tiredness and the associated feelings of depression. Therefore, eliminating these substances may also eliminate the energy and tension cycles that create depression.

If you answer yes to the fourth item, being sedentary versus active, it may or may not indicate tense-tiredness. Energy feelings are closely tied to the motor system (Chapter 7) and when you get up and move about, your energy rises as well. Conversely, inactivity often leads to lower energy, but not always. That is, you may feel energetic even while sitting. But even though that is true, if negative thoughts enter your mind and you have been sedentary for some time, you may be experiencing a tense-tired mood because of your inactivity.

Health, the fifth item, is a good indication of energy level. Research shows that reduced health is directly associated with tiredness and low energy (Chapter 3). On the other hand, optimal health produces energy during normally energetic times of the day.

Stress level, the sixth item, provides information about how tense you feel. Stress increases tension, and high levels of tension are associated with decreased energy and tiredness (Chapter 6). Of course, moderate levels of tension can increase energy, and both tense-energy and tense-tiredness can be the direct result of stress. But continued stress over time may deplete your resources to a point that even low levels of tension can result in fatigue. Moreover, even a small amount of tension makes older people and those in poor physical condition tired.

Premenstrual tension, the seventh item, is applicable to only some women, either each month or only some months (Chapter 5). Although the evidence regarding PMS is mixed, it appears that some women experience heightened tension for several days immediately before menstruation (and sometimes during the first days). If nothing else, the unpleasant physical sensations associated with this cycle can elevate tension, and with this elevated tension, tense-tiredness is often the result.

Psychoactive drugs, the eighth item, can be associated with tense-tiredness, particularly some time after they are ingested. An energy-enhancing drug such as caffeine can have the delayed effect of reducing energy to levels below those before taking the drug. Often this is a natural physiological reaction or a rebound to the initially heightened energy. Similarly, alcohol may initially elevate mood, probably by lowering tension. But ultimately this drug is a depressant and reduces energy in the long run.

Tense-tiredness also frequently occurs during periods of withdrawal from psychoactive drugs. For example, a person addicted to nicotine begins to feel more tension (and often tense-tiredness) when he or she has been without a cigarette for a certain number of minutes (e.g., a two-pack-a-day smoker often needs a cigarette every half hour or so). With a greater passage of time, the tension may mount until it reaches agitation. When personal resources are low, tense-tiredness is the result. Cocaine, opiates, and other powerful psychoactive drugs produce similar mood reactions.

The ninth and tenth items, energy and tension levels, are included in this index to cover various other influences on tense-tiredness that are too numerous to detail. Energy and tension levels are readily apparent to many people, but not always. Tense-tiredness may have a characteristic feeling, or it may be manifested mainly in the behaviors that it produces. Generally, people have a good deal of experience with identifying energy and tiredness, and so it is relatively easy to notice this state. But anxiety, tension, or nervousness is often more difficult to identify. Many of us must observe our behavior systematically (e.g., Are you tapping your fingers or moving a leg? Are your shoulders tight) in order to realize we are tense. (In Chapter 17, I discuss the issue of awareness.)

This index of tense-tiredness can predict negative thoughts. Even one of these items—such as lack of sleep—may indicate a tense-tired condition, and should be a warning that your thoughts and decisions may be unreliable. If several of your answers indicate a tense-tired state, negative thoughts will be the natural result. I advise your taking this self-inventory, at least mentally, every time that you have a negative thought or a negative thought-related behavior.

As I have indicated repeatedly throughout this book, tense-tiredness is a state that occurs periodically in a person under stress within the natural cycles of energy and tiredness. Understanding its immediate effects in everyday experience provides some control. Although stress is often difficult or impossible to eliminate, its bad effects are more manageable when you understand that this negative tense-tired state is tied to your changing personal resources. With this understanding and some systematic self-observation, it should become apparent that these resources are related to such things as deficits in sleep, health, and nutrition, and even to times of day. At the very least, you will know that your tiredness will disappear after a night's sleep or with the passing of a few hours. Depressing thoughts can at times be distressing because one is so tired and tense—they seem insurmountable. And we all experience such moments. But the mood does not indicate permanent defects; rather, it is a barometer of that moment's resources.

If you observe yourself, you will see that your negative thoughts are quite often changeable. They have their own pattern throughout the day, reflecting all the biological factors related to mood. Once you become aware of these patterns, you will have more control over your habits, both the good and the bad ones.

14

Overcoming Tense-Tiredness by Increasing Energy

Much evidence indicates that tense-tiredness helps create the most undesirable moods and probably underlies depression, low self-esteem, negative thoughts of all sorts, and many kinds of dysfunctional behavior, including the use of drugs and alcohol to alter mood. When we say we are in a bad mood, chances are that it is some form of tense-tiredness. This mood probably has a clear biological function: It signals the need for rest and recuperation, together with caution— we sense potential danger, and tension is the result. As functional as it may be, however, tense-tiredness is unpleasant, and most people try to avoid it whenever possible. Unfortunately, their method of avoidance is often some form of substance use, or if avoidance doesn't work, depression may ensue.

Accordingly, we should look for healthier ways of avoiding or changing tense-tiredness. In the first part of this book I suggested a number of good general strategies. I refer to them as general because within a strategy, many specific methods can be used. The best one depends on the particular person, because so many experiences and biological predispositions make mood highly individual. For example, some of us like tension; others require a great deal of sleep; and still others can skip meals without great consequence. A person's physiology is important as well.

Tense-tiredness is best avoided or altered by increasing energy or reducing tension. Either strategy works, but a combination of increased energy and reduced tension works best of all. In this and the following chapters, I shall describe the most effective methods that are supported by scientific research, and ones that my students find especially useful.

Increasing Energy and Reducing Tension Through Exercise

For most people, exercise is the most effective and natural way to raise energy and reduce tension. Exercise produces rapid and reliable results, and it changes mood immediately. Any sort of movement that engages the larger skeletal–muscular system increases general bodily arousal, and the immediate manifestation of that arousal is a feeling of increased energy.

This pattern of arousal change and energy enhancement works in predictable ways. The best evidence indicates that moderate exercise is enough to raise energy and that the boost in energy can last for as much as 2 hours. More intense exercise initially raises energy, but depending on the intensity, it may result in a temporary decline in energy after the exercise. Intense exercise frequently causes a kind of energy rebound after initially declining. For example, 30 minutes of aerobic exercise produces fatigue and lowers tension immediately afterward but often substantially increases energy an hour or so later.

Tension frequently is eased by moderate exercise, but this effect is not as certain as the energy enhancement. Whether or not tension reduction is apparent from exercise, however, the practical effect of increased energy is that the existing tension is less unpleasant. When your energy is high, you can better handle whatever tension, anxiety, or nervousness you may feel. Much of the time, with moderate exercise, you at least move from a tense-tired state to a tense-energetic state.

Another important point to know about exercise is that intense forms, as opposed to moderate forms, have the primary effect of reducing tension.[1] This fact is quite useful if you are especially tense. An anxious person can vigorously exercise and often feel completely relaxed afterward.

Let us look at a case involving the practical use of moderate exercise. Remember that Rhonda, the 23-year-old elementary teacher, spoke of the tense-tiredness that she felt during a demanding day and that she could no longer be pleasant and polite when she felt this way. Regarding one incident she remarked, "When it was time for my break, I took a quick walk around the building. The walk helped me boost my energy level. I was then ready for combat the rest of the day."

It may be hard to imagine that something as simple as a short brisk walk can increase energy, but some very reliable scientific research now indicates that as little as 5 minutes of brisk walking can have exactly this effect.[2] In addition, often just walking around can have a tension-reducing effect, probably through enhanced energy. This is revealed in the pacing back and forth we often see in an anxious person. When someone is worried about something, a small amount of exercise can feel good, which is why it is unpleasant for an agitated person just to sit quietly. As I noted in Chapter 7, this is probably an elemental biological impulse to reduce the muscular freeze response that occurs initially with feelings of danger.

An example of the mood change that comes from only a little exercise is shown in the following case:

> Jeff is a 23-year-old graduate student pursuing a degree in physical therapy. He has a great fear of public speaking which has clearly interfered with his class work because the students often are required to make oral presentations. Jeff spoke about using the ideas he learned in my mood class to deal with his fear. "I would be so afraid to receive any criticism or negative response that I tended to mumble most of the time. The more tense I felt, the more I looked down on my notes instead of maintaining eye contact. A technique that I now use is walking around in front of the room while I give my speech. I am not as anxious when I do this, and it makes the speech go much better."

Walking around just a little can have an immediate, often quite positive, effect but a brisk 5- or 10-minute walk has a very reliable mood-enhancing effect. A psychiatrist who reviewed one of my scientific papers was impressed with the experimental results and adopted the procedure for himself. He sees a number of clients each day, and he told me that every couple of hours, between clients, he puts on his tennis shoes and walks quickly down the hall, up the stairs to the next floor, down that hall, and so on. He is convinced that a 10-minute walk of this kind enables him to focus better on what his clients are saying and to react more effectively. One of my former students, Debra, is a 39-year-old real estate negotiator. At about the time of day when she usually is in a tense-tired mood (3:00 to 4:00 in the afternoon), she told me "If I take time for a brief walk, I come back refreshed, and in a more calm-energetic state." Carolyn, a 24-year-old graduate student in clinical psychology, is another former student who has gone on to apply these mood concepts to both herself and her practice. She told me that when she enters a midafternoon slump she finds that taking a walk, or just stretching, improves her mood (one increases energy, and the other reduces tension).

In a sense, a walk is a natural energy booster with the net effect of a mild tranquilizer, although unlike those drugs that primarily affect tension, a walk probably tranquilizes by enhancing energy. And a walk can be taken at any time.

> Jim is a 42-year-old minister who leads a quiet but often demanding life. He read my earlier book and applied some of these concepts. "I sometimes have depressing thoughts for no reason I can think of. When this happens, I have gotten into the habit of grabbing my keys, and taking a brisk walk around the neighborhood (the advantage of having an office in a neighborhood church). By the time I get back, the depressing thoughts are gone!"

What kind of walking is best to improve mood? In our earlier experiments, we told our subjects to walk about as rapidly as they would if they were late for an appointment. The pace should be fast, but not so fast as to result in exhaustion. Unlike being late and tense, however, the walker should be erect, relax those muscles not necessary for walking, breathe smoothly and naturally, and swing the arms in a natural motion. One probable effect of this arm swing is a kind of biomechanical relaxation of the muscles in the arms, shoulders, back, and neck; tension in these muscle groups is often a central part of anxiety. In addition, the arm swing arouses the entire body—and increases energy because of greater skeletal–muscular activation.

Although a short brisk walk works well and fast, longer exercise sessions are even better and produce more long-lasting effects. Again, I am not talking about the benefits of long-term physical conditioning often reported in both scientific papers and the popular literature. Instead, I am speaking of the immediate effects of each exercise episode.

We can learn a lot of psychology from watching children and adolescents, since their reactions are less disguised. If you have ever watched young children fidget after sitting quietly for a long time, you will understand the body's natural reaction to lengthy sedentary behavior. That is why playtimes are routine fixtures in most classes with young children.

Adolescents and adults have similar needs for physical activity. Christina, the rehabilitation aid at an adolescent center, gives us a good look at how young people respond to exercise:

"At my work we have several physical activities that we use for groups (e.g., sports, body fitness, walking and jogging, outings, and aerobics). I feel that these activities are important because they not only reduce stress but also reduce tension and raise energy for both the kids and myself. For example, I often lead an aerobics class for eight children. Before the exercise, the kids are agitated about having to do aerobics, and also, I am sometimes frustrated and tense. However, after the aerobics the kids are in much better spirits. Also I have much more energy and my tension has ceased."

One session of exercise also can improve cognitive perspectives so that people feel greater self-esteem. These benefits and changes occur every time that one exercises, not just over time with increased physical conditioning. The practical value of these immediate exercise effects is apparent in the following case:

Carol is a 39-year-old law school student. She decided to go back to school after a successful business career, and she took my Psychology of Mood class because she told me, she wanted to learn more about depression, a condition that she had suffered from for many years. The ideas she learned in this class, together with other lifestyle changes, led her to enroll in a gym and to go there for workouts many times a week. "Once I realized that my feelings of depression were directly related to my energy level and that energy could be changed immediately with exercise, I headed for the gym whenever I was depressed. For example, in the mornings I often wake up feeling depressed. Since my early mornings are relatively free, I just go to the gym if those depression feelings are there. Late afternoons and evenings (low-energy times) also are prime times for gym attendance. The results are fantastic. Within minutes of beginning my workout, the depression usually is gone. I have stopped using my antidepressants and have begun to use exercise as their replacement."

Carol discovered an important reason why exercise is likely to be known in the future mainly for its ability to control mood. Moreover, since energy level is known to follow a predictable circadian rhythm (Chapter 2), the fact that Carol's depressed feelings appeared at certain times of the day suddenly was clear. Tying exercise to feelings of low energy at certain times of day makes sense. In Carol's case, it immediately allayed her depression. Moreover, these changes are likely to prevail for a time, as we know from our studies of how long energy remained high after only 10 minutes of brisk walking.[3]

In regard to Carol's admission that she gradually stopped using her antidepressants, I must caution anyone who may be tempted to do the same. For a seriously depressed person, it often is necessary to intervene with close supervision and appropriate drug treatment. Furthermore, suicide is an all too frequent outcome of nontreatment or of inappropriate self-remedies. Therefore, I would not have advised Carol to stop her medication, even though she was exercising. In her case, her feelings of depression may not have been serious, but in any event, I would have told her to make the decision about reducing her antidepressant medication together with her physician.

Carol's reference to exercise as a tranquilizer reminds me of many such reports by my former students.[4] Whether it is short brisk walks, or more intense exercise, this physical activity can have an immediate mood-enhancing effect. The walks are especially useful because they can be employed easily, and any time that minor psychological crises occur. As I have already stated, I do not believe that the walks act as tranquilizers because they do not directly reduce tension, as tranquilizing drugs apparently do. Instead, the walks appear to control anxiety, tension, or nervousness primarily through their energy-enhancing effects.

You can readily observe the effect on mood of different kinds of exercise if you simply repeat the activity a number of times and rate the change in your energy and tension levels. In one of my classes I assign students to do a short self-study that lasts only a couple of weeks but that can provide information that lasts for a lifetime. For example, Steve, a 26-year-old former student, describes a self-study in which he compared running and sugar snacking:

> "The data, which I agree with, showed that after running a half hour I felt energized psychologically, physically, and biologically. This high feeling went on for hours after a relatively brief jog. What's more exciting was that I got rid of tension that was built up in my body from the earlier part of the day. I also felt less tired and less agitated internally and more relieved of daily stress. For example, I didn't look at people or the environment in a negative way. I felt more upbeat and seemed to accomplish the goals that I had."

However, the sugar-snacking condition also produced these results:

> "After I ate a piece of apple pie, I felt great for about 15 minutes, meaning my body felt like it could get up and run a few miles. In spite of feeling more energy and less tension, the effect only lasted for about 15 minutes. Later the sugar made me moody, agitated, and grumpy."

Steve rated his energy and tension immediately after running or snacking, as well as an hour later. From the research we reviewed in class, he knew that an immediate measure gives only part of the picture.[5] The initial effect on mood, as in Steve's positive reaction to sugar, tends to motivate us to continue the behavior. But the longer-term effect—for Steve, moodiness, agitation, and grumpiness—is often quite negative. To realize how sugar affects our mood, we must consider both the short-and long-term reactions.

Steve's example brings up another point from our research. The urge to snack can sometimes be lessened with moderate exercise.

> Margaret is a 43-year-old housewife who returned to school when her children had grown. After taking my mood class, she began adopting some of the principles in her continuing struggle to avoid good-tasting food, and to keep her weight down. "My diet usually goes fine, but once in a while (a tense-tired period) I get an over-

whelming urge for something sweet. If I give in, my diet is gone for a week or more. From your experiments, I learned that on those occasions if I just take a short-brisk walk, I don't need the sugar snack as much. The urge seems to be much weaker."

Margaret's experience with reducing her urge to snack by short brisk walks corresponds well to our findings in two experiments.[6] Recall that we studied frequent sugar snackers in one experiment and addicted smokers in the other. In these experiments, the walks significantly lessened the urge both to snack and to smoke. In addition, after the walk, the subjects waited longer before indulging than they did if they had merely been seated. In sum, exercise not only boosts our energy better than the candy we normally reach for does, but it also often eases the tension we all experience during the day. As the many examples in this chapter show, walks or other forms of exercise can become part of our daily routine and can alter our mood in significant ways.

A Practical Look at Exercise for Mood Control

The evidence of the general health benefits of exercise is abundant. A few years ago, a major scientific paper was published in the *Journal of the American Medical Association* reporting the results of a large-scale study (13,334 participants) of the health of American adults in relation to their lifestyle habits.[7] What was already clear about the value of exercise was confirmed in these research results: Adults who exercise regularly live longer and are much healthier.

Most researchers understand these statistics to mean that cardiovascular fitness and other positive effects of physical conditioning influenced the health of people who regularly exercise. I believe that in the future we will understand even better a second and related value of exercise: its effect on mood. This may be of even greater immediate benefit to most people. In the next decade, as the relationship of exercise and mood is fully revealed, health clubs will begin advertising this benefit, as well as physical health and weight control. And eventually, they will educate their members about the immediate mood-enhancing effects of exercise, including reduced anxiety and depression. We might see advertising campaigns that emphasize one session of exercise in replacement of a pep pill or a tranquilizer. "Any time that you are anxious, depressed, or you just need a lift, visit our health club for a needed pick-me-up!" This is not as far-fetched as it might sound.

Lack of Motivation to Exercise

Although it may be perfectly clear that negative moods can be directly reduced by exercise, it is hard to get motivated. In fact, when you are depressed, the very idea of exercise may be discouraging because you already feel tired. This illustrates clearly the strong influence of moods. They have the power to prevent behavior, or to compel it. This is especially true if we think of this motivation over time, and not just on a single occasion.

In the case of depression, and related tense-tired states, the individual often is especially reluctant to do the necessary exercise. This point was made clear to me from one study of moderately depressed women that my student Renee Bassin and I conducted.[8] Sixteen volunteers enthusiastically began the experiment, which consisted of 15-minute brisk walks on depressed days and comparable walks on nondepressed days, on three separate occasions. Most of the women who completed at least one of the walks experienced the expected energy increases and tension decreases and most important, their depression was reduced.

Although it was clear that the walks diminished the unpleasant depression that these women were experiencing, only 7 of the 16 who began the experiment were able to complete the study. Ironically, those who dropped out were simply too depressed to take the walks. Notice the irony in this. These women were too depressed to do the activity which would be most beneficial for their condition. The power of their depressed mood was too strong and prevented them from completing the study.

If you think about why exercise is so difficult when you are depressed, the answer may become clear. As one student told me, "When I'm depressed, I'm too tired to exercise." Of course, depression is a condition in which fatigue and lack of energy is predominant.

What can be done under these circumstances? Based on my discussions with students, I have found that it is possible to use cognitive override in this condition. That is, the knowledge that exercise will reduce the fatigue and alleviate the depression enables one to exercise a kind of teeth-gritting self-control, and the anticipated results make this much easier than otherwise it would be. In other words, this cognitive override is facilitated if the person remembers that the tiredness, which makes exercise so unappealing, will be immediately lifted once the exercise begins.

Thoughts about a long exercise session are often counterproductive here. So in this circumstance, my advice to students is not to think about extended exercise before beginning.[9] Instead, begin very slowly and hold the thought that the exercise can be brief if necessary. For example, begin with a slow-paced stroll, just down the street. The chances are that just getting moving will energize you a little, at which point your greater energy will make it easier to pick up your pace. After beginning slowly, you often will feel like walking faster. With such a beginning, a 20-minute brisk walk becomes quite possible, even·for a depressed person. If you try this strategy, remember to remind yourself about how exercise will change your negative feelings. A bit of systematic self-observation is very convincing here. If you notice how exercise leads to increased energy on a few occasions, you will be able to use cognitive override on those days when thoughts or fatigue seem to sabotage your best efforts.

Why People Get into Shape, Feel Good, and Then Stop Exercising

I have been speaking here of the immediate benefits of exercise to deal with a negative mood, but regular exercise should become part of your lifestyle if you want a positive mood to prevail most of the time. Once again, the problem of motivation can prevent this kind of change, and of course, it is difficult to find time to exercise regularly. Nevertheless, with all the information now available about the benefits of regular exercise, it should be clear, even to a Type A personality, that exercise is worth the time.

Nonetheless, most people do not exercise regularly. Let me suggest a reason that may account in part for this mistake. This reason has to do with what exercise routines are chosen, and particularly the negative consequences of certain kinds of exercise. Here, I'm not referring to the types of exercise that will provide the biggest health benefits based on well-known principles of exercise physiology. Instead, I'm talking about what motivates us to exercise or not.

I begin with the question, "If moderate exercise is mood enhancing and pleasurable, why don't people exercise more?" I started thinking about this some time ago when it occurred to me that one of the most interesting psychological questions is Why do people get into good physical condition, feel wonderful, and then stop? That this happens quite regularly is evident to anyone who has observed people trying to get themselves into shape. I have often spoken to students who were engaged in demanding conditioning routines and enthusiastically described their progress. They told me about how wonderful they felt and how the exercise improved their mood. But a few months later, when I asked about the exercise, they would tell me that they had stopped. Why would anyone who felt so good from the exercise give it up?

I believe that one part of the answer lies in the kind of exercise. We know that at the most basic level of motivation, people do things that are immediately pleasurable and that they avoid things that are painful. Therefore, people stop exercising—and give up all the wonderful elements of being in excellent physical condition—because the exercise no longer is fun. This is usually because the conditioning is not moderate; instead, the temptation is to get into shape as fast as possible. To condition yourself too fast is often a grueling and painful experience.

True, intense exercise may not be painful for long and may result in a state of pleasure once one has broken through "the wall" during the exercise or after it is over. Certainly, the long-term effects of exercise are quite pleasurable. Many people have enough self-discipline to endure the pain temporarily for the ultimate pleasure that exercise can provide. But eventually most will give up the pain—and give up the exercise—because in the final analysis they have a natural tendency to seek immediate pleasure and avoid immediate pain. This is one of the most enduring messages of behavioral scientists from Pavlov to Skinner: The immediate positive and negative consequences of a behavior (sometimes called *reinforcements*) control the behavior in the future. What this means in the case of stopping exercise is that over time, if it hurts while we do it, we will eventually stop doing it. And it doesn't matter if good feelings follow later. It is the immediate pain that counts.

To apply this theory to yourself, think about the feelings that accompany your regular exercise. If you look forward to doing it and enjoy the exercise while you are doing it, you don't have a problem. But if it frequently takes an act of will to begin exercising and if the exercise hurts, this is a sign of trouble. You will soon abandon the program. Perhaps you won't stop immediately; you may continue the routine even for years. But exercise programs that aren't fun are poor risks.

When I observe people in what I call terminal exercise programs, my usual advice is to slow down and enjoy it more. Of course, if it takes 6 months to reach a conditioning goal that could be achieved in 1 month, one could say that 5 months were wasted. But suppose that the intense exercise program lasts only a year or two, whereas the more moderate program continues for a lifetime. How much time has been wasted then?

Thirty minutes a day or every other day for a mere 6 months can have a remarkable effect. I usually advise prospective exercisers to set aside the same time period every exercise day so that it becomes a habit. The first thing in the morning is an excellent time because energy is increasing in its natural cycle, which tends to increase motivation during the exercise. Also, activities that take precedence over the exercise are less likely to interfere early in the morning. On the other hand, late afternoon—another popular exercise time—is when energy and motivation are low. The benefit of regular exercise during this time is that the activity can be a natural antidote for afternoon tense-tired periods.

Let us use running or fast walking as an example of an exercise program. Once you have decided on an exercise time, you should start with 30 minutes of slow walking or running and then gradually increase the speed. The time that it takes to walk or run a certain distance should not be of paramount importance; instead, continuous activity for 30 minutes should be your goal. As you become better conditioned, you will naturally increase the speed of your walking or running, especially if you push yourself just a little. The optimal rate of increase is an important point to consider. The exercise always should be fun, and the exerciser should stay within his or her readily available energy reserves. These rather nebulous concepts will become clearer with practice, but several tests can be used if you are uncertain about the rate. For example, is energy the predominant feeling that accompanies the exercise, or is it exhaustion? And do you eagerly anticipate the exercise, or do you dread it?

These ideas may not be embraced enthusiastically by some exercise purists. Many have a kind of macho pride that they can endure pain. And of course, there is always the puritan belief that if it doesn't hurt a little it can't be doing much good. Some exercise physiologists also may object on the basis of commonly cited statistics about how much heart rate must be raised above resting levels, and assertions that there must be optimal stress for cardiovascular fitness. But without the motivation to exercise, these physiological principles are useless. Knowing how quickly and efficiently conditioning can be achieved is one thing, but knowing how to get people to exercise as a lifelong activity is quite another.

The methods I suggest should eventually result in a good physical condition, and with these methods, daily moods will be regulated to much more optimal levels. Of course, physical conditioning will take longer to achieve with this approach, but if I am right about these motivational principles, regular exercise will still be an integral part of life at 80 years of age, because it is fun each time it occurs.

15

Reducing Tension to Overcome Tense-Tiredness

As we have seen in previous chapters, tense-tiredness is the mood that brings with it undesirable feelings as well as negative thoughts. We found in our research, and the research of others, that this mood can be counteracted by enhancing energy and that some of the most effective methods include the various forms of exercise that I described in the last chapter.

Because tense-tiredness represents a dynamic balance between energy and tension, this negative state also may be eliminated by reducing tension and related states such as anxiety and nervousness. Depending on the degree of energy that is naturally present (e.g., at certain times of day), lowering tension leaves a person in either a calm-energetic or a calm-tired state. Either state is preferable to the bad mood of tense-tiredness.

The following example is a practical use of some of these principles:

Mary is a 36-year-old teacher. Her inner-city class is much too large, and her students are difficult to control, much less to teach. She wrote about a relaxation technique that she experimented with while taking my mood class and that has helped her since then. "Late in the morning I have a break. While many other teachers use their breaks to visit the lounge for some coffee and sweets, I spend 15 minutes meditating. Although by that point of the morning my tension level is high, this brief meditation period refreshes me. When I next meet my students I am in more of a calm-energetic state."

The calm-energy that Mary experiences after 15 minutes of meditation illustrates the dynamic balance of tension and energy. Before the meditation, she feels tense-energy, or on very stressful days, she may feel tense-tiredness. Although some people like a little tension, Mary is not one of them. Even so, tense-tiredness is never pleasant. Furthermore, Mary probably appreciates calm states because she has meditated for some time, which has the effect of lowering her tension level and permitting her rhythms of energy and tiredness to vary according to their natural cycle.

This example also shows that meditation is most effective in producing calm-energy at certain times of day. For example, Mary practices meditation in the late morning, a time during her circadian rhythm of energetic arousal when her energy is high. Therefore, as her tension subsides, calm-energy replaces it. On the other hand, if she were to meditate late at night or late in the afternoon on a day following a poor night's sleep, the effect could be calm-tiredness, and she might end up falling asleep. Again, the dynamic balance between tension and energy governs this outcome.

There is no clear consensus on why meditation reduces tension.[1] But in my view, the tension probably is reduced for two reasons: Meditation simultaneously controls anxiety-producing thoughts and relaxes unnecessarily tense muscles. Negative thoughts are controlled because the mind is occupied with a nonstressful attentional focus during meditation, which is incompatible with anxious thoughts. It is almost as though the mind is unable to devote adequate attention and energy to both.

The mental activity during mediation may be counting breaths, repeating a phrase, observing a candle, or some other way of directing one's attention. The focus of attention can be nearly anything. For example, some forms of meditation, such as Tai Chi, may concentrate on bodily movements. In all meditation, this focused attention enables the meditator to clear his or her mind of other thoughts, particularly anxiety-producing thoughts.[2]

This kind of mental control is not achieved the first time it is practiced, which is probably why meditation is not widely employed. There is a learning curve associated with it. At first, attempts to focus attention lead easily to distraction, but like learning to ride a bicycle or play tennis, learning to focus attention gradually improves. It is useful to keep track of one's progress in doing this over several weeks because this gradual but continuous improvement motivates one to continue. Eventually, the meditator can focus attention for long periods of time, and this seems to have the added benefit of providing some self-control of anxiety-producing thoughts on other occasions when stress is present.

A second reason for the effectiveness of meditation is muscular relaxation, an essential requirement to meditate successfully. If the meditator sits in an erect but relaxed posture, muscular tension is naturally reduced. Certain forms of yoga and other schools of meditation have developed particular methods of sitting while meditating. For example, the lotus posture enables the meditator to remain alert and also relax. If one assumes the correct posture, only the muscles that maintain erectness will be activated; all others will be relaxed. For a meditation in movement, like Tai Chi, those muscles not necessary for the various ritualized movements are relaxed as well.

In addition, most forms of meditation are enhanced by smooth, regular breathing. Besides oxygenating the whole body, this also facilitates muscular relaxation, especially relaxation of the chest muscles. You will notice that when you are under stress, you usually breath with short panting breaths but that when you are exercising, your breathing involves your whole chest.[3] In the first case, the muscles throughout your body are tight, including those in the chest area—a typical tension response. But with exercise and the associated calm-energy, the muscles throughout your body that are not necessary for the activity are relaxed, including the muscles in your chest area that are not required for efficient breathing.

Proper breathing is basic to all forms of stress management and, therefore, to tension reduction. Unlike many involuntary physiological functions, breathing can be consciously controlled. An interesting anecdote demonstrating the ease with which breathing can be controlled comes from Johnny Carson, the famous late-night talk-show host. He used to say that before beginning a performance—at which time his heart rate would rise to near maximal levels—two or three deep breaths would enable him to deal with the sudden and intense stress that occurred at the beginning of his performance.

Proper breathing can be learned in a relatively small amount of time, and once learned, it can have great effects. Think, for example, of the pain that millions of women have learned to control by using Lamaze breathing exercises for childbirth. Since pain is a clear cause of increased tension, this is a good example of how breathing techniques can control that tension.[4]

Many other techniques also are effective, including both active and passive progressive relaxation.

A former student named Michael is a 29-year-old business man. He practices active progressive muscle relaxation to avoid tense-tiredness, having learned this technique in a stress management course that his firm provided. When he has a few minutes alone, he systematically tightens and relaxes certain muscles in his body that he knows become tense when he is under stress. "I find that if I spend just 5 minutes doing this, and particularly working on the muscles that are usually tight—those of my shoulders, neck, and face—I will feel much more energized. I often try to do this kind of relaxation just before an important conference, and it increases my alertness and energy."

Muscle relaxation is a good way of controlling anxiety. Some years ago, a physician named Edmond Jacobson extensively studied this form of relaxation, and published his observations in a series of popular books.[5] Basically, he maintained that anxiety and nervousness invariably involve muscular tension and that relaxing these muscles alleviates the negative mood. These ideas are compatible with the mood theory described here. Jacobson's books were read and used by a large number of people, and although they may now be out of print, they continue to be a valuable resource. Based on Jacobson's work and similar work by others, muscle relaxation has become a widely practiced technique often used by behavior therapists when the goal is to reduce anxiety.[6]

I believe that one reason for the effectiveness of muscle relaxation is that it counteracts the freeze response that invariably accompanies most kinds of threat, danger, or stress. Recall from Chapter 7 that this elemental biological response typically occurs before the well-known fight-or-flight response. It is a core element of anxiety. Thus any activity that relieves this muscular tension also relieves anxiety and other related states.

Even something as simple as worry beads seems to have the effect of lessening the muscular freeze response. As when one continuously fingers one's beads, this simple act appears to achieve a degree of general relaxation. I was reminded of the value of this once while traveling by taxi in busy afternoon traffic in Washington, D.C. The driver, a Middle Eastern man of about 40, was steering with one hand and fingering his beads with the other (probably an unsafe practice). He held a circle of beads, each of which was about a half-inch thick and, stretched out, would probably measure less than a foot. He slowly fingered each bead before going on to the next. In a short time, he was back to the first bead again. I asked him about what he was doing, and he said he is never bothered by traffic when he uses his beads. I was intrigued because of my theoretical work and some supportive experimental work that I knew about, but especially because he did appear exceptionally relaxed.[7]

The same principle of reducing the skeletal–muscular freeze response probably is at the base of nervous mannerisms such as pacing, tapping fingers, or wiggling a foot by which means, the person is alleviating unpleasant muscular tension. Although the muscles that are primarily affected may be limited, the tendency of the body to act in general arousal patterns results in broader skeletal–muscular relaxation. Usually this seems to happen without any real awareness of the motivation for the nervous mannerism, and yet the continued occurrence indicates that the mannerism is satisfying.

There are many other proven techniques for reducing tension and thus eliminating tense-tiredness in addition to meditation, proper breathing, and progressive muscle relaxation. Visualization is a proven part of the stress management armamentarium and is usually taught in various forms in stress management courses.

Earlier when I spoke of why meditation is effective I said that controlling attention is an essential part of this practice. Visualization accomplishes the same purpose. Again, any benign focus of attention enables one to stop thinking about anxiety-producing matters, which in turn lowers one's overall tension level.

In my experience with mood management, I have found that some people are very good at visualization and that others are less good, but that everyone can become reasonably proficient. Visualizing a place where one was relaxed and happy—say a beach during a vacation or a pleasant forest area where one has hiked—is a good way of focusing attention. Good visualizers can often picture a great deal of detail, including colors and other subtle variations. Those who are less good can at least approach this kind of focused attention, but even a somewhat unsuccessful visualization can minimize thoughts about anxious subjects.

Another excellent way to reduce tension, readily available to most people, is a warm bath or shower. This is an excellent muscle relaxant. The water of a warm bath should not be too hot, probably no more than 102° or 103°. Some research suggests that hotter water shocks the system and although it relaxes muscles, it has negative effects as well.

One of the self-study projects that my students have occasionally performed is measuring mood reactions to different lengths of time in a jacuzzi. Based on these informal results, people should not stay in a jacuzzi, which is often hotter than 103°, for very long. In one study, for example, 10 minutes had the mood effect of reduced tension and increased energy, but a longer time reduced both tension and energy, leaving the occupant in a somewhat lethargic state.

Massage is also an excellent muscle relaxant, and it has the advantage of directly attending to those muscles that are most affected by stress. Notwithstanding the common stereotype that commercial massage is a front for illicit sexual activity, this form of body manipulation has recently become popular because it eases muscular tension directly. After a half hour or hour of massage, a person feels refreshed and often quite energized. It is a good example of how tense-tiredness can be eliminated directly by tension reduction and how this reduced tension often results in enhanced energy.[8]

Of course we should mention the time-honored practice of yoga. These various ritualized movements that stretch the muscles, together with focused attention, is an excellent means of reducing tense-tiredness. Moreover, this form of activity represents a kind of physical exercise that is very beneficial.

I have found that all these ways of reducing tension directly are effective. But their effectiveness depends on the individual person, probably because of personality or temperament differences. Accordingly, some people will find visualization useful, but others will not. Likewise, meditation may be good for some, whereas progressive muscle relaxation may be best for others.[9]

Anyone deciding to use one of these techniques regularly should try as many of them as possible and keep track of their moods after each. It soon will become apparent which one is best. The mood theory that I have been describing—with particular attention to energy and tension levels and to states such as tense-tiredness and calm-energy—is an excellent means of judging the effectiveness of different techniques.

16

Moods at Different Times of Day

People, consciously or not, self-regulate their bad moods (tense-tiredness) by means of various activities, from exercise and specific methods of reducing tension to smoking, eating, and drinking alcohol. Self-regulating everyday moods is at once both a simple and a complex process. In some cases, moods can be changed by uncomplicated activities such as taking a walk, chatting with a friend, or eating something if a meal is missed. A bit more complicated are the various stress management techniques such as meditation or deep muscle relaxation. Still more complicated is an informed and subtle self-regulation based on a knowledge of which moods occur at different times of day and the appropriate activities for those moods.

All self-regulation of mood takes place against a background of biologically based cycles of energy (Chapter 2) and the dynamic interactions between energy and tension (Chapter 6). With a little self-observation, these energy cycles can easily be predicted. But even without systematic self-observation, most people have a sense of their basic cycle characteristics (e.g., whether they are morning or night types), and with just a little self-study of the interaction of energy and tension, it is relatively easy to identify the optimal and poor hours of the day.

Once it is clear how the time of day and mood are associated, self-regulation becomes a matter of matching activities with naturally occurring moods. For example, during the day you will have low-energy states, times when stress should be minimized (frequently in the late afternoon and evening). Stressful activities that can't be avoided should be scheduled at other high-energy times (often in the late morning). At certain times it is risky to have family arguments (late afternoon or late at night), and other times are more suitable for discussions that are sensitive but necessary (e.g., late morning or any time when energy is high). There are times when demanding intellectual work should be done (hours associated with calm-energy) and other times of day when poor intellectual performance can be expected (periods of tense-tiredness). Sometimes feelings of slight depression are not unusual just on the basis of rhythmic energy cycles (e.g., when awakening in the morning or late in the day). At other times good moods should be expected, and interactions with significant others might be encouraged. There even are times when sexual activity is more likely to be positive (high-energy periods) and times when it is not (low-energy periods).

This chapter deals with these kinds of issues. I begin by sketching the general outlines of moods that may be predicted at different times of day. Of course, as I frequently stated thus far, because of individual differences in these mood cycles, you can be sure of optimal and poor times for yourself only by self-observation (see Chapter 17). Nevertheless, the characteristics of the daily periods that I describe apply to the majority of people.

Morning Awakening

Upon awakening in the morning, most people are at one of their lowest energy points of the day. The only lower time in the diurnal rhythm is just before going to sleep at night (see Figure 1). Morning awakening is a vulnerable period because feelings of depression are apt to well up during this time. Indeed, feelings of depression in the morning are sometimes viewed as symptoms of serious clinical disorders. On the other hand, because morning awakening is one of the lowest points of the energy cycle, feelings of slight depression at this time may not be unusual because of their relationship to the natural energy cycle.

Recall the case of Mark, the 45-year-old businessman, who sometimes awakens at 3:00 A.M. and thinks about his life in very negative terms. The same phenomenon may occur during the low-energy time of morning awakening and also in the low-energy times of the late afternoon and late at night. The common element in these different times of day is that they all represent a low point in the energy cycle.

Under certain conditions, tension can be moderately high at morning awakening, perhaps because a potentially depressed person has been somewhat tense throughout the night. This person probably awakens early from sleep, sometimes with troubling dreams and maybe with pain in the jaw or other parts of the body. Or the heightened anxiety at awakening could be caused by personal problems sufficiently severe that they create tension immediately upon awakening. In any event, this early morning period may be characterized by the predominance of tense-tiredness. In this case, self-regulating activities that heighten energy and reduce tension would be the best antidotes.

For most people, however, tension is not the problem first thing in the morning. For them, the characteristic arousal pattern upon awakening is both low energy and low tension (calm-tiredness). In this more usual condition, tension begins at a low point and mounts slowly during the day as stress builds. When people awaken in this calm-tired pattern, they move and act more slowly, and their thoughts are not yet fully coherent. This low energy ensures that they operate at half speed, so to speak. Accordingly, activities that require more speed and alertness are likely to be stressful (e.g., being late for work).

Night types, or so-called owls, are particularly groggy and tired upon awakening, which may present problems if they have to interact with people. This inability to function well in the early morning can lead to some interesting social problems. For example, one of my students, a classic night type, described to our mood class his basic incompatibility with his girlfriend, a classic morning type. She frequently wanted to talk over some of the problems in their relationship first thing in the morning, and when she tried, he reacted badly, as he couldn't concentrate on the problems, let alone come up with any solutions. On the other hand, his girlfriend felt sharp and coherent at that early morning time. For her, early mornings are periods of good mood. Not surprisingly, her boyfriend preferred talking over problems at night. But this was a time when she had the same negative reaction that he had in the early morning. The main solution for this kind of incompatibility is knowing the characteristic energy patterns of your mate and yourself, in order to negotiate better times for activities together and for important talks.

The girlfriend in this example is similar to other people who have high levels of energy soon after awakening. In my experience, fewer than 15 percent of the population have this pattern (the percentages are comparable for extreme night types). Another of my former students with this energy pattern learned to match her behavior to her characteristic cycle. Kim is a 21-year-old full-time student: "After learning about circadian energy rhythms in your class, I decided to experiment with the best time of day to study. I found mornings, just after I wake up, to be the best. Perhaps this is because I am an extreme morning type. At that time, my head is clear, and I seem to retain ideas much better."

People's cognitive performance varies widely just after awakening. For example, Kim's experience and my own are somewhat different, probably reflecting stable and biologically based individual differences. Unlike her, I am a moderate or weak morning type, and so I can do only certain kinds of intellectual work just after awakening. More complicated work that requires a great deal of concentration I can do better later in the morning when I have more energy. I have found that matching tasks to my energy level puts me in a better mood.

Most of us are in a better mood in the morning than at other times of day partly because our energy is rising. At some level of consciousness, we are aware of this; that is, most people feel more energetic at 8:00 A.M than they do at 7:00 A.M., and so on. This perception of increasing energy in the morning contrasts with the relative unawareness of decreasing energy at some point in the afternoon.

In the morning, something about this awareness of energy level, of positive change, creates a better frame of mind and greater optimism, probably because of the feeling that one will have more resources to deal with whatever might come up. Recognition of these kinds of changing energy levels at different times of day is useful for mood regulation. If for no other reason, it is useful because it provides an explanation for otherwise mysterious behavior that can be troubling.

Middle to Late Morning

At some time in the late morning or early afternoon, most people's energy reaches a peak. Note in Figure 1 the high point for energetic arousal at point B, an optimal time. Energy has risen sharply, but tension still is relatively low. Of all the times of day, this period is most likely to be characterized by calm-energy. One of my former students, Jennifer, a 28-year-old middle-level manager in a small company, described her later mornings in very positive terms: "I find that I can accomplish a great deal. Although there are many distractions, I am able to stay focused. I can juggle many things at once. I tend to put off my important decisions until this time. It seems as though I am more realistic then, and my decisions are better." Jennifer's experience is not unusual; many people like mornings best. These time periods are high in energy, and relatively low in tension. As Jennifer said, she can accomplish a great deal and "juggle many things at once." Spreading work out so that one can do most of it, or the most difficult part, in the morning (or other high-energy times) is likely to be best for mood regulation.

People who are aware of these concepts often intentionally schedule their most demanding activities in the mornings; indeed, unavoidable activities that are known to be stressful probably are best scheduled during this period. For example, one of my students talked about making difficult telephone calls only in the morning. Another person, who has two workers reporting to him, tries to deal with any problems that they might have at this morning time, which, he believes, results in better communication and fewer arguments. Stress in general is best handled during high-energy periods, especially times of calm-energy. Since most people experience these states in the late morning or early afternoon, it makes a great deal of sense to schedule stressful activities for this time whenever possible. This isn't always easy, but after thinking about it, most people find that they have some flexibility in scheduling their day.

In Jennifer's case, she mentions that she makes important decisions during the mornings. This is a notable point. Although many people do not have the option of scheduling stressful activities at particular times of day, nonetheless, they have some choice about when they will make their own personal decisions. It is logical to make decisions during the time when there is the most accurate perception of personal issues.

Late morning and early afternoon aren't always the times when we have our most accurate perceptions. Remember the series of studies showing that personal problems appear less serious at late morning than they do in the mid-to late afternoon (Chapter 2). Note, however, that these studies did not show that the late afternoon time is associated with the least accurate perception, only that problems appear to be more serious then. Nevertheless, my sense from numerous discussions about this is that one has a less accurate perception of personal problems during tense-tired times: Problems seem worse, and so tension runs high. Thus it makes sense to assume that when we are under less tension our decisions will be more sound.[1]

The occasional family dispute, which everyone has, probably should be dealt with during the late morning or whenever the persons involved feel the most energetic and least tense. This may be difficult to schedule if they are working during those times of day.[2] But often it is possible to put off a discussion until a better time, perhaps a weekend. This shouldn't be done as a means of avoiding the discussion because it is too unpleasant. Instead, it should be a conscious choice of the best natural time to resolve a conflict. Such scheduling is likely to pay off in a better overall mood for all involved.

In Kim's case, she observed that her head was clearest and that she had the best intellectual retention just after she awoke. She mentioned that she is an extreme morning type, and in my view, that probably is the reason that she studies best early in the morning. On the other hand, in Chapter 6, I described a study showing that calm-energy is the best predictor of the effectiveness of recent mental work. Calm-energy can occur at various times of day, depending on individual differences in energy cycles, but most people experience this state in the late morning and early afternoon.

Mid- to Late Afternoon

For many people, mid- to late afternoon is a time when their energy dips to a low point in its cycle and when their vulnerability to tension is especially great. Some of the highest tension of the day often occurs during this period (see Figures 2 and 3). All sorts of negative psychological reactions can be expected at mid to late afternoon. For example, it is a time when negative thoughts can predominate, family or coworker disputes frequently surface, and diets are easily broken. For most people, this is a time of tense-tiredness.

I am often struck by this late-afternoon effect when I walk by the snack area at my university at around 3:00 or 4:00 P.M. It is crowded with people buying muffins, cookies, ice cream, and other snacks, probably trying to self-regulate their mood, although they may not be aware that that is what they are doing. From long experience, people who are tense and tired, sense that sugar will make them feel better. The fact that the good feelings may only be temporary seems to have little effect. Not only does eating sugar at this tense-tired time probably put these people in a worse mood an hour or so later (greater tense-tiredness), but the act of breaking a diet just by itself can make them depressed.

Carol is a 48-year-old former businesswoman who is now retired and going to school to complete a degree. Whenever possible, she schedules her classes in the mornings and leaves her afternoons free for studying and personal business. She told me about her battle to avoid sweets. "I noticed that the afternoons and evenings are the times when I'm most tempted to snack. It seems that it is worse if I haven't slept well the night before and if I'm a little tense. Sometimes just a little frustration from a difficult textbook or problems with a paper that I'm writing will set me off. Thoughts about the cookies in the cupboard or of something else I have in the house that's good to eat, will be very persistent. I used to succumb, and sometimes I wouldn't stop with just eating a little. One of the worst parts was that after breaking my diet, I would feel terrible about myself. But after realizing the way that my tense-tiredness and these urges are related, I try to be vigilant in these times of day. I try to do something else to counteract the dangerous mood. A walk or some other exercise often helps."

In Carol's case, timing her snacks in the afternoon and the connection with poor sleep the night before make low energy the likely reason for the urge. Her energy pattern is typical of that of most people:

highest in the morning, lower in the afternoon, slightly higher in the early evening, and again lower until bedtime. Moreover, her experience with poor sleep also is typical. A lack of sleep affects people in the low points of their energy cycle.

Her subsequent bad mood was also likely to be influenced by her diminished self-esteem, which probably was manifested as heightened tension. The reduced self-esteem which stemmed from breaking her diet occurred because she went against her resolve not to eat the forbidden food. It was a powerful indication that she couldn't even control herself in this simple way. But she shouldn't have blamed herself too much. An often unnoticed point here is that self-esteem is closely related to energy level.

In one study that a graduate student and I conducted, energy level and self-esteem were reliably correlated over several weeks.[3] When energy was low, self-esteem also was low, and vice versa. Interestingly enough, level of tension was less related to self-esteem. If self-esteem seems lower at certain times and doesn't appear to be caused by any recent event, energy level is probably low as well.

Other research that I have described revealed the mid- to late afternoon as the time when personal problems seem to be most serious. Remarkable as it may appear, the way we look at our problems subtly changes with different energy and tension levels. Recall that I suggested this may happen because low present energy levels are used to assess reserves in the future. But instead of being aware that the necessary energy to solve the problem may be higher at other times, the present low energy, coupled with moderate tension, leads to the conclusion that the problems are indeed serious, and will not be manageable.

A useful way of counteracting these negative thoughts is to become aware of this relationship. I have found that it is moderately easy to stop thinking about bothersome things if I know there is an obvious biological reason for the troubling thoughts, such as little energy. It is much more difficult to control thoughts under other circumstances. It is as though control somehow is gained over thoughts if you can see the basis of their irrationality. Thus, at certain times of day, it's worthwhile to keep in mind that this may be a bad period to be thinking about a personal problem.

The siesta that many people in Latin countries take seems to be an excellent way of counteracting this tense-tired time. One of the most pleasurable scientific conferences I attended took place in Spain in the summer. Papers were given and lively discussions held in the mornings and the evenings, but the afternoons were devoted to a nice meal followed by a nap or other ways of relaxing. Unlike the case at many other conferences, everyone was in an excellent mood throughout the proceedings.

If tense-tiredness is the basis of negative moods, then naps or other forms of relaxation in the lowest energy times would seem to be a good method of self-regulation. Some of my students report that naps can be very effective mood regulators in this afternoon time. Short naps also seem to counteract a deficit in sleep the night before. And a short nap can result in a positive mood for the rest of the day.

In my experience, it is necessary to be careful about how naps are taken, however. A nap that is too long or taken at the wrong time of day can disrupt sleep that night. For me, the best method is to sleep 30 minutes at the low point of the afternoon. Also I know that when I wake up from a nap, I will feel low in energy for a time, much as I do when I wake up in the morning. I suspect that people who do not nap because it leaves them feeling out of sorts may be sleeping too long or at the wrong time of day. Or they are not aware of the time necessary to recover their energy following a nap, and they are paying too much attention to the low-energy period when they wake up. Once again, a little experimentation, together with systematic self-observation, is the best way to proceed with naps.

Compare the relaxation of siesta time, or the slowed and leisurely activity of afternoon naps, with the hectic high intensity of the Type A corporate lifestyle, in which no time is allotted to rest in the low-energy periods of the day. Instead, these driven people must push ahead, even though they may be in an unpleasant tense-tired state, further exacerbated by the low value they place on sleep. It is seen as a waste of precious time. These conditions seem to be a prescription for depression, alcohol and other substance use, or other negative mood states such as anxiety. This is not even to mention the likely physical debilitation of such a lifestyle.

Evening

In the early evening, people's energy often slightly rises, and their tension slightly drops, perhaps as a result of having dinner. Then, in the typical cycle, energy declines continuously until it reaches the lowest point of the day just before the night's sleep. All the negative psychological reactions associated with the low energy of late afternoon also may occur in the later evening. This easily can be a period of tense-tiredness, although for many, early evening is a time of some calm-energy. Incidentally, I have found that meditation practiced just before dinner often extends and enhances this early evening calm-energy and also has the added benefit that one is less hungry for unhealthy foods at dinnertime.

Optimal mood regulation in this period requires scheduling activities that are not very demanding, perhaps some light work or a hobby. It is no accident that many people watch television at this time, as their energy level is too low to do anything else and the television keeps them awake long enough so as not to disrupt their nightly sleep patterns. This is a somewhat different way of interpreting the motivation for watching TV than the idea that interesting programs motivate the audience to tune in. Rather, TV viewing is seen as a way of self-regulating mood and, in particular, of maintaining behaviors consistent with energy level.

One of the most notable effects of dysphoric, or bad, moods during this time of day is the tendency to eat forbidden foods or abuse alcohol or other substances. Tense-tiredness leads many people to snack. Others may resort to alcohol use (Chapter 11). These behaviors, in turn, result in temporarily positive moods, but ultimately they result in negative moods.

Like the late afternoon, the late evening can also be a time of negative thoughts, if not depression. Low energy is the common factor, although for many people, tense-tiredness is not as great in the late evening as it is in late afternoon, maybe because they are more tired as bedtime nears. At this phase of their energy cycle, many people are bordering on exhaustion, a state in which tension diminishes. Also, their tension may be diminished because late evening usually has fewer lifestyle demands that require alertness.

Optimal mood regulation at this time of the day and especially late in the evening should center on relaxation in preparation for sleep. Activities such as progressive muscle relaxation, visualization, hot baths, soft music, and quiet reading are good choices. Since our energy cycle is nearing its lowest point of the day, the self-management problem for this period is to reduce tension so that we can enjoy a refreshing sleep.

If you do not reduce your tension, you can expect insomnia. Assuming you are not trying to sleep more than you need to, the usual cause of insomnia is tension. Unfortunately, the result of insomnia is the loss of needed sleep and less energy the following day, and so in a vicious cycle, you are left vulnerable to even more tension. Ultimately, a bad mood is produced by a cycle of lack of sleep, loss of energy, and increased tension.

One last point worthy of comment concerns the timing of sexual activity. Most sexual encounters take place in late evening, for many people only after all the necessary tasks are finished and they fall into bed near exhaustion. But this seems to be a particularly poor time for such high-energy activity. Intense sexual arousal and orgasm require mobilizing and expending massive amounts of energy. During orgasm, heart rate has been found to climb to nearly 200 beats per minute, and respiration rate, depth of breathing, and body heat increase greatly as well.[5] In addition to the likely difficulties of expending so much energy in the low-energy period of late evening, another problem may be vulnerability to anxiety in low-energy periods. And since anxiety is frequently a significant cause of sexual dysfunction, this time of day would not seem to bode well for good sex.[6] The high-energy periods of the day probably are better alternatives.

On the other hand, some data that a colleague and I collected on the immediate mood effects of sexual activity suggest that the reduction of tension is the primary mood change that follows satisfactory sexual activity.[7] If this finding proves to be reliable, it means that sexual activity has the benefit of leaving the participants in a calm state so that they can fall asleep easily. Although our research is only at the preliminary stages at this time, it poses several interesting questions.

17

Systematic Self-Observation:
The First Step in Mood Change

Most of us can improve our daily moods if we have accurate information about why they occur. Knowing what to look for is often the most difficult part of obtaining this information. But with a few basic variables to monitor, self-study yields immediate information about how to make changes in our daily life that can lead to a better mood, more energy, and less tension. Moreover, your behavior is most likely to remain changed if insights about it are discovered in your own self-analyses. Advice from experts certainly is useful. But finding something out for yourself is particularly motivating.

Another reason I advocate self-discovery is that experts have varying points of view. I am particularly aware of this in lecturing to my classes. Consequently, on matters of practical application, I advise my students to find out for themselves and not to trust any single expert. Naturally, I want them to understand my point of view, but in the final analysis, when considering their own mood variations, there is no substitute for systematic self-observation. Such self-observation soon reveals if an idea is valid, or if it is suspect.

A third reason for systematic self-observation is the principle that all aspects of mood have individual differences. All the characteristics that I have already mentioned, from energy cycles to exercise effects, involve individualized ways of responding. Some are morning people, and others are night people. Some people feel energized after only five minutes of brisk walking, and others require longer periods. Sleep loss affects some people substantially, and others to a lesser extent. Each person is different, and so in any practical application of these ideas, the remedial actions must be tailored to the individual. In order to take account of these differences, self-studies of each characteristic are essential.

Systematic Studies of the Causes and Effects of Mood

A cardinal rule for a change in mood is that awareness must come first. Often a cause for a particular mood is unmistakable, but we just don't notice it. But once we are aware of the processes involved, we wonder why we didn't see it before. A common example of this occurs when something quite obvious is overlooked in everyday situations only to be noticed frequently once awareness about it occurs. When we learn a new word or a concept that we previously didn't know, we seem to see it everywhere. It was always there; we just didn't notice it.

The same thing happens with everyday moods. Simple relationships exist, but most people are unaware of them. But if awareness occurs, a kind of control is possible that previously didn't seem to exist. Everyday moods can be anticipated and their causes manipulated. The behavioral effects of moods, such as eating, also can be controlled. In my experience, most adults are remarkably good at changing their moods once they realize what causes them.

To see how this works, let us first consider important mood-related behaviors like sugar snacking or substance use. The first thing to notice is the association between the behavior and the feelings immediately before and after it. Usually a behavior like snacking is at least partially controlled by feelings. As I indicated in Chapter 9, we continuously monitor ourselves and make changes in order to feel better.[1] These changes frequently involve food or some other substance that we ingest.

As an example, to control your sugar snacking, first notice the sequence of events and feelings that lead to a snack. When do you crave a snack, and what other feelings do you have, especially your mood preceding the snack. Your thoughts are important too, but as we have seen, mood and thoughts often are integrally related.

It is equally important to notice what feelings occur immediately after the snack and your feelings about a half hour, an hour, or 2 hours afterward. Frequently, you will find that you don't want to snack because of hunger but because of your emotional state. You may also find that your negative mood improves immediately after you eat but then gets worse some time later. This pattern of feelings tends to entrap a person in a cycle of maladaptive behavior that seems impossible to change.

Some of these matters are illustrated in the following case. As you will see, the process of self-understanding is fairly complicated but not unmanageable.

Mary is a 23-year-old student who supports herself as a secretary while attending college. She spoke about learning to discriminate moods, causes of moods, and subsequent behaviors, as part of a multiweek exercise for one of my classes. "As I did my self-observational study concerning unmindful snacking during work, I noticed that I would get an urge to eat when I had anxiety or slight depression feelings (tense-tired). Immediately after the snack, I felt better, although this didn't last long. Then I noticed that much of the time the feelings that came before my desire to snack were related to the stress I was under, particularly from my boyfriend. They also were related to whether I slept well the night before and how healthy I felt. These were important new insights."

Because of careful self-monitoring, Mary was able to see that a behavior, almost unconscious, was actually quite predictable. Perhaps the most important thing that she learned was the relationship between her energy and tension levels and her urge to snack. In other words, she learned how these moods influenced her craving and how they changed after her snack. Once she recognized these relationships, she was able to anticipate when she would crave a snack and so take action to change the motivating moods in ways other than snacking.

Table 4 Mood Test

	Definitely do not feel			Definitely feel
Energetic	1	2	3	4
Vigorous	1	2	3	4
Lively	1	2	3	4
Active	1	2	3	4
Full of pep	1	2	3	4
	Add together scores for energy			
Tense	1	2	3	4
Jittery	1	2	3	4
Fearful	1	2	3	4
Intense	1	2	3	4
Clutched-up	1	2	3	4
	Add together scores for tension			

Sources: Robert E. Thayer, Activation–Deactivation Adjective Check List: Current Overview and Structural Analysis. *Psychological Report 58*, 607–617; Robert E. Thayer, *The Biopsychology of Mood and Arousal*. New York: Oxford University Press, 1989, App.1.

For a systematic study of an undesirable behavior, rate your energy and tension (see Table 4) before and after each time that the behavior occurs. It is best to record these mood levels in a diary and, if possible, to graph them. In addition, the more times you observe the relationship, the more reliable the results will be.

To control our general moods, we need to study certain primary variables such as sleep, time of day, exercise, food ingestion, health, and stress. For an easy study, I suggest observing the immediate effects of exercise. To reveal the mood effects of exercise, try this simple experiment. After you have been sitting for a while (e.g., 45 minutes), rate your energy level. Next take a brisk, 10-minute walk, and then rate yourself again using the same scale. Follow this procedure on a number of occasions and at different times of day. Almost always, you will see a change in energy. Usually this effect is apparent on the first occasion but, if not, then after only a few occasions.

In additional self-studies you can rate your overall mood or other kinds of feelings. After these ratings, take a brisk walk, and then make the same ratings a second time. It should soon become clear that the exercise produces all kinds of mood changes, but usually energy is the most obvious. Your findings in these studies should lead you to understand one easy way of effectively self-regulating your mood.

If you want to try a more sophisticated experiment, add a control, or comparison, condition. This means that sometimes you do something else in order to compare the mood effects with those coming from exercise, for instance, sitting and watching TV for the same length of time. Then compare the before-and-after exercise ratings with those made before and after sitting. Again, making several comparisons is better than just one.

You can add still other variations to determine what exercise level is best for you. For example, you might try a 5-minute walk and, at other times, 10 or 15 minutes. Record your energy and tension levels together with these variations in exercise times, and you will soon establish your optimal exercise time to produce the desired mood effect.

In conducting research like this, one difficulty may become apparent: You might be expecting certain results. In the long run, however, this will not be a great problem. I have found that when you repeatedly observe a relationship, your expectations tend to diminish and soon will no longer influence your observations enough to matter.

A practical self-study concerning moderate exercise is suggested by two experiments discussed in Chapter 12 in which we showed that the urges to snack and to smoke were lessened by short brisk walks. To do this kind of experiment on yourself, follow a set procedure on a number of occasions. Whenever you feel an urge to snack or smoke, rate the urge (strong, moderate, weak) and also your energy and tension levels. Now take a brisk 5- to 10-minute walk, or try a control condition by replacing the walk with a sedentary activity for 5 or 10 minutes, such as watching TV or reading a magazine. After the walk or alternative activity, rate yourself again.

After you have walked, do you feel less urge to smoke or snack? If less, how much time elapses before the original urge returns? Are your energy and tension levels different after the walk? We found that after walking, most people waited twice as long to snack or smoke than they did after a sedentary activity, and that their ability to wait seemed to be related to the increased energy from the walk.

Time of day is a variable that can give you an excellent appreciation of the good and bad hours of the day for different kinds of activities and the hours when you must compensate for higher levels of stress. A favorite exercise of my students is to chart their energy cycles and changes in tension throughout the day. For women, it may be interesting to rate some typical days just before menstruating and compare them with days in the middle of their cycle.

To chart your energy and tension cycles, choose at least three typical days when your waking and sleeping times are the same (and with a similar amount of sleep for the previous night), days on which nothing unusual occurs. Rate your energy and tension levels (Table 4) at the beginning of every hour, from waking until sleep. After the first time or two, it will take only a few seconds for each hourly rating and no more than a half hour in all for the day.[2] The graphed results easily reveal periods of tense-tiredness and calm-energy. If the days are sufficiently representative, the energy measures will indicate your personal internal cycle.

To illustrate how useful such a study can be, consider Carolyn, the 24-year-old doctoral student in clinical psychology whom I mentioned earlier. She first learned about charting her energy and tension levels throughout the day while she was a student in one of my classes. Later in her clinical training, she adapted this technique to use with her clients.

"I have been seeing adolescent clients at my practicum placement, and have incorporated your mood concepts into my group work with eating-disordered girls. In addition to the fairly standard insight-oriented self-esteem work and cognitive techniques with this population, I chose to integrate the use of a daily log. Clients were instructed to note their moods and energy levels at various points of their day. They also noted how this was related to their body image (self-esteem) and eating behaviors or urges. After several weeks of self-monitoring and discussion, the clients were able to see how patterns of mood/energy were related to not only their eating habits but also their self-esteem and self-efficacy, which in turn dictated whether they would use food for reasons other than nourishment."

Systematic self-observation is the best way to develop self awareness. If energy and tension levels are rated repeatedly, it will soon become second nature to you to notice patterns in all kinds of situations. Although an individual may sense energy and tension as part of ongoing behaviors, these feelings often are not the most salient things in a situation. Your mind is on other things. But a systematic self-study changes this.

Indirect Avenues to Awareness: When Energy and Tension Are Recognized Through Other Reactions

High levels of energy and tension are fairly easy for most of us to recognize. But moderate tension levels and slight declines in energy are not so obvious, and so it may be easier to gauge energy and tension through the behaviors that they influence.

One problem is that most people have little experience in identifying tension, nervousness, or anxiety. Parents usually do not teach their children to recognize the telltale signs of these negative conditions. Nor is there any systematic instruction given in the school system or anywhere else for recognizing these feelings. This shortcoming in instruction is compounded for many young boys who from the earliest age are taught, indirectly or otherwise, that fear is unmasculine. Even though a young man may be very anxious, and the effects quite extensive, the feeling of tension is ignored. Only sissies succumb to pressure, or so they are taught.

In cases like this, it may be necessary to develop an awareness of tension by learning its common effects. For example, skeletal–muscular tightness is a clear indication of nervousness, anxiety, or fear, and it is readily observable. In particular, tapping fingers, shaking a leg or a foot, and pain in the neck, shoulders, back, or jaw frequently are signs of tension. Impatience or irritability also is an indication and, as we have seen from earlier chapters, urges for food or various kinds of undesirable substances may reveal tension as well as low energy.

Of the two states, energy is usually the more readily recognized, maybe because we talk more about energy and it is not socially undesirable, as tension is. Moreover, most of us receive some early training in recognizing signs of energy and fatigue, even if indirectly. For example a child rubs his eyes, and the attentive parent comments, "Are you tired?" "Time for bed." Or the child romping around the house is told that she has "energy to burn." Such training seldom occurs with anxiety or tension.

The ease of recognizing tiredness, as compared with tense-tiredness, can be seen with regard to depression. Many experts believe that a decline in energy is the primary indication of depression (a tense-tired mood). The psychiatrist Willard Gaylin made this point when he noted that depressed patients may be unaware of their condition. Rather than depression, they often complain of exhaustion, fatigue, and boredom. "When a patient states that he is chronically tired, and then describes the fact that he has had a precipitous weight loss and insomnia, the psychiatrist knows that—barring physical illness—he is getting a classical description of depression."[3]

Mood-related bodily conditions may be revealed in such common social reactions as irritability. For example, skipping a meal probably results in a subtle energy decline, but this may be noticed only in terms of how someone reacts to others. My 19-year-old daughter Kara, a full-time college student, explained, "I have been interested in the effects of food for some time. After repeatedly observing myself in relation to eating, I am aware that if I miss a meal, sometimes I will not feel especially hungry. But then I notice unusual irritability. After I eat something, the irritability will be gone, and it is replaced by a feeling of well-being."

Most people feel a skipped meal does little harm, and in fact, many do not get hungry when they miss a meal. But I am convinced that careful study would find various mood shifts, such as a drop in energy and a slight increase in tension, along with increased irritability. As I have indicated in previous chapters, the tense-tired state causes not only irritability but negative thoughts and other subtle changes. If this is true, we can recognize energy and tension by seeing their manifestations—jitteryness, impatience, irritability, and other secondary effects of our basic energy and tension cycles.

Once you begin to recognize your mood-related behavioral reactions, such as reaching for a sugar snack or a glass of wine, your reactions to your energy and tension levels also will become apparent. The times when you want to eat, when you feel crabby, and even when you feel most like making love will become apparent and will give you a greater degree of self-control.

18

A Review of the Origin and
Self-Regulation of Everyday Moods

Understanding and controlling everyday moods can add substantially to the pleasure of living. Our moods determine whether or not we are satisfied with our lives, whether we are productive or unproductive, whether we live each day with enthusiasm or give up in despair. Our moods are more important than the personal issues and other events that confront us daily. For, in the final analysis, it is our reactions to life events, not the events themselves that count the most. And these reactions are filtered through our prevailing moods.

It is easy to think of everyday moods as mysterious and unknowable. When asked about the origin of these subjective states, many people go no further than the conclusion that "It's all biochemical." Others harbor the implicit belief that if they just had more money, a better car, or a nicer house, their moods would be predominantly positive. Essentially, these ideas are admissions that mood control is difficult or impossible because the causes of these moods are mostly beyond our understanding.

What I have tried to show in this book is that everyday moods are not mysterious and unknowable, especially if you know what to look for. Moods do have biochemical bases, and life events do affect these moods. But all of this takes place in the context of natural biological processes such as sleep, activity, food, and general health.

Knowing what to look for is half the battle in understanding mood. We have seen in this book that moods come from general states of bodily arousal, primarily variations in energy and tension. Scientists may differ on whether these arousal states account for all moods, but most agree that significant elements of everyday moods can be attributed to energy and tension, or at least to the largely synonymous categories of positive and negative affect or feeling.

Viewing moods as underlaid by energy and tension states, allows us an intuitive grasp of what is involved. We all experience these states day in and day out. At some level of understanding, we all know what makes us energetic and tired, and why we may become fearful, anxious, or tense. These processes are not mysterious, but important matters must be considered before real understanding and control can take place.

It is vital, for example, to be aware of the most significant causes of variations in subjective feelings of energy. Here the daily cycle of energy is particularly important. Energy changes should be viewed as reflecting a kind of biological clock. Energy is low at morning awakening, and for most people it gradually increases to a daily high point sometime in the late morning or early afternoon. In a typical cycle, energy next declines to a low point in the mid- to late afternoon. It increases again slightly after dinner before falling to the lowest point of the day just before bedtime. Although there are many individual differences in the shapes of these energy cycles, each person's cycle is nonetheless somewhat fixed.

Tension, the other major component of mood, often has its own daily pattern. The average person under stress begins with little tension upon awakening. Then as the stress-filled day progresses, this tension gradually mounts, often reaching a high level in the late afternoon when energy has dropped to one of its lowest daily points.

Tension may continue to increase into the evening, but usually it diminishes and is influential mainly because of the low levels of energy during that period.

Besides daily biological cycles, the most important causes of the variations in energy and tension are health, sleep, exercise, food, thoughts, and stress. Each of these variables exerts significant influence on energy and tension, and therefore, on mood. Energy level is something like a barometer of the state of our body in relation to these variables and usually, is directly affected when any of them change. Tension is the elemental mood reaction to danger or threat and has an important cognitive basis. It is very much related to our interpretation of events.

The subjective experience of these two major components of mood can be readily explained using some simple concepts. For example, consider calm-energy. In the middle to the late morning, this pleasant state often represents the predominant mood. Or for the person who lives a 90-mile-an-hour lifestyle, this may be the time of a moderately exciting mood state of tense-energy. But tension for too long a period, even if it seems pleasant for a while, will take a toll, and tense-energy will give way to the markedly unpleasant state of tense-tiredness. In a typical day, tense-tiredness may reach a high point in the late afternoon and continue until bedtime, producing insomnia and only a fitful sleep.

Energy and tension have an interesting relationship to each other. If the person under stress has an increase in either tension or energy, the other component (energy or tension) will also rise, but only to moderate levels. After this moderate level is passed, any more increases in either energy or tension will lead to decreases in the other. For example, tense-tiredness is the inevitable result of too much tension or of too little energy in relation to existing tension. On the other hand, if energy increases beyond a moderate level, tension will begin to diminish. Thus, activities that increase energy, such as exercise, often produce calm-energy.

To understand how tension and energy combine to create what we call moods, think of depression. Although tense-tiredness is not equivalent to depression, it usually underlies it. But in depression, a variety of thoughts accompany this tense-tiredness and in part are stimulated by it. Sadness, hopelessness, and low self-esteem are some of these cognitive reactions.

We know that energy and tension influence our immediate thoughts, but they also have a wider influence on cognitive and behavioral processes. For example, the apparent seriousness of our problems and our degree of optimism or pessimism about the future are directly related to these elemental moods. Indeed, many behaviors, including social interactions and even sexual functioning, are probably affected by levels of energy and tension.

The relationship among moods, thoughts, and behaviors points to the biopsychological nature of these states of energy and tension, joining biology and psychology with behavior. In other words, the body operates as a holistic unit, and so we cannot separate thoughts from feelings or feelings from physical condition. Biochemical and basic metabolic processes are integrally coupled with subjective feelings and thoughts. Functions so diverse as brain neurotransmitters, heart activity, blood pressure, respiration, blood sugar level, and immune system activity are a part. The whole body in fact is involved in mood.

General states of tension and energy are very much like wide-ranging stop and go systems in the body. Energy prompts alertness, physical movement, and an active engagement with the environment. On the other hand, tension produces caution, signaling danger and a need to stop and evaluate the situation.

Illustrating this tendency to stop and evaluate, the tension-related states of fear, anxiety, or nervousness are associated with a kind of muscular tightness that inhibits movement. At its most elemental level, this is a freeze response that evolved through millions of years as the best way of evaluating and reacting to potential danger. Today, we can most often recognize this state because our neck and back tightens up, or we might be tapping our fingers or wiggling a foot in a slight discharge of this tension.

One of the most interesting aspects of everyday moods—and in many respects the heart of this book—is the knowledge that moods motivate us. We regulate our moods semiconsciously every day, even moment by moment. The impulse to do something to improve our moods is the basis of self-regulation, whether we sense a negative mood or seek a positive one.

The negative moods that incline us to self-regulate generally involve some variation of tense-tiredness. This state is unpleasant, and people try to avoid it. Anything that raises energy or reduces tension can be the means of regulation. For example, sugar is a common substance of choice, a kind of self-medication. The process by which this occurs is subtle. It may not even involve a conscious urge for a snack; it may simply be persistent thoughts about that good-tasting food—which lead eventually to eating.

Seeking the pleasant state of calm-energy also is important. Most of us sense its attractiveness even if we don't experience it very much. Exercise, a pleasant social interaction, a snack, some wine, or a cigarette—these and many other behaviors enable us to achieve calm-energy, at least temporarily. In sum, behaviors that produce calm-energy and reduce tense-tiredness account for most of the self-controlled process of mood regulation.

Our recent research yields a reliable picture of the ways that most people self-regulate their moods. In other words, we now know the most common ways of changing a bad mood, raising energy, and reducing tension. In addition, we have evidence of how successful these various behaviors and strategies really are in regulating mood. This complex picture includes important individual differences. For example, men and women use different strategies to regulate their moods. But even with this complexity, the findings offer a great deal of information we can all use.

When noticing a bad mood, people usually try to control or to change their thoughts in some way, such as calling, talking to, or being with other people. Less frequent but still commonly used ways that people try to change a bad mood are listening to music, being alone, resting or sleeping, exercising, eating something, and watching TV. Based on this research, we found that the single best thing to do when experiencing a bad mood is to exercise. It also is quite effective to listen to music and to interact with other people or just to do chores. Less effective ways of changing a bad mood include avoiding the cause of the mood and being alone. Drugs and alcohol are among the worst ways—not in the short run but over time.

Besides evaluating individual behaviors, we identified broad general strategies commonly used to regulate moods. This means attacking the bad mood not in a single way but in a number of ways. The best overall strategy for changing a bad mood is simultaneously controlling many aspects of bodily functioning, by combining exercise, thought control, stress management, and relaxation. Other common but less effective strategies are eating, watching TV, and related activities. The poorest strategies are drinking and using drugs.

The best general strategy to change bad moods supports the theory that energy and tension are central to these negative states. Because the primary mood effect of exercise is increasing energy and reducing tension, it should be no surprise that it is the best way of altering a bad mood. But in addition to that, all the best ways of changing a bad mood raise energy and reduce tension, either directly or indirectly.

These general strategies for changing bad moods may be different for men and women. For example, although professional women tend to use the very best strategy, compared with men, women in general are more likely to use less effective passive strategies, including eating. On the other hand, men as a whole are more likely than women to use effective distraction strategies when they are in a bad mood. These findings relate directly to medical evidence that depression is twice as common among women than among men. Use of poor mood-change strategies could be a reason for the increased depression among women. Men do not always fare better than women, however. Some men are more likely to use the poorest strategy of all for dealing with a bad mood: using alcohol or drugs.

Another aspect of mood regulation is that when people are trying to break a habit like drinking, smoking, or illicit drug use, they often substitute other ways of creating the good mood that these substances provide. At Alcoholics Anonymous meetings, for example, people trying to avoid alcohol turn to smoking and eating sugar. Or those trying to stop smoking start eating more, and so gain weight. A very similar kind of substitution occurs with abstinent drug users.

The best kind of substitution to achieve a good mood and to escape a bad habit is something that raises energy and reduces tension in a longer-lasting way. It turns out that exercise has exactly this effect, and moreover, we have discovered that short periods of exercise can be surprisingly effective in reducing all kinds of undesirable appetites. Short brisk walks, for example, seem to have a positive effect on mood, and just 5 or 10 minutes of brisk walking can enhance mood for an hour or more. These walks seem to reduce the appetite for food and other substances, at least long enough to get over the peak of the urge.

One of the most important findings from our research is that tense-tiredness is the mood that most people try to escape. Certain times of day, lack of sleep, inactivity, and stress all contribute to this mood. Recognizing tense-tiredness by its many unpleasant reactions, including negative thoughts, feelings of depression, and urges to eat or use other substances, is one of the crucial steps you can take in curbing bad habits and boosting your energy. By overcoming tense-tiredness, you can experience moods that are energizing rather than fatiguing.

Although there are many ways of overcoming a tense-tired mood, exercise is the most valuable in this respect. Moderate exercise, such as short brisk walks, works well to raise energy, and often can reduce tension. More intense and longer sessions of exercise are especially valuable if high levels of tension are the problem. Keep in mind that more intense activity will raise energy at a later time but might be fatiguing directly afterward.

A very interesting question—given the mood-enhancing effect of exercise—is why most people don't do more of it. I advise students to start an exercise program that is enjoyable. If it isn't fun while you are doing it, you won't stick with it. Many people begin with programs that are too difficult, because they want to see fast results. Unfortunately, these people quit even though they get into shape and feel great for a short while. I think that the reason they quit stems from the residual effects of exercise programs that are just too onerous.

Besides exercise and other activities that raise energy, methods of reducing tension also improve moods. Stress management techniques usually work, although they require regular practice. For example, various forms of meditation produce calm-energy directly, by controlling anxiety-producing thoughts and encouraging general bodily relaxation. Other activities ranging from yoga to massage, and even hot baths, can also lower tension.

Another important consideration in optimizing mood is to be able to predict your mood at different times of the day. When possible, you should schedule activities for optimal periods based on what you have learned from studying your own daily energy cycle. Knowing what mood effects to expect also provides some comfort when negative moods take charge. For example, rather than thinking of yourself as troubled and tired all the time, use this knowledge to become aware of when you are most vulnerable to negative moods and to understand that this doesn't mean your life is bad. You can also use exercise, meditation, or some positive social activity to temporarily raise your energy.

Finally, the first step in optimal mood regulation is systematic self-observation. Individual differences require that you observe yourself.

Although the general processes may be the same, the moods of each of us are likely to be somewhat different. Some individuals require more exercise to achieve a certain effect, and others less. Sleep needs vary for each person. Sugar affects some people more strongly than others. Systematic self-observations of all these matters may seem overwhelming, but actually they are not difficult if you know what to look for, and how to do it.

So what is the optimal mood we all should aim for, and what should we expect? I have argued that through countless years of evolution we have inherited the means to be happy and satisfied with our lives. All the tools are readily available to us. An optimal mood is free of depression and anxiety with few negative thoughts. We look at ourselves in a positive light and with satisfaction.

In this optimal mood state, we have energy at our disposal at the high times of day and untroubled tiredness when rest and sleep are required. During our active hours, calm-energy predominates, which leads us to full involvement in whatever we are doing. We are not distracted by tension-related demands; rather, each activity receives our full attention. In this calm-energetic mood, the state of our bodies and all our thoughts make us feel good. In this optimal mood, when it is time for rest and sleep, our relaxation is complete. We have no urgent thoughts of things left undone, of future problems that have not yet materialized. As we gently sink into deep sleep, we feel calm and tired from the activities of the day and pleasure as our cheek hits the pillow.

APPENDIX

Beyond Stress Management to Calm-Energy

The following is a set of simple suggestions that I sometimes give my students when they ask me how they can achieve more calm-energy, but I don't pretend that this course of action is the only way of achieving that mood. To many people, some of these suggestions may seem to be extreme departures from their current lifestyle, and it may not be possible to follow them exactly. But if more calm-energy is the goal, I believe that these ideas may help.

• Allocate at least two hours each day entirely for yourself. These are times to be used for your own pleasure.

In this fast-paced achievement-oriented society, people often crowd in much more than they should for optimal mental health. We get the message implicitly and explicitly that we are failing if we aren't doing something productive, which often means something that isn't fun. Consequently, many people find themselves trying to do more and more in less and less time. This frenetic pace will not produce calm-energy; at best, it will lead to tense-energy. This is a moderately positive state but inevitably will result in tense-tiredness and sometimes in depression.

• Modify your schedule and personal problems to manageable proportions. Your goal should be to eliminate or reduce stress.

This advice is easy to give but hard to accomplish. Nevertheless, it is good to have a goal in mind so that when you decide on schedules, you will know which direction to take. Personal problems also are difficult to manage. Is this job too stressful? Should we abandon a relationship? Should we seek professional guidance? These aren't easy questions to answer, but once again, it often comes down to a matter of priorities. Is achieving calm-energy sufficiently important to do what is necessary to make the needed changes?

• Set aside 7 to 8 hours each night for sleep.

Too little sleep inevitably contributes to negative moods. The National Commission on Sleep Disorders (Chapter 3), is probably correct that Americans are usually sleep deprived. Based on my personal experiences with college students, I agree. Students are among the most sleep-starved people in the population, along with high achievers with Type A lifestyles.

• Eat three nutritious and balanced meals each day. Try to reduce your intake of fat and avoid simple sugars and caffeinated beverages. Also avoid snacking between meals, but eat often enough to maintain your energy.

No one knows exactly what foods are best for mood management because the scientific literature is unclear on this matter. The mood effects of different kinds of food are extremely subtle, and for the average person they tend to be important mainly in a cumulative way. You must determine for yourself exactly how different foods cause your moods to change, through systematic self-observation (Chapter 17).

• Follow a regular exercise program that lasts 15 to 30 minutes each day or at least every other day (an hour of moderate exercise every day pays great dividends). In addition to the mood benefits of general physical conditioning, use moderate exercise (e.g., short brisk walks) often as a short-term energy booster and as a kind of tranquilizer at times when tension is moderately high.

• Develop expertise with one or more stress reduction exercises (e.g., diaphragmatic breathing, muscle relaxation, meditation, visualization), and practice them daily, immediately upon arising in the morning and just before going to sleep at night (for 15 to 30 minutes each time). An excellent alternative evening period is just before dinner, a time that has the added benefit of reducing undesirable food urges. Stress management procedures have great benefits when they are well learned and applied on a regular basis. There is a learning curve involved in all these skills, and they take practice. But once mastered, they can bring us much calm-energy.

• Schedule demanding activities during calm-energetic times, and avoid these activities, including arguments and unpleasant social interactions, during tense-tired times.

Although we can't always schedule our stress for a particular time, most people find that some degree of control is possible. It may be something as simple as when we think about problems that must be solved or when we make a difficult telephone call. Or if we must talk to a mate about a problem, we should do it during calm-energetic times, not tense-tired ones.

• Anytime that you have negative thoughts, remember to ask yourself questions like What time of day is it, have I eaten recently, when did I exercise last, and how much sleep have I had? Learn to stop these negative thoughts and to think instead about something neutral if any of these questions indicate a deficit or a low-energy time.

It isn't easy to stop negative thoughts, but it is a skill that can be learned. After a time of observing yourself in this way, you will find that negative thoughts frequently occur during periods of low energy and heightened tension, a pattern related to one of the preceding questions. There is something about this knowledge that makes it easier to stop the thoughts. Probably this is because you realize that there is a reason for your negative thoughts that can be corrected with the passage of a few hours, some exercise, a good night's sleep, or a meal.

• Systematically observe and record your energy, tension, and general stress levels. Pay particular attention to your daily cycles, to optimal and poor hours, and to your reactions to exercise, sleep, and various foods. At first, this may require a diary that you carry with you, but later, a continuing awareness is sufficient.

To achieve optimal mood management, there is no substitute for systematic self-observation. We all are different, but at a basic level most thoughtful adults will know how to achieve calm-energy if they just pay attention to the right things. But what to attend to is the key. Energy and tension are critical variables in this respect. Attending to general stress levels in this self-observation has another benefit, as we soon find that feelings of stress are equivalent to heightened tension and too little energy.

• Use systematic self-observation to become aware of how you self-regulate your daily moods. Choose effective behaviors and strategies to do this, and carefully avoid ineffective ones.

As is apparent from earlier parts of this book, we all self-regulate our moods in a number of ways, but many people regulate their bad moods in less effective ways. For example, snacking, drinking, and using other kinds of drugs are particularly ineffective. Also, isolating yourself and using passive self-regulation strategies is less good. The most effective self-regulation strategy involves a combination of relaxation, stress management, cognitive control, and exercise. And of all the individual behaviors that can be employed, exercise is the best.

• To conclude, several simple matters of lifestyle yield great mood benefits. Always allow yourself plenty of time for each thing that you do, and complete each task with undivided attention before going on to the next. Cultivate an attitude of patience.

Time demand is a major source of stress, and the effects of this are directly experienced as increased tension. Undivided attention is especially important to a calm mind. The attitude of patience is one in which the hassles of everyday life are approached with calmness. Think of necessary delays (e.g., traffic lights, long lines) as opportunities to practice stress-reduction exercises and to fully experience calm-energy. Some may know these lifestyle practices as a kind of Zen way of living—not the religious part, but the general demeanor. This is an excellent approach to calm-energy.

NOTES

CHAPTER 1   Mood and Its Meanings

1. In PsychLIT, the scientific abstracting data base for over 1300 scientific journals related to psychology, mood references usually are found under the general descriptor, *emotional state*. More than a thousand scientific articles on mood have been published in the past 10 years.

2. See G. Ryle, *The Concept of Mind* (New York: Barnes and Noble, 1949).

3. See R. Ketai, "Affect, Mood, Emotion, and Feeling: Semantic Considerations," *American Journal of Psychiatry* 132 (1975): 1215–1217; and H. Owens and J. S. Maxmen,. "Mood and Affect: A Semantic Confusion," *American Journal of Psychiatry* 136 (1979): 97–99.

4. D. Watson and A. Tellegen, "Toward a Consensual Structure of Mood," *Psychological Bulletin* 98, (1985) 219–235. For example, self-ratings using many mood-descriptive adjectives can be factor analyzed, yielding a small number of factors or dimensions that can account for the variability of the larger number of adjective ratings, or variables.

5. For other conceptions of mood, see: R. J. Larsen and E. Diener "Promises and Problems with the Circumplex Model of Emotion," in *Emotion*, ed. M. S. Clark (Newbury Park, CA: Sage,1992), 25–59; G. Matthews, D. M. Jones, and A. G. Chamberlain, "Refining the Measurement of Mood: The UWIST Mood Adjective Checklist," *British Journal of Psychology* 81 (1990) 17–42; and J.A. Russell,. "A Circumplex Model of Affect," *Journal of Personality and Social Psychology* 39 (1980) 1161–1178.

6. A couple of questions may arise about this two-dimensional model. First, if all moods are related to energy and tension, together with thoughts and interpretations, what about sexual and angry moods? Where do they fit in? Some researchers think of sex and anger as independent of other emotions or feelings. I will be discussing these moods to some degree in various parts of the book, but for now let me say that the evidence isn't entirely clear. These emotional states have some unique neuroanatomy—for example, genital structures and related brain areas—but they also have energy and tension components, and therefore they are related to the kinds of general moods I will be discussing. In fact, it is probable that both sexual and angry moods have a predominant energy component and varying degrees of tension. In other words, when you feel very sexual

or very angry, you also feel energetic; this is a core element of these feelings. But you may or may not feel particularly tense.

The second question concerns some kinds of pleasurable or even euphoric moods such as those associated with intense happiness or with certain kinds of drug experiences. These states can be so strong that they appear to be more than just combinations of energy, tension, and thoughts. Future research may indicate that intense pleasure is generated in certain parts of the brain, for example, the so-called pleasure center and the associated catecholamine activity (see Chapter 8). But whether that is true or not, energy and tension in different amounts are likely to be present as well. In other words, energy and tension are likely to be central components of all moods, but some moods may involve additional interactions with specialized areas of the brain and body.

CHAPTER 2   A Theory of Mood

1. S. Suzuki, *Zen Mind, Beginner's Mind* (New York: Weatherhill, 1970), 46.

2. R. E. Thayer, P. J. Takahashi, and J. A. Pauli, "Multidimensional Arousal States, Diurnal Rhythms, Cognitive and Social Processes, and Extraversion." *Personality and Individual Differences* 9 (1988): 15–24.

3. R. E. Thayer, *The Biopsychology of Mood and Arousal* (New York: Oxford University Press, 1989).

4. R. E. Thayer, "Problem Perception, Optimism, and Related States as a Function of Time of Day (Diurnal Rhythm) and Moderate Exercise: Two Arousal Systems in Interaction," *Motivation And Emotion* 11 (1978) 19–36.

5. Alternative explanations for these findings, such as subjects' expectation effects, as well as important methodological issues, such as the need for multiple observations of subtle mood changes, are discussed in Thayer, "Problem Perception," and *Biopsychology*.

6. See Thayer, "Problem Perception," and Thayer et al., "Multidimensional Arousal States."

7. For example, see C. S. Carver and M. F. Scheier, "Control Theory: A Useful Conceptual Framework for Personality—Social, Clinical, and Health Psychology," *Psychological Bulletin* 92 (1982): 111–135.

CHAPTER 3   Moods as Barometers of Well-Being

1. See the reviews in R. E. Thayer, *The Biopsychology of Mood and Arousal* (New York: Oxford University Press,1989), and R. E. Thayer, D. P. Peters, P. J. Takahashi and A. M. Birkhead-Flight, "Mood and Behavior (Smoking and Sugar Snacking) Following Moderate Exercise: A Partial Test of Self-Regulation Theory," *Personality and Individual Differences* 14 (1993): 97–104.

2. See R. E. Thayer, Toward a Psychological Theory of Multidimensional Activation (Arousal)," *Motivation and Emotion* 2, (1978): 1–34.

3. See W. Revelle, "Manipulations and Measurement of Arousal: Within and Between—Subject Evidence for Two Components of Arousal," paper presented at the meeting of the International Society for the Study of Individual Differences, Baltimore, 1993; and D. H. Saklofske, G. C. Blomme, and I. W. Kelly, (1992). "The Effect of Exercise and Relaxation on Energetic and Tense Arousal." *Personality and Individual Differences* 13 (1992): 623–25.

4. See L. A. Slauson, "The Effects of Exercise and the Relationship of Personality Factors on Arousal Levels, Optimism, and Self-Esteem in Adults." (master's thesis, California State University at Long Beach, 1989).

5. R. E. Thayer. "Energy, Tiredness, and Tension Effects of a Sugar Snack Versus Moderate Exercise." *Journal of Personality and Social Psychology* 52 (1987): 119–25.

6. R. E. Thayer, "Walking: Mood Modulator," address delivered to the National Press Club, Washington, DC, May 27, 1987.

7. For research and review see Thayer et al., "Mood and Behavior."

8. For a relevant study, see J. D. Flory and D. S. Holmes "Effects of an Acute Bout of Aerobic Exercise on Cardiovascular and Subjective Responses During Subsequent Cognitive Work," *Journal of Psychosomatic Research* 35 (1991): 225–230.

9. For example, see C. J. Hardy and W. J. Rejeski, "Not What, But How One Feels: The Measurement of Affect During Exercise," *Journal of Sport and Exercise Psychology* 11 (1989): 304–17.

10. A. Keys, J. Brozek, A. Henschel, O. Mickelsen, and H. L. Taylor, *The Biology of Human Starvation* (Minneapolis: University of Minnesota Press, 1950).

11. See, for example, B. Spring, R. Pingitore, K. H. Kessler, and E. Bruckner, "The Effects and Non-Effects of Skipping Breakfast: Results of Three Studies," paper presented at the annual meeting of the American Psychological Association, Washington, D.C., 1992; A. Smith, A. Kendrick, and A. Maben, "Effects of Breakfast and Caffeine on Cognitive Performance, Mood and Cardiovascular Functioning," *Appetite 22* (1994): 39–55; and A. Smith, A. Maben, and P. Brockman, "Effects of Evening Meals and Caffeine on Cognitive Performance, Mood and Cardiovascular Functioning," *Appetite 22* (1994): 57–65.

12. D. S. King, and P. Wisocki, "A Survey About the Effects of Food on Behavior," paper presented at the annual convention of the American Psychological Association, San Francisco, 1991.

13. For a further discussion of these methodological issues, see Thayer, *Biopsychology*, chap. 7.

14. In *blind* experiments, the subjects do not know whether they are ingesting the experimental substance or a placebo control. In *double-blind* experiments, the experimenter also does not know. Such procedures make it unlikely that the results are due to expectations.

15. Thayer, "Energy, Tiredness, and Tension Effects."

16. M. M. Tuckerman and S. J. Turco, *Human Nutrition* (Philadelphia: Lea and

Febiger, 1983); and S.C. Woods, "The Eating Paradox: How We Tolerate Food," *Psychological Review* 98 (1991): 488–505.

17. For example, see B. Spring, J. Chiodo, and D.J. Bowen, "Carbohydrates, Tryptophan, and Behavior: A Methodological Review," *Psychological Bulletin* 102 (1987): 234–256.

18. R. J. Wurtman and J. J. Wurtman, *Food Constituents Affecting Normal and Abnormal Behaviors*, vol. 7 of *Nutrition and the Brain Series* (New York:Raven Press, 1986).

19. R. E. Thayer, M. L. Valek, and S. Peck, "When Alertness is Required, a Sugar Snack Causes Tension," paper presented at the American Psychological Society, Dallas, 1990.

20. For example, L. Christensen, and R. Burrows, "Dietary Treatment of Depression," *Behavior Therapy* 21 (1990): 183–194.

21. Consider, for example, the excellent research by C. M. Grilo, S. Shiffman, and R. R. Wing, "Relapse Crises and Coping Among Dieters," *Journal of Consulting and Clinical Psychology* 57 (1989): 488–495; and the review of multiple studies by R. M. Ganley, "Emotion and Eating in Obesity: A Review of the Literature," *International Journal of Eating Disorders* 8 (1989), 343–61. These and other studies are discussed more fully in Chapter 11.

22. L. Christensen, "Effects of Eating Behavior on Mood: A Review of the Literature," *International Journal of Eating Disorders* 14 (1993): 171–183; and A. J Ruderman, "Dietary Restraint: A Theoretical and Empirical Review," *Psychological Bulletin* 99 (1986): 247–62.

23. D. A. Hepburn, I. J. Deary, M. Munoz, and B. M. Frier, "Physiological Manipulation of Psychometric Mood Factors Using Acute Insulin-Induced Hypoglycemia in Humans," *Personality and Individual Differences* 18 (1995): 385–91.

24. D. S. King, "Can Allergic Exposure Provoke Psychological Symptoms? A Double-Blind Test," *Biological Psychiatry* 16 (1981): 3–19.

25. For example, D. J. Bowen, and N. E. Grunberg,. "Variations in Food Preferences and Consumption Across the Menstrual Cycle." *Physiology and Behavior* 47 (1990): 287–91; and C. Hellekson "Phenomenology of Seasonal Affective Disorder: An Alaskan Perspective," In *Seasonal Affective Disorders and Phototherapy*, ed. N. E. Rosenthal and M. C. Blehar (New York: Guilford Press, 1989), pp. 33–45.

26. Ruderman, "Dietary Restraint."

27. D. Buchwald, J. L. Sullivan,and A. L. Komaroff, "Frequency of 'Chronic Active Epstein-Barr Virus Infection' in a General Medical Practice," *Journal of the American Medical Association* 257 (1987): 2303–7.

28. J. K. Dixon, J. P. Dixon, and M. Hickey, "Energy as a Central Factor in the Self-Assessment of Health," *Advances in Nursing Science* 15 (1993): 1–12.

29. S. R. Cramer, D. C. Nieman and J. W. Lee, "The Effects of Moderate Exercise

Training on Psychological Well-Being and Mood State in Women," *Journal of Psychosomatic Research* 35 (1991): 437–49.

30. J. A. Harrigan, J. R. Kuess, D. Ricks, and R. Smith, "Moods that Predict Coming Migraine Headaches," *Pain* 20 (1984): 385–96.

31. P. Blanchet and G. P. Frommer, "Mood Change Preceding Epileptic Seizures," *Journal of Nervous and Mental Disease* 174 (1986): 471–76.

32. King, "Can Allergic Exposure Provoke Psychological Symptoms?"

33. M. W. Linn, B. S. Linn, and J. Jensen, "Stressful Events, Dysphoric Mood, and Immune Responsiveness," *Psychological Reports* 54 (1984): 219–22.

34. A. A. Stone, D. S. Cox, H. Valdimarsdottir, L. Jandorf, and J. M. Neale, "Evidence that Secretory IgA Antibody Is Associated With Daily Mood," *Journal of Personality and Social Psychology* 52 (1987): 988–93; A. A. Stone, J. D. Neale, D. S. Cox, A. Napoli, H. Valdimarsdottir, and E. Kennedy-Moore, "Daily Events Are Associated With a Secretory Immune Response to an Oral Antigen in Men," *Health Psychology* 13 (1994): 440–46.

35. Although Berry and Webb's 1985 research cast doubt on the relationship between sleep and mood, more recent research such as that by Totterdell and his associates has supported that relationship. See D. T. R. Berry and W. B. Webb, "Mood and Sleep in Aging Women," *Journal of Personality and Social Psychology* 49 (1985): 1724–27; P. Totterdell, S. Reynolds, B. Parkinson, and R. B. Briner, "Associations of Sleep With Everyday Mood, Minor Symptoms, and Social Interaction Experience," *Sleep* 17 (1994): 466–75. Moreover, the integral relationship between sleep and general bodily process, of which mood is a part, is clearly demonstrated in the research by Irwin and his associates on sleep deprivation and immune system functioning. See M. Irwin, A. Mascovich, J. C. Gillin, R. Willoughby, J. Pike, and Tom L. Smith, "Partial Sleep Deprivation Reduces Natural Killer Cell Activity in Humans," *Psychosomatic Medicine* 56 (1994): 493–98.

36. *Wake Up America: A National Sleep Alert*, vol. 1 of *Report of the National Commission on Sleep Disorders Research*, submitted to the United States Congress and to the Secretary, U.S. Department of Health and Human Services (Washington DC: January 1993), 22.

37. Ibid.

38. T. A. Wehr, "Effects of Wakefulness and Sleep on Depression and Mania," in *Sleep and Biological Rhythms*, ed. J. Montplaisir and R. Godbout (New York: Oxford University Press 1990), pp. 42–86.

CHAPTER 4 The Relationship Between Mood and Thoughts

1. For two good analyses of an alternative viewpoint that emphasizes body and mind integration, see M. J. Mahoney, "Psychotherapy and the Body in the Mind," in *Body Images: Development, Deviance, and Change*, ed. T. F. Cash and

T. Pruzinsky (New York: Guilford, 1990), pp. 316–33; and A. C. Papanicolaou, *Emotion: A Reconsideration of the Somatic Theory* (New York: Gordon and Breach Science Publishers, 1989).

2. Compare N. V. Peale, *The Power of Positive Thinking* (New York: Prentice Hall, 1952).

3. In one study, we obtained multiple ratings of self-esteem, energy, and tension over a 7-week period. When tension was high, self-esteem was low, but the best predictor of self-esteem was energy level. High levels of energy predicted high self-esteem. See J. Rubadeau and R. E. Thayer "The Relationship of Self-Esteem and Self-Reported Activation Level over a Seven Week Period," paper presented at the Western Psychological Association, Los Angeles, 1976.

4. To understand this type of response better, consider that a leading cognitive psychologist, Richard Lazarus, views cognitive science as involving the way that environmental displays are attended to, registered, encoded, transformed, stored, and retrieved. This leads to decision making. See R. J. Lazarus, *Emotion and Adaptation* (New York: Oxford University Press, 1991).

5. See the excellent analysis of stress in R. S. Lazarus and B. N. Lazarus, *Passion and Reason: Making Sense of Our Emotions* (New York: Oxford University Press, 1994).

6. For example, see D. S. King, "Can Allergic Exposure Provoke Psychological Symptoms? A Double-Blind Test," *Biological Psychiatry* 16 (1981): 3–19 and E. J. Rogers and B. Vilkin, "Diurnal Variations in Sensory and Pain Thresholds Correlated with Mood States," *Journal of Clinical Psychiatry* 39 (1978): 431–38. Indeed, increased tension is a common reaction to pain, B. Sofaer and J. Walker, "Mood Assessment in Chronic Pain Patients," *Disability and Rehabilitation* 16 (1994): 35–38.

7. Of course, one may be argued that not all interpretations of bodily condition are conscious, that the brain probably makes interpretations on many levels of consciousness, even during sleep.

8. Compare R. B. Zajonc, "Feeling and Thinking: Preferences Need No Inferences," *American Psychologist* 35 (1980): 151–75 and R. B. Zajonc, "On the Primacy of Affect," *American Psychologist* 39 (1984): 117–23.

9. Mood congruence has been fairly well documented in a large body of research, although there are still some questions about it, for instance, congruence involving both positive and negative moods. See P. H. Blaney, "Affect and Memory: A Review," *Psychological Bulletin* 99 (1986): 229–46; and W. N. Morris, *Mood: The Frame of Mind* (New York: Springer-Verlag, 1989).

10. A. T. Beck, *Cognitive Therapy and the Emotional Disorders* (New York: International Universities Press, 1976).

11. Beck *Cognitive Therapy*, and other cognitive mood therapies use this approach.

12. This should be regarded only as a loose analogy used to show the rela-

tionship. The limits of this analogy become clear with newer conceptions of computer science.

13. D. A. Overton, "Major Theories of State Dependent Learning," in *Drug Discrimination and State Dependent Learning*, ed. B. T. Ho, D. W. Richards, and D. L. Chute (New York: Academic Press, 1978), pp. 283–318.

14. Compare M. S. Clark, S. Milberg and J. Ross, "Arousal Cues Arousal-Related Material in Memory: Implications for Understanding Effects of Mood on Memory," *Journal of Verbal Learning and Verbal Behavior* 22 (1983): 633–649.

15. H. Weingartner, H. Miller and D. L. Murphy, "Mood-State-Dependent Retrieval of Verbal Associations," *Journal of Abnormal Psychology* 86 (1977): 276–84.

16. See Blaney, "Affect and Memory"; and Morris, *Mood*.

CHAPTER 5 PMS, Drugs, Social Interaction, Weather, and Life Events

1. D. Asso, "A Reappraisal of the Normal Menstrual Cycle," *Journal of Reproductive and Infant Psychology* 10 (1992): 103–9; and R. E. Thayer, *The Biopsychology of Mood and Arousal* (New York: Oxford University Press, 1989.)

2. For example, R. DeJong, D. R. Rubinow, P. Roy-Byrne, C. Hoban, G. N. Grover, and R. M. Post, "Premenstrual Mood Disorders and Psychiatric Illness," *American Journal of Psychiatry* 142, 1359–61; and P. P. Schnurr, "Some Correlates of Prospectively-Defined Premenstrual Syndrome," *American Journal of Psychiatry* 145 (1988): 491–94.

3. Compare B. Olasov and J. Jackson, "Effects of Expectancies on Women's Reports of Moods During the Menstrual Cycle," *Psychosomatic Medicine* 49 (1987): 65–78. Also see, J. M. McFarlane and T. M. Williams, "Placing Premenstrual Syndrome in Perspective," *Psychology of Women Quarterly* 18 (1994): 339–73.

4. The American Psychological Association took the position that there isn't sufficient scientific evidence for this kind of classification and protested its inclusion. See *Monitor* (Washington, D.C.: American Psychological Association, September 1993), 32–33.

5. D. Asso, "Psychology Degree Examinations and Premenstrual Phase of the Menstrual Cycle," *Women and Health* 10 (1985/86): 91–104; S. L. Black and C. A. Koulis, "The Menstrual Cycle and Typing Skill: An Ecologically-Valid Test of the 'Raging Hormones' Hypothesis," *Canadian Journal of Behavioural Science* 22 (1990): 445–55; and P. Patkai, "The Menstrual Cycle," in *Hours of Work*, ed. S. Folkard and T. H. Monk (Chichester: Wiley, 1985), pp. 87–96.

6. See Thayer, *Biopsychology*, chap. 7.

7. Technically speaking such a definition would not hold. A common pharmacological definition of drugs is "any substance, other than food, that by its chemical and physical nature alters structure and function in the living organism."

See O. S. Ray, *Drugs, Society, and Human Behavior* (St. Louis: Mosby, 1972), 50. Although this definition excludes food—and, accordingly, sugar—sugar is often used for its psychoactive function, just as some drugs are.

8. R. M. Julien, *A Primer of Drug Action* (New York: W.H. Freeman, 1992); and O. S. Ray and C. Ksir, *Drugs, Society, and Human Behavior*, 5th ed. (St. Louis: Mosby, 1990).

9. For example, D. G. Gilbert, "Paradoxical Tranquilizing and Emotion-Reducing Effects of Nicotine," *Psychological Bulletin* 86 (1979): 643–61.

10. Ray and Ksir *Drugs, Society, and Human Behavior*.

11. F. F. Ikard, D. E. Green, and D. Horn, "A Scale to Differentiate Between Types of Smoking as Related to the Management of Affect," *International Journal of Addictions* 4 (1969): 649–59.

12. E. F. Domino, "Neuropsychopharmacology of Nicotine and Tobacco Smoking," in *Smoking Behavior: Motives and Incentives*, ed. W. L. Dunn (New York: Wiley, 1973), pp. 5–31.

13. J. G. Hull and C.F. Bond, "Social and Behavioral Consequences of Alcohol Consumption and Expectancy: A meta-Analysis," *Psychological Bulletin* 99 (1986): 347–60.

14. For example, K. Gilliland, and D. Andress, "Ad Lib Caffeine Consumption, Symptoms of Caffeinism and Academic Performance," *American Journal of Psychiatry* 138 (1981): 512–14; and K. Gilliland and W. Bullock, "Caffeine: A Potential Drug of Abuse," *Advances in Alcohol and Substance Abuse* 3 (1983/84): 53–73.

15. The effect of coffee is a favorite self-study project of my students in an advanced research methods class. Some of them experience increased energy and no change in tension from one cup, whereas others have an increase in tension but none in energy. The most common effect is tense-energy, a result that has been observed in empirical studies. For example, see W. A. Bullock and K. Gilliland, "Eysenck's Arousal Theory of Introversion-Extraversion: A Converging Measure of Investigation," *Journal of Personality and Social Psychology* 64 (1993): 113–23; and K. Anderson, "Impulsivity and Caffeine: A Within and Between Subjects Test of the Yerkes-Dodson Law," paper presented at the annual meeting of the Society for the Study of Individual Differences, Toronto, Canada, 1987.

16. S. D. Iversen and L. L. Iversen, *Behavioral Pharmacology* (New York: Oxford University Press, 1975).

17. R. E. Thayer, J. R. Newman, and T. M. McClain, "The Self-Regulation of Mood: Strategies for Changing a Bad Mood, Raising Energy, and Reducing Tension," *Journal of Personality and Social Psychology* 67 (1994): 910–25.

18. D. Watson, L. A. Clark, C. W. McIntyre, and S. Hamaker, "Affect Personality and Social Activity," *Journal of Personality and Social Psychology* 63 (1992): 1011–25.

19. S. Cohen, and T. A. Wills, "Stress, Social Support, and the Buffering Hypothesis," *Psychological Bulletin* 98 (1985): 310–57.

20. R. C. Kessler, K. S. Kendler, A. Heath, M. C. Neale, and L. J. Eaves, "Social Support, Depressed Mood, and Adjustment to Stress: A Genetic Epidemiological Investigation," *Journal of Personality and Social Psychology* 62 (1992): 257–72.

21. T. J. Bouchard, D. T. Lykken, M. McGue, N. L. Segal, A. Tellegen, "Sources of Human Psychological Differences: The Minnesota Study of Twins Reared Apart," *Science* 250 (1990): 223–28; and J. L. Eaves, H. J. Eysenck, and N. G. Martin, *Genes, Culture and Personality: An Empirical Approach* (New York: Academic Press, 1988).

22. G. G. Globus, R. L. Drury, E. C. Phoebus, and R. Boyd, "Ultradian Rhythms in Human Performance," *Perceptual and Motor Skills* 33 (1971): 1171–74; D. L. Kripke, "An Ultradian Biological Rhythm Associated with Perceptual Deprivation and REM Sleep," *Psychosomatic Medicine* 34 (1972): 221–34; D. Kripke and D. Sonnenschein, "A Biologic Rhythm in Waking Fantasy," in *The Stream of Consciousness*, ed. D. Pope and J. L. Singer (New York: Plenum Press, 1978), pp. 321–32; P. Lavie and A. Scherson, "Ultrashort Sleep-Wake Schedule 1: Evidence of Ultradian Rhythmicity in 'Sleep-Ability.' " *Electroenchephalography and Clinical Neurophysiology* 52 (1981): 163–74; and E. L. Rossi, *Dreams and the Growth of Personality: Expanding Awareness in Psychotherapy*, 2nd ed. (New York: Brunner/Mazel, 1985).

23. N. E. Rosenthal, D. A. Sack, S. P. James, B. L. Parry, W. B. Mendelson, L. Tomarkin, and T. A. Wehr, "Seasonal Affective Disorder and Phototherapy," *Annals of the New York Academy of Sciences* 453 (1985): 260–69; N. E. Rosenthal and M. C. Blehar, eds. *Seasonal Affective Disorders and Phototherapy* (New York: Guilford Press, 1989).

24. For example, seasonal pattern depression. See American Psychiatric Association, *Diagnostic and Statistical Manual of Mental Disorders*, 3rd ed., rev. (Washington, DC: American Psychiatric Association, 1987).

25. T. A. Wehr, D. A Sack, and N. E. Rosenthal, "Seasonal Affective Disorder with Summer Depression and Winter Hypomania," *American Journal of Psychiatry* 144 (1987); 1602–3.

26. Consistent with this, melatonin appears to be useful in alleviating jet lag, especially if taken at certain times in relation to time shifts. See B. Claustrat, J. Brun, M. David, G. Sassolas, et al., "Melatonin and Jet Lag: Confirmatory Result Using a Simplified Protocol," *Biological Psychiatry* 32 (1992): 705–11; and K. Petrie, A. G. Dawson, L. Thompson, and R. Brook, "A Double-Blind Trial of Melatonin as a Treatment for Jet Lag in International Cabin Crew," *Biological Psychiatry* 33 (1993): 526–30.

27. See the review of melatonin and circadian rhythm hypotheses by A. J. Lewy, R. C. Sack, C. M. Singer, D. M. White, and T. M. Hoban, "Winter Depression and the Phase-Shift Hypothesis for Bright Light's Therapeutic Effects: History, Theory, and Experimental Evidence," in Rosenthal and Blehar, eds., *Seasonal Affective Disorders*, pp. 295–310.

28. See the related chapters in, Rosenthal and Blehar, eds., *Seasonal Affective Disorders*

29. See R. A. Depue, P. Arbisi, M. R. Spoont, A. Leon, and B. Ainsworth, "Dopamine Functioning in the Behavioral Facilitation System and Seasonal Variation in Behavior: Normal Population and Clinical Studies," in Rosenthal and Blehar, eds., *Seasonal Affective Disorders*, pp. 230–59.

30. N. Mrosovsky, "Seasonal Affective Disorder, Hibernation, and Annual Cycles of Animals: Chipmunks in the Sky," in Rosenthal and Blehar, eds., *Seasonal Affective Disorders*, pp. 127–48.

31. A. Haggag, B. Eklund, O. Linaker, and K. G. Gotestam, "Seasonal Mood Variation: An Epidemiological Study in Northern Norway," *Acta Psychiatrica Scandinavica* 81 (1990): 141–45; L. N. Rosen, S. D. Targum, M. Terman, M. J. Bryant, et al., "Prevalence of Seasonal Affective Disorders at Four Latitudes," *Psychiatry Research* 31 (1990): 131–44; and M. Terman, "On the Question of Mechanism in Phototherapy for Seasonal Affective Disorder: Considerations of Clinical Efficacy and Epidemiology," in Rosenthal and Blehar, eds., *Seasonal Affective Disorders*, pp. 357–76.

32. M. A. Persinger, "Winter Blahs and Spring Irritability: The Chronic but Subtle Behavioral Observations," *Perceptual and Motor Skills* 57 (1983): 496–98.

33. F. Soyka and A. Edwards. *The Ion Effect* (New York: Bantam Books, 1976).

34. For example, R. A. Baron, G. W. Russell, and R. L. Arms, "Negative Ions and Behavior: Impact on Mood, Memory, and Aggression Among Type A and Type B Persons," *Journal of Personality and Social Psychology* 48 (1985): 746–54.

35. For example, D. E. Campbell, "Lunar-Lunacy: When Enough is Enough," *Environment and Behavior* 14 (1982): 418–24; and S. Garzino, "Lunar Effects on Behavior: A Defense of the Empirical Research," *Environment and Behavior* 14 (1982): 395–417.

36. J. Rotton and I. W. Kelly, "Much Ado About the Full Moon: A Meta-Analysis of Lunar-Lunacy Research," *Psychological Bulletin* 97 (1985): 286–306.

37. P. M. Lewinsohn, M. Weinstein, and D. Shaw, "Depression: A Clinical-Research Approach," in *Advances in Behavior Therapy*, ed. R. D. Rubin and C. M. Frank (New York: Academic Press, 1968), pp. 231–40.

38. For example, P. M. Lewinsohn and C. S. Amenson, "Some Relations Between Pleasant and Unpleasant Mood-Related Events and Depression," *Journal of Abnormal Psychology* 87 (1978): 644–54.

39. L. A. McArthur, "The How and the Why: Some Determinants and Consequences of Causal Attribution," *Journal of Personality and Social Psychology* 22 (1972): 171–93.

CHAPTER 6 How Energy and Tension Interact

1. In today's scientific analyses of mood, many researchers think of positive and negative affect as independent, or in scientific terms, *orthogonal*. If they are

independent, it means that an individual could experience both Positive and Negative Affect at the same time, a mixture that appears unlikely. Because energy and tension are important elements of positive and negative affect, this theory would also hold that energetic and tense arousal are independent as well. I believe that this analysis is correct in that there are two separate arousal dimensions. See D. Watson and A. Tellegen, "Toward a Consensual Structure of Mood," *Psychological Bulletin* 98 (1985): 219–35.

2. R. E. Thayer and L. E. Moore, "Reported Activation and Verbal Learning as a Function of Group Size (Social Facilitation) and Anxiety-Inducing Instructions," *Journal of Social Psychology* 88 (1972): 277–87.

3. We expected this because of an early theory that there is only one general arousal continuum, and that all arousal states change more or less in the same way, although to different degrees. See E. Duffy, *Activation and Behavior* (New York: Wiley, 1962).

4. The originators of the concept of Type A personality have described this tense-energetic profile. See M. Friedman and R. H. Rosenman, *Type A Behavior and Your Heart* (New York: Knopf, 1974); in addition, systematic empirical research has documented this tendency of Type A personalities to have both higher tension and energy than others. See R. A. Hicks, T. Green, and J. Haleblian, "The Thayer Scale Response Patterns of Type A and Type B College Students," *Psychological Reports* 65 (1989): 1167–70.

5. R. H. Rosenman, "The Interview Method of Assessment of the Coronary-Prone Behavior Pattern," In *Coronary-Prone Behavior*, ed. T. M. Dembrowski, S. M. Weiss, J. L. Shields, S. G. Haynes, and M. Feinleib (New York: Springer-Verlag, 1978), 55–69.

6. R. A. Sternbach, *Principles of Psychophysiology: An Introductory Text and Readings* (New York: Academic Press, 1966).

7. P. R. Robbins and R. H. Tanck, "A Study of Diurnal Patterns of Depressed Mood," *Motivation and Emotion* 11 (1987): 37–49.

8. L. A. Clark and D. Watson, "Tripartite Model of Anxiety and Depression: Psychometric Evidence and Taxonomic Implications," *Journal of Abnormal Psychology* 100 (1991), 316–36.

9. R. B. Bassin and R. E. Thayer, "Self-Reported Depression, Moderate Exercise, and Arousal Level," paper presented at the Western Psychological Association, Seattle, 1986; and R. E. Thayer and A. Wettler, "Activation Patterns in Self-Reported Depression States," unpublished manuscript, California State University at Long Beach, 1975.

10. American Psychiatric Association, *Diagnostic and Statistical Manual of Mental Disorders*, 3rd ed., rev. (Washington, DC: American Psychiatric Association, 1987).

11. Clark and Watson, "Tripartite Model."

12. H. H. W. Miles, E. L. Barrabee, and J. E. Finesinger, "Evaluation of Psychotherapy, with a Follow-up Study of 62 Cases of Anxiety Neurosis," *Psychosomatic*

Medicine 13 (1951): 83–105; and E. O. Wheeler, P. D. White, E. W. Reed, and M. E. Cohen, "Neurocirculatory Asthenia (Anxiety Neurosis, Effort Syndrome, Neurasthenia)," *Journal of the American Medical Association* 142 (1950): 878–89.

13. R. E. Thayer, "Energy, Tiredness, and Tension Effects of a Sugar Snack Versus Moderate Exercise," *Journal of Personality and Social Psychology* 52 (1987): 119–25.

14. H. J. Eysenck and M. W. Eysenck, *Personality and Individual Differences: A Natural Science Approach* (New York: Plenum Press, 1985); M. Zuckerman, *Sensation Seeking: Beyond the Optimal Level of Arousal* (Hillsdale, NJ: Erlbaum, 1979); and F. Farley, "The Big T in Personality," *Psychology Today* 20 (1986): 44–52.

15. See R. E. Thayer, D. P. Peters, P. J. Takahashi, and A. M. Birkhead-Flight, "Mood and Behavior (Smoking and Sugar Snacking) Following Moderate Exercise: A Partial Test of Self-Regulation Theory," *Personality and Individual Differences* 14 (1993): 97–104.

16. W. P. Morgan and M. L. Pollock, "Psychologic Characterization of the Elite Distance Runner," *Annals of the New York Academy of Science* 301 (1978): 382–403.

17. E. H. Wughalter and J. G. Gondola, "Mood States of Professional Female Tennis Players," *Perceptual and Motor Skills* 73 (1991): 187–90; and J. V. Mastro, C. Sherrill, B. Gench, and R. French, "Psychological Characteristics of Elite Visually-Impaired Athletes," *Journal of Sport Behavior* 10 (1987): 39–46.

18. Also see S. E. Frazier, "Mood State Profiles of Chronic Exercisers with Differing Abilities," *International Journal of Sport Psychology* 19 (1988): 65–71.

19. Although the literature showing that elite athletes have an iceberg profile compared with others is logical, at this point it is not definitive. The problem concerns the way that comparisons with the mood profiles of others (control subjects) are performed. This requires more attention to measurement than has been paid until now.

20. F. M. Docuyanan and R. E. Thayer, "Effectiveness of Study Time as a Function of Transitory Moods," paper presented at the annual convention of the American Psychological Association, Toronto, 1993.

21. R. M. Julien, *A Primer of Drug Action* (New York: W. H. Freeman, 1992); and O. S. Ray and C. Ksir, eds., *Drugs, Society, and Human Behavior*, 5th ed. (St. Louis: Mosby, 1990).

22. My thanks to Kara Thayer and Retha Evans for their insights into this activity.

23. N. Kleitman, *Sleep and Wakefulness*, rev. and enlarged ed. (Chicago: University of Chicago Press, 1963).

24. B. Bettelheim, "Individual and Mass Behavior in Extreme Situations," *Journal of Abnormal and Social Psychology* 38 (1943): 417–52.

CHAPTER 7   The Evolutionary Biology of Moods

1. R. W. Sperry, "Neurology and the Mind-Brain Problem," *American Scientist* 40 (1952): 291–312, 297.

2. R. B. Malmo, *On Emotions, Needs, and Our Archaic Brain* (New York: Holt, Rinehart and Winston, 1975).

3. N. Kleitman, *Sleep and Wakefulness*, rev. and enlarged ed. (Chicago: University of Chicago Press, 1963), 369.

4. W. B. Cannon, *Bodily Changes in Pain, Hunger, Fear and Rage* (New York: Harper & Row, 1929/1963); and M. B. Arnold, "Physiological Differentiation of Emotional States," *Psychological Review* 52 (1945): 35–48.

5. The muscle pattern of REM sleep shows an interesting parallel to this tension-induced bodily pattern of inactivity of the large muscles and activity of the peripheral muscles of the fingers and feet. If these two patterns were found to be similar in other respects, they would suggest some potential hypotheses for the bases of REM sleep.

6. Most of the body's systems operate reciprocally. As we walk, for instance, extensor muscles alternatively contract with each push and then relax. Then reciprocally acting flexor muscles bring the leg into place for the next push. Neurons in the brain bathe synapses with molecules that facilitate neural transmission, and other molecules are alternatively released that facilitate the uptake of the first neurotransmitter. Examples of these kinds of reciprocal systems abound throughout the body. Therefore, considering tension and energy as stop and go systems is consistent with known principles of bodily functioning, although these systems occur at another level of generality.

7. Compare A. Appels, "Vital Exhaustion and Depression as Precursors of Myocardial Infarction," in *Stress and Anxiety*, vol 11, ed. P. D. Defares (Washington, DC: Hemisphere Books, 1991), pp. 143–150.

8. In fact, early studies of mine indicated that self-report may be a better indication of general bodily activation than any single physiological index, probably because someone describing his or her arousal state is sensing and integrating many physiological systems. For example, if intelligent adults are asked about their current state of excitement, they may evaluate their heart and respiration rate, sweating, muscle tension, and even their metabolism and blood glucose levels. Research on the awareness of these systems is not advanced, however. See R. E. Thayer, "Activation States as Assessed by Verbal Report and Four Psychophysiological Variables," *Psychophysiology* 7 (1970): 86–94.

CHAPTER 8   The Physiology and Anatomy of Mood

1. See footnote 8, Chapter 7, for further discussion of this matter.

2. See R. E. Thayer, "Activation States As Assessed by Verbal Report and Four Psychophysiological Variables," *Psychophysiology* 7 (1970): 86–94.

3. This wider pattern of physiological arousal when demands were placed on a person was not an original observation from our laboratory work; rather, it had often been observed before, with a variety of activating conditions and with many different physiological functions. See E. Duffy, *Activation and Behavior* (New York: Wiley, 1962); R. A. Sternbach, *Principles of Psychophysiology: An Introductory Text and Readings* (New York: Academic Press, 1966); and J. T. Cacioppo, B. N. Uchino, S. L. Crites, M. A. Snydersmith, G. Smith, and G. G. Berntson, "Relationship Between Facial Expressiveness and Sympathetic Activation in Emotion: A Critical Review, with Emphasis on Modeling Underlying Mechanisms and Individual Differences," *Journal of Personality and Social Psychology* 62 (1992): 110–28.

4. Although there are exceptions to this general arousal response, by and large these general bodily responses occur in many different activating circumstances. See P. Ekman, R. W. Levenson, and W. V. Friesen, "Autonomic Nervous System Activity Distinguishes Among Emotions," *Science* 221 (1983): 1208–10; and J. I. Lacey, "Somatic Response Patterning and Stress: Some Revisions of Activation Theory," in *Psychological Stress*, ed. M. Appley and R. Trumbull (New York:Appleton-Century-Crofts, 1967), pp. 14–42.

5. For example, animal research provides evidence that one or more parts of the brain and their neurochemical systems are associated with wakefulness, compared with sleep, activity versus inactivity, different aspects of sensory arousal, pleasurable stimulus seeking, and strong emotions. Little certainty exists beyond these general characterizations, and all these elemental processes involve states of general bodily arousal, as opposed to quiescence. Pharmacological evidence concerning specific drugs in the treatment of states such as depression gives us other evidence, but nonetheless, our understanding of the underlying anatomy and neurochemistry of these mood disorders is still unclear.

All these elemental processes and mood disorders may be subsumed under the two mood dimensions described in this book. For example, energetic arousal underlies approach or appetitive tendencies of all sorts, and tense arousal mediates caution, inhibitory, and defensive processes in general. Wakefulness, motor activity, pleasure, and positive emotions are associated with high energetic arousal. Conversely, tense arousal, includes fear, anxiety, caution, inhibition, and stress reactions in general. Depression is a mixed arousal state of low energy and moderate tension. Therefore, the same central neurochemical processes and behavior connections that scientists have reliably identified also may underlie energetic and tense arousal.

6. A. Baum, N. E. Grunberg, and J. E. Singer, "Biochemical Measurements in the Study of Emotion," *Psychological Science* 3 (1992): 56–59.

7. J. P. J. Pinel, *Biopsychology*, 2nd ed. (Boston: Allyn & Bacon, 1990).

8. Another possibility is that slowly changing densities and sensitivities of brain receptor systems could be the basis of drug efficacy. See E. T. McNeal and

P. Cimbolic, "Antidepressants and Biochemical Theories of Depression," *Psychological Bulletin* 99 (1986): 361–74.

9. M. McGuire, and A. Troisi, *Evolutionary Psychiatry* (Cambridge: Harvard University Press, in press). Also see J. Panksepp, "Neurochemical Control of Moods and Emotions: Amino Acids and Neuropeptides," in *Handbook of Emotions*, ed. M. Lewis and J. M. Haviland (New York: Guilford Press, 1993), pp. 87–107, for a brief but excellent discussion of a wide variety of neurochemical systems that might affect mood, including systems that are often overlooked in this regard.

10. C. P. Ransford, "A Role for Amines in the Antidepressant Effect of Exercise: A Review," *Medicine and Science in Sports and Exercise* 14 (1982): 1–10; and B. D. Hatfield, "Exercise and Mental Health: The Mechanisms of Exercise-Induced Psychological States," in *Psychology of Sports, Exercise, and Fitness*, ed. L. Diamant (New York: Hemisphere Books, 1991), pp. 17–49 .

11. E. D. Abercrombie, and B. L. Jacobs, "Single Unit Response of Noradrenergic Neurons in The Locus Coeruleus of Freely Moving Cats. I. Acutely Presented Stressful and Non-stressful Stimuli," *Journal of Neuroscience* 7 (1987): 2837–43.

12. R. M. Julien, *A Primer of Drug Action*, 6th ed. (New York: W. H. Freeman, 1992).

13. R. N. Golden and D. S. Janowsky "Biological Theories of Depression," in *Depressive Disorders: Facts, Theories, and Treatment Models*, ed. B. B. Wolman and G. Stricker (New York: Wiley, 1990), pp. 3–21; and N. Iqbal, W. Bajwa, and G. M. Asnis, "The Role of Norepinephrine in Depression," *Psychiatric Annals* 19 (1989): 354–59.

14. Golden and Janowsky, "Biological Theories."

15. Julien, *Primer*.

16. M. Le Moal, and H. Simon, "Mesocorticolimbic Dopaminergic Network: Functional and Regulatory Roles," *Physiological Reviews* 71 (1991): 155–234.

17. Ibid.

18. E. R. Kandel, J. H. Schwartz, and T. M. Jessell, *Principles of Neural Science*, 3rd ed. (Norwalk, CO: Appleton & Lange, 1991); Pinel, *Biopsychology*.

19. Le Moal and Simon, "Mesocorticolimbic Dopaminergic Network."

20. Ibid.; and R. A. Wise, and M. A. Bozarth, "A Psychomotor Stimulant Theory of Addiction," *Psychological Review* 94 (1987): 469–92.

21. R. A. Depue, M. Luciana, P. Arbisi, P. Collins, and A. Leon, "Dopamine and Structure of Personality: Relation of Agonist-Induced Dopamine Activity to Positive Emotionality," *Journal of Personality and Social Psychology* 67 (1994): 485–98.

22. Le Moal and Simon, "Mesocorticolimbic Dopaminergic Network."

23. An interesting theory was proposed by Tucker and Williamson, in which dopamine projections result in a kind of tonic activation similar to tense arousal and interact with norepinephrine projections that produce phasic arousal (like energetic arousal). If this theory is correct, the interaction of these two neuro-

chemical systems could be a basis for the reciprocal interaction of energy and tension. See D. M. Tucker and P. A. Williamson, "Asymmetric Neural Control Systems in Human Self-Regulation," *Psychological Review* 91 (1984): 185–215; and also D. Derryberry and D. M. Tucker, "The Adaptive Base of the Neural Hierarchy: Elementary Motivational Controls on Network Function," in *Nebraska Symposium on Motivation*, ed. R. Dienstbier (Lincoln: University of Nebraska Press, 1990), pp. 289–342.

24. On the other hand, serotonin appears to suppress certain kinds of dopamine-facilitated motor activity. But such suppression would be consistent with Tucker and Williamson's view that dopamine-facilitated motor activity is characteristic of vigilance and motor readiness, a state similar to tense arousal. See B. L. Jacobs, "Serotonin, Motor Activity and Depression-Related Disorders," *American Scientist* 82 (1994): 456–63; B. L. Jacobs, and E. C. Azmitia, "Structure and Function of the Brain Serotonin System," *Physiological Reviews* 72 (1992): 165–229; and R. A. Depue, and D. H. Zald, "Biological and Environmental Processes in Nonpsychotic Psychopathology: A Neurobehavioral Perspective," In *Basic Issues in Psychopathology*, ed. C. G. Costello (New York: Guilford Press, 1993), pp. 127–237.

25. G. F. Weiss, P. Papadakos, K. Knudson, and S. F. Leibowitz, "Medial Hypothalamic Serotonin: Effects on Deprivation and Norepinephrine-Induced Eating," *Pharmacology, Biochemistry, and Behavior* 25 (1986): 1223–30.

26. Jacobs and Azmitia, "Structure and Function"; Depue, and Zald, "Biological and Environmental Processes"; and R. A. Depue and M. R. Spoont, "Conceptualizing a Serotonin Trait: A Behavioral Dimension of Restraint," *Annals of the New York Academy of Sciences* 487 (1986): 47–62.

27. Several popular books discuss various aspects of Prozac, and each is informative in its own way. In addition to Peter Kramer's book that will be discussed below, Ronald Fieve offers a general description of the values and drawbacks of Prozac, together with a brief explanation of the underlying physiology. Peter Breggin provides a cautionary analysis of this drug, emphasizing particularly the problems associated with its approval by the FDA and with its use by some patients. Michael Norden provides an analysis of natural and prescription alternatives to the drug and focuses particularly on how these alternatives are related to the serotonin system, which Prozac affects. See R. R. Fieve, *Prozac* (New York: Avon Books, 1994); P. R. Breggin and G. R. Breggin, *Talking Back to Prozac: What Doctors Won't Tell You About Today's Most Controversial Drug* (New York: St. Martin's Press, 1994); M. J. Norden, *Beyond Prozac: Brain-Toxic Lifestyles, Natural Antidotes and New Generation Antidepressants* (New York: Regan Books 1995).

28. This is sometimes referred to as an SSRI, or a seratonin selective re-uptake inhibitor

29. P. E. Stokes, "Fluoxetine: A Five-Year Review," *Clinical Therapeutics* 15 (1993): 216–43.

30. P. Stark and C. D. Hardison, "A Review of Multicenter Controlled Studies of Fluoxetine vs. Imipramine and Placebo in Outpatients with Major Depressive Disorder," *Journal of Clinical Psychiatry* 46 (1985): 53–58.

31. *Physicians' Desk Reference* 45th ed. (Oradell, NJ: Medical Economics Company, 1991).

32. Stark and Hardison, "Review.".

33. *Physicians' Desk Reference.*

34. Speculating broadly, a possible explanation for this combination of primary effects and side effects may be derived from the model described in this book. This model predicts that increased energy raises tension at lower levels and reduces it at higher levels. The differential drug effect on energy for various people could be the basis of both the positive effects of Prozac (calm-energy) and the side effects on some people (tense-energy).

35. P. Kramer, *Listening to Prozac* (New York: Viking, 1993).

36. Panksepp offered a plausible hypothesis: "A unitary functional principle underlying opioid function in the brain is the homeostatic reestablishment of baseline conditions in many types of neuronal circuits following stressful perturbations." See J. Panksepp, "The Neurochemistry of Behavior," *Annual Review of Psychology* 37 (1986): 77–107, 82.

37. For example, M. N. Janal, E. W. D. Colt, W. C. Clark, and M. Glusman, "Pain Sensitivity, Mood and Plasma Endocrine Levels in Man Following Long-Distance Running: Effects of Naloxone," *Pain* 19 (1984): 13–25; and Hatfield, "Exercise and Mental Health."

38. I believe that we will understand the central neurochemistry of everyday moods when we have done more extensive research with humans, systematically exploring conscious mood changes, together with the relevant neurochemistry. A few studies on humans now offer a good beginning for this kind of research. See Depue et al., "Dopamine and Structure of Personality."

39. Personal communication; September 2, 1994.

40. R. A. Dienstbier, "Arousal and Physiological Toughness: Implications for Mental and Physical Health," *Psychological Review* 96 (1989): 84–100.

41. R. A. Dienstbier, "Mutual Impacts of Toughening on Crises and Losses," in *Life Crises and Experiences of Loss in Adulthood*, ed. L. Montada, F. Sigrun-Heide, and M. J. Lerner (Hillsdale, NJ: Erlbaum, 1992), pp. 367–84.

42. W. D. McArdle, F. I. Katch, and V. L. Katch, *Exercise Physiology: Energy, Nutrition, and Human Performance* (Philadelphia: Lea & Febiger, 1991).

43. R. A. Dienstbier, "Behavioral Correlates of Sympathoadrenal Reactivity: The Toughness Model," *Medicine and Science in Sports and Exercise* 23 (1991): 846–52.

44. For example, see M. M. van Eck and N. A. Nicolson, "Perceived Stress and Salivatory Cortisol in Daily Life," *Annals of Behavioral Medicine* 16 (1994): 221–27.

45. E. R. Kandel, (1991). "Disorders of Mood: Depression, Mania, and Anxiety Disorders," in Kandel et al., eds., *Principles of Neural Science*, pp. 869–86.

46. G. M. Pepper and D. T. Krieger, "Hypothalamic-Pituitary-Adrenal Abnormalities in Depression: Their Possible Relation to Central Mechanisms Regulating ACTH Release," in *Neurobiology of Mood Disorders*, vol. 1, ed. R. M. Post and J. C. Ballenger (Baltimore: Williams and Wilkins, 1984), pp. 245–70.

47. W. A. Brown, "Use of Dexamethasone Suppression Test in Test of Depression," in Post and Ballenger, eds., *Neurobiology of Mood Disorders*, pp. 290–96.

48. D. Benton and D. Owens, "Is Raised Blood Glucose Associated with the Relief of Tension?" *Journal of Psychosomatic Research* 37 (1993): 723–35.

49. A. C. Gold, K. M. MacLeod, B. M. Frier, and I. Deary, "Changes in Mood During Acute Hypoglycemia in Healthy Subjects," *Journal of Personality and Social Psychology* 68 (1995): 498–504; and D. A.Hepburn, I. J. Deary, M. Munoz, and B. M. Frier, "Physiological Manipulation of Psychometric Mood Factors Using Acute Insulin-Induced Hypoglycemia in Humans," *Personality and Individual Differences* 18 (1995): 385–91.

50. Derryberry and Tucker, "The Adaptive Base of the Neural Hierarchy."

51. Ibid.

52. J. A. Gray, *The Neuropsychology of Anxiety* (London: Oxford University Press, 1982); and N. H. Kalin, "The Neurobiology of Fear," *Scientific American*, May 1993, 94–101.

53. Derryberry and Tucker, "The Adaptive Base of the Neural Hierarchy."

54. For example, R. G. Robinson, "Investigating Mood Disorders Following Brain Injury: An Integrative Approach Using Clinical and Laboratory Studies," *Integrative Psychiatry* 1 (1983): 35–39.

55. H. Leventhal and A. J. Tomarken "Emotion: Today's Problems," *Annual Review of Psychology* 37 (1986): 565–610

56. For example, N. A. Fox, "If It's Not Left, It's Right: Electroencephalography Asymmetry and the Development of Emotion," *American Psychologist* 46 (1991): 863–72.

57. Derryberry and Tucker, "The Adaptive Base of the Neural Hierarchy."

58. J. Dodd, and L. W. Role, (1991). "The Autonomic Nervous System," in Kandel et al., eds. *Principles of Neural Science*, pp. 761–75; and W. B. Cannon, *The Wisdom of the Body* (New York: Norton, 1932).

59. H. A. de Vries, *Physiology of Exercise for Physical Education and Athletics* 4th ed. (Dubuque, IA: Brown, 1986); and R. J. Shephard, *Physiology and Biochemistry of Exercise* (New York: Praeger, 1982).

60. F. N. Pitts, and J. N. McClure, "Lactate Metabolism in Anxiety Neurosis," *New England Journal of Medicine* 227 (1967): 1329–36.

CHAPTER 9   Self-Regulation: Why, How, and How Effective

1. For an interesting indication of the motivation of negative moods, consider a study by Osmond, Mullaly and Bisbee. They interviewed 30 depressed psychiatric inpatients who had previously experienced severe physical pain from injury, illness, or surgery. When asked to compare the two conditions, they stated that the depression was worse, and that they would rather reexperience pain than the depression. See H. Osmond, R. Mullaly, C. Bisbee, "Mood Pain: A Comparative Study of Clinical Pain and Depression," *Journal of Orthomolecular Psychiatry* 14 (1985): 5–12.

2. Shiffman offers persuasive evidence that in most cases, substance users who are trying to stop usually do not relapse because of physiological withdrawal symptoms but, instead, because of dysphoric moods. See S. Shiffman, "Coping With Temptations to Smoke," in *Coping and Substance Use*, ed. S. Shiffman and T. A. Wills, (Orlando: Academic Press, 1985), pp. 223–42.

3. For example, one estimate was 55 hours per week for the average household, "1986 Nielsen Report on Television" (New York: A. C. Nielsen and Company).

4. Compare C. S. Carver and M. F. Scheier, "Control Theory: A Useful Conceptual Framework for Personality—Social, Clinical, and Health Psychology," *Psychological Bulletin* 92 (1982): 111–35.

5. V. Rippere, " 'What's the Thing to do When You're Depressed'—A Pilot Study," *Behaviour Research and Therapy* 15 (1977): 185–91.

6. G. B. Parker and L. B. Brown, "Coping Behaviors That Mediate Between Life Events and Depression," *Archives of General Psychiatry* 39 (1982): 1386–91.

7. G. Gallup, Jr. and J. Castelli, *The People's Religion* (New York: Macmillan, 1989).

8. Polls like this have limitations and are not as rigorous as scientific studies, but this was a good start.

9. On the other hand, within these 32 categories, many different behaviors that we thought were similar are grouped together, so there are a larger absolute number of commonly used behaviors than 32.

10. These three items included one for energy enhancement, "Go outside for some fresh air," and two for tension reduction, "Engage in nervous behavior" (e.g., pacing, biting nails, biting pencil) and "Don't drink coffee or caffeinated beverage."

11. J. Dollard, and N. Miller, *Personality and Psychotherapy* (New York: McGraw-Hill, 1950).

12. P. M. Lewinsohn, M. Weinstein, and D. Shaw, "Depression: A Clinical-Research Approach," in *Advances in Behavior Therapy*, ed. R. D. Rubin and C. M. Frank (New York: Academic Press, 1968), pp. 231–40.

13. Such agreement is considered valid in scientific research because it establishes what is called *construct validation.*

14. The exact wording in this part of the questionnaire concerning energy was, "indicate what activities you usually use to prepare yourself if you are tired (fatigued), and in a short while (within 30 minutes) you have something to do that requires alertness and attention (energy)."

15. S. Sethi and M. E. P. Seligman, "Optimism and Fundamentalism," *Psychological Science* 4 (1993): 256–59.

16. S. N. Blair, H. W. Kohl, III, R. S. Paffenbarger. Jr., D. G. Clark, K. H. Cooper, and L. W. Gibbons, "Physical Fitness and All-Cause Mortality: A Prospective Study of Healthy Men and Women," *Journal of the American Medical Association* 262 (1989): 2395–2401. For a good study on the usual motivations for exercise, see C. Davis, J. Fox, H. Brewer, and D. Ratusny, "Motivations to Exercise as a Function of Personality Characteristics, Age, and Gender," *Personality and Individual Differences* 19 (1995): 165–74.

17. Since 1987, I have given lots of interviews for newspapers and magazines, and I often ask my interviewer whether he or she exercises regularly. If the answer is yes, the interviewer will understand what I am talking about. Most regular exercisers know about these matters, but they have yet to be fully disseminated to the general public.

18. Although the literature is not large, a certain number of experiments demonstrate the positive mood benefits of music. But these mood effects may be mixed, depending on the type of music and lyrics employed. See, for example, S. B. Hanser and L. W. Thompson, "Effects of a Music Therapy Strategy on Depressed Older Adults," *Journal of Gerontology* 49 (1994): 265–69; V. N. Stratton and A. H. Zalanowski, "Affective Impact of Music vs. Lyrics," *Empirical Studies of the Arts* 12 (1994): 173–84.

19. S. Cohen and T. A. Wills, "Stress, Social Support and the Buffering Hypothesis," *Psychological Bulletin* 98 (1985): 310–57.

20. A. T. Beck, *Cognitive Therapy and the Emotional Disorders* (New York: International Universities Press, 1976).

CHAPTER 10   Individual Differences in Mood-Regulating Strategies

1. For example, D. Tannen's *You Just Don't Understand* (New York: Morrow, 1990); and J. Gray's *Men Are from Mars; Women Are from Venus* (New York: HarperCollins, 1993).

2. Our findings about the effectiveness of shopping are mixed. Among the few respondents in our study who indicated that they use shopping as their number-one way of changing a bad mood, this activity was rated as among the most effective. In the wider sample, however, shopping was part of a not very effective general strategy.

3. There is good evidence that in regard to both positive and negative emotions, females characteristically show more emotional intensity than males do. Thus, the tendency for women to engage in emotional activity as a way of chang-

ing a bad mood could be a manifestation of their greater emotional intensity in general. See F. Fujita, E. Diener, and E. Sandvik, "Gender Differences in Negative Affect and Well-Being: The Case for Emotional Intensity," *Journal of Personality and Social Psychology* 61 (1991): 427–34.

4. Aside from the small number rating this behavior by itself, sex is combined with the general strategy Direct Tension Reduction (alcohol, drugs, and sex), and this strategy is rated as the least effective.

5. Or perhaps it is the type of person who becomes a prefessional. There may be strong genetic control of this matter.

6. R. Herrington, "Alcohol Abuse and Alcohol Dependence: Treatment and Rehabilitation," in *Alcohol and Drug Abuse Handbook*, ed. R. E. Herrington, G. R. Jacobson, and D. G. Benzer (St. Louis: Warren H. Green, 1987), pp. 180–217; and K. C. Dube, A. Kumar, N. Kumar, and S. P. Gupka, "Prevalence and Pattern of Drug Use Amongst College Students," *Acta Psychiatrica Scandinavica* 57 (1978): 336–56.

7. E. McGrath, *"When Feeling Bad is Good"* (New York: Holt, 1992); and E. McGrath, G. P. Keita, B. R. Strickland, and N. F. Russo, *Women and Depression: Risk Factors and Treatment Issues* (Washington, DC: American Psychological Association, 1990), 1.

8. For a discussion of the pros and cons of the various explanations of women's greater tendency to develop depression, see S. K. Nolen-Hoeksema, *Women and Depression* (Stanford, CA: Stanford University Press, 1990).

9. Compare G. Winokur, and P. Clayton, "Family History Studies: 2. Sex Differences and Alcoholism in Primary Affective Illness," *British Journal of Psychiatry* 113 (1967): 973–79.

10. S. K. Nolen-Hoeksema, "Sex Differences in Unipolar Depression: Evidence and Theory," *Psychological Bulletin* 101 (1987): 259–82.

11. National Public Radio, *Morning Edition*, February 13, 1992.

12. Herrington, "Alcohol Abuse"; and B. J. Bushman, "Human Aggression While Under the Influence of Alcohol and Other Drugs: An Integrative Research Review," *Current Directions in Psychological Science* 2 (1993): 148–52.

13. N. E. Grunberg, and R. Straub, "The Role of Gender and Taste Class in the Effects of Stress on Eating," *Health Psychology* 11 (1992): 97–100.

14. G. L. Hsu, "The Gender Gap in Eating Disorders: Why Are the Eating Disorders More Common Among Women?" *Clinical Psychology Review* 9 (1989): 393–407.

15. H. J. Eysenck and M. W. Eysenck, *Personality and Individual Differences: A Natural Science Approach* (New York: Plenum Press, 1985).

16. A more conservative estimate is half and half, but even this attributes much more influence to genes and less to learning and experience than most people realize. See T. J. Bouchard, D. T. Lykken, M. McGue, N. L. Segal, and A. Tellegen, "Sources of Human Psychological Differences: The Minnesota Study of Twins Reared Apart," *Science* 250 (1990): 223–28; and J. L. Eaves, H. J. Eysenck, and

N. G. Martin, *Genes, Culture and Personality: An Empirical Approach* (New York: Academic Press, 1988).

17. W. H. Sheldon, *The Varieties of Temperament* (New York: Harper, 1942).

18. A. J. Ruderman, "Dietary Restraint: A Theoretical and Empirical Review," *Psychological Bulletin* 99 (1986): 247–62.

CHAPTER 11 Mood Substitution

1. S. N. Rosenfield and J. S. Stevenson, "Perception of Daily Stress and Daily Coping Behaviors in Normal, Overweight, and Recovering Alcoholic Women," *Research in Nursing and Health* 11 (1988): 165–74.

2. J. S. Verinis, "Caffine Use in the Recovering Alcoholic," *Alcohol Health and Research World*, Fall (1986): 64. My thanks to Retha Evans for her observation from studies of alcoholics that other mood-enhancing behaviors are also commonly substituted by those in recovery. Many of them become "meeting junkies," for instance, and in this case it is the increased frequency of social interactions that substitutes for the lost alcohol.

3. S. M. Hall, R. McGee, C. Tunstall, J. Duffy, and N. Benowitz, "Changes in Food Intake and Activity After Quitting Smoking," *Journal of Consulting and Clinical Psychology* 57 (1989): 81–86.

4. Other reasons for the weight gain have also been suggested, including changes in resting metabolic rate. See P. H. Blitzer, A. A. Rimm, E. E. Giefer, "The Effect of Cessation of Smoking on Body Weight in 57,032 Women: Cross-Sectional and Longitudinal Analyses," *Journal of Chronic Diseases* 30 (1977): 415–29; and K. A. Perkins, L. H. Epstein, and S. Pastor, "Changes in Energy Balance Following Smoking Cessation and Resumption of Smoking in Women," *Journal of Consulting and Clinical Psychology* 58 (1990): 121–25.

5. S. Shiffman and T. A. Wills, eds, *Coping and Substance Use* (Orlando, FL: Academic Press, 1985)

6. Given the obvious similarities of the withdrawal effects of various drugs, biological scientists have, surprisingly, avoided speculating about cross-substance commonalities. This is partly because of the difficulty of identifying physiological mechanisms that are the same for the various drugs and withdrawal processes. The principle that general mood effects are the causes of these substance addictions and withdrawals has lagged far behind the logic of the idea, and behind the experimental evidence. However, there has been some speculation in addition to my own work. See for example L. Christensen, "Effects of Eating Behavior on Mood: A Review of the Literature," *International Journal of Eating Disorders* 14 (1993): 171–83; N. E. Grunberg and A. Baum, "Biological Commonalities of Stress and Substance Abuse," in Shiffman and Wills, eds., *Coping and Substance Abuse*, pp. 25–61; and R. E. Thayer, *The Biopsychology of Mood and Arousal* (New York: Oxford University Press, 1989).

Wise offered an intriguing neurobiological theory concerning the similarity of various drugs on the basis of their psychomotor stimulant effects (positive reinforcement mediated by the dopaminergic system) or their ability to suppress pain and distress (negative reinforcement). See R. A. Wise, "The Neurobiology of Craving: Implications for the Understanding of Treatment of Addiction," *Journal of Abnormal Psychology* 97 (1988): 118–32.

7. G. A. Marlatt, and J. R. Gordon, *Relapse Prevention* (New York: Guilford Press, 1985); and S. Shiffman, "Coping With Temptations to Smoke," in Shiffman, and Wills, eds., *Coping and Substance Use*, pp. 223–42.

8. C. Cummings, J. R. Gordon, and G. A. Marlatt, "Relapse: Prevention and Prediction," in *The Addictive Behaviors*, ed. W. R. Miller, (New York: Pergamon Press, 1980), pp. 271–321.

9. N. E. Rosenthal, M. J. Genhart, B. Caballero, F. M. Jacobsen, R. G. Skwerer, S. Rogers, R. D. Coursey, B. J. Spring, "Psychobiological Effects of Carbohydrate and Protein-Rich Meals in Patients with Seasonal Affective Disorder and Normal Controls," *Biological Psychiatry* 25 (1989): 1029–40.

10. J. J. Wurtman, A. Brezezinski, R. J. Wurtman, and B. Laferrere, "Effect of Nutrient Intake on Premenstrual Depression," *American Journal of Obstetrics and Gynecology* 161 (1989): 1228–34.

11. Grunberg and Baum, "Biological Commonalities"; and A. J. Ruderman, "Dietary Restraint: A Theoretical and Empirical Review," *Psychological Bulletin* 99 (1986): 247–62.

12. C. Johnson and R. Larson, "Bulimia: An Analysis of Moods and Behavior," *Psychosomatic Medicine* 44 (1982): 341–51.

13. By necessity, this modest conceptualization deals with only some of the issues here. Numerous studies and many theories account for the observed phenomena. See J. D. Kassel and S. Shiffman, "What Hunger Can Teach Us About Drug Craving? A Comparative Analysis of the Two Constructs," *Advances in Behavioral Research and Therapy* 14 (1992): 141–67; and R. S. Niaura, D. Rohsenow, J. Binkoff, P. Monti, M. Pedraza, and D. Abrams, "Relevance of Cue Reactivity to Understanding Alcohol and Smoking Relapse," *Journal of Abnormal Psychology* 97 (1988): 133–52.

14. As I noted earlier, even though alcohol is a central nervous system depressant, in the initial stages, small amounts tend to improve mood. For a review of studies of this, see J. G. Hull and C. F. Bond, "Social and Behavioral Consequences of Alcohol Consumption and Expectancy: A Meta-Analysis," *Psychological Bulletin* 99 (1986): 347–60.

15. This kind of analysis is valuable for those people to use when learning about self-regulation, as it pertains to feelings in the seconds before a thought or an actual behavior. Although this kind of self-analysis is difficult, it is not impossible.

16. C. M. Grilo, S. Shiffman, and R. R. Wing, "Relapse Crises and Coping Among Dieters," *Journal of Consulting and Clinical Psychology* 57 (1989): 488–95.

17. Compare N. A. Fox, "If It's Not Left, It's Right: Electroencephalograph Asymmetry and the Development of Emotion," *American Psychologist* 46 (1991): 863–72. An alternative interpretation of anger as a stimulus to mood regulation is that the angry person experiencing tense-energy is seeking calm-energy.

18. Willard Gaylin offered a good description of being upset, albeit one based on psychoanalytic theory. See W. Gaylin, *Feelings: Our Vital Signs* (New York: Harper and Row, 1979).

19. A. J. Ruderman, "Dietary Restraint: A Theoretical and Empirical Review," *Psychological Bulletin* 99 (1986): 247–62.

20. D. J. LaPorte, "A Fatiguing Effect in Obese Patients During a Partial Fasting: Increase in Vulnerability to Emotion-Related Events and Anxiety," *International Journal of Eating Disorders* 9 (1990): 345–55.

21. This is perhaps the basis of the difficulty of discriminating between anxiety and depression, a pattern of tense-tiredness. Compare L. A. Feldman, "Distinguishing Depression and Anxiety in Self-Report: Evidence from Confirmatory Factor Analysis on Nonclinical and Clinical Samples," *Journal of Consulting and Clinical Psychology* 61 (1993): 631–38.

22. R. M. Ganley, "Emotion and Eating in Obesity: A Review of the Literature," *International Journal of Eating Disorders* 8 (1989): 343–61.

23. Compare D. E. Berlyne, *Conflict, Arousal, and Curiosity* (New York: Mc-Graw-Hill, 1960).

24. Shiffman, "Coping with Temptations to Smoke."

25. T. P. Carmody, "Affect Regulation, Smoking Addiction, and Smoking Cessation," *Journal of Psychoactive Drugs* 21 (1989): 331–42.

26. D. Cappell and S. Greely, "Alcohol and Tension Reduction: An Update on Research and Theory," in *Psychological Theories and Drinking and Alcoholism* ed. H. T. Blane and K. E. Leonard (New York: Guilford Press, 1987), pp. 15–54.

27. J. A. Neff and B. A. Husaini, "Life Events, Drinking Patterns and Depressive Symptomatology: The Stress Buffering Effect of Alcohol Consumption," *Journal of Studies on Alcohol* 43 (1982): 301–18.

28. E. E. Chaney and D. K. Roszell, (1985). "Coping in Opiate Addicts Maintained on Methadone," in Shiffman and Wills, eds., *Coping and Substance Use*, pp. 267–93.

29. T. B. Baker, E. Morse, and J. E. Sherman, "The Motivation to Use Drugs," in *The Nebraska Symposium on Motivation: Alcohol Use and Abuse*, ed. C.Rivers (Lincoln: Univ. of Nebraska Press, 1987), pp. 257–323.

CHAPTER 12   Rational Mood Substitution

1. As Garrow argued, "Obesity arises when energy intake exceeds energy expenditure over a long period." See J. S. Garrow, "Is Obesity an Eating Disorder?" *Journal of Psychosomatic Research* 32 (1988): 585–90, 585.

2. For example, J. Mayer, N. B. Marshall, J. J. Vitale, J. H. Christensen, M. B. Mashayekhi, and F. J. Stare, "Exercise, Food Intake and Body Weight in Normal Rats and Genetically Obese Adult Mice," *Journal of Physiology* 177 (1954): 544–48.

3. C. A. Titchenal, "Exercise and Food Intake: What Is the Relationship?" *Sports Medicine* 6 (1988): 135–45.

4. My thanks to Retha Evans for this observation.

5. The two exercise conditions included 50 percent VO_2MAX and 30 minutes alternating 15 seconds at 100 percent with 105 seconds at 40 percent. See W. E. Reger and T. G. Allison, "Exercise and Appetite," *Medicine and Science in Sports and Exercise* 19 (1987): 226. Another experiment by these researchers provided less support for the appetite suppression idea: W. E. Reger, T. G. Allison, and R. L. Kurucz, "Exercise, Post-Exercise Metabolic Rate, and Appetite," in *Sport, Health, and Nutrition. The 1984 Olympic Scientific Congress Proceedings*, vol. 2, ed. F. I. Katch (Champaign, IL: Human Kinetics, 1986), pp. 115–23.

6. R. M. Julien, *A Primer of Drug Action* (New York: W. H. Freeman, 1992).

7. B. B. Hoffman and R. J. Lefkowitz, "Catecholamines and Sympathomimetic Drugs," in *The Pharmacological Basis of Therapeutics*, 8th ed., ed. A. J. Gilman et al. (New York: Pergamon Press, 1990), pp. 187–220.

8. R. E. Thayer, D. P. Peters, and A. M. Birkhead-Flight, "Mood and Behavior (Smoking and Sugar Snacking) Following Moderate Exercise: A Partial Test of Self-Regulation Theory," *Personality and Individual Differences* 14 (1993): 97–104.

9. The 5-minute brisk walk was taken at a relatively fast pace, but not so fast as to result in exhaustion. The subjects were instructed to walk about as fast as they would if late for an appointment. However, they were instructed to walk with a relaxed and erect posture, unlike that if they were late. They also were instructed to allow their arms to swing in a natural motion. The brisk pace was intended to activate the subjects physiologically. The arm swing was intended not only to activate but also to relax muscles in the shoulders and neck, which often are significant sources of anxiety and nervousness.

10. Subjects rated their own mood with a small checklist of adjectives called the AD ACL, short for Activation-Deactivation Adjective Check List. I developed this measure some years ago in conjunction with my physiological research. Since then it has been translated into many languages and is used all over the world in research on mood. Self-ratings on this checklist correlate moderately well with physiological measures of arousal and quite well with general biological variations. In this case, we were interested in self-ratings of energy (energetic, lively, active, vigorous, full of pep) and tension (tense, clutched-up, fearful, jittery, intense). The urge to snack was rated on a 7-point scale that ranged from extreme to none at all. See R. E. Thayer, "Activation-Deactivation Adjective Check List: Current Overview and Structural Analysis," *Psychological Reports* 58 (1986): 607–14; and R. E. Thayer, *The Biopsychology of Mood and Arousal* (New York: Oxford University Press, 1989), Appendix I.

11. Additional details of the experiment include the following. The subjects were not aware of the purposes of this experiment or about our research and theory concerning mood. On another point, the mood effects of moderate exercise are most detectable when the experimental subject has been sitting down for a while. Therefore, in this study subjects had to be sitting for at least 40 minutes before beginning the experiment. During the five minutes of the control or no-walk condition, 27 percent of the time the subjects read, studied, or did paperwork; 29 percent of the time they watched TV; 24 percent of the time they talked or listened to the radio, music, or college lectures; and 21 percent of the time they did other sedentary activities. The snack was one of several standard-sized candy bars, supplied by the experimenters after preferences were noted.

Finally, one great problem with previous research on mood is that these feelings are so subtle and ephemeral that they are difficult to measure in a scientific study, particularly in regard to food influences on mood. When asked to self-rate their mood, the subjects are so influenced by the conditions of the experiment that the subtle mood effects are lost. Just being in a scientific study is exciting to some extent, and this excitement may wash out more natural mood effects. A practical implication of this problem is that the experimenter studying the mood effects of sugar may find no effect and so conclude that sugar does not influence mood. In everyday life, however, sugar might have real influences on mood, although on any one occasion these are so subtle that they don't show up. This problem is sufficiently important that in my opinion, much of the research on mood and food is flawed because it has not taken these matters into consideration, because the relationship between sugar and mood was measured on only one occasion. See Thayer, *Biopsychology*, chap. 7.

To counteract this problem, we used a procedure that was successful in several of my previous experiments on mood. We repeated over and over the main conditions of the experiment for 3 weeks, and then averaged the results. In this way, we increased the reliability of the measurement because the subtle mood effects produced by the sugar snacks were repeated and so the 3-week averages were more accurate, even though the effects were small. In addition, other, occasional influences (e.g., something unusual that raises or lowers mood but happens only once in a while) don't affect mood because they are averaged out. (For everyday mood issues, people should apply these same procedures. For example, if a person is interested in sugar effects, sugar should be eaten on a number of occasions, with the mood noted each time, and the results averaged.)

The problem with this design is that it is difficult to control the effects of the subjects' expectations. We have some evidence about these, however, because we were able to determine statistically if the difference across the two conditions (walk/no walk) grew larger as the subject completed more trials. This would be likely if the subjects discovered the purpose of the experiment and somehow were making consistent self-ratings. The results of this statistical analysis showed no change.

12. O. F. Pomerleau, H. H. Scherzer, N. E. Grunberg, C. S. Pomerleau, J. Judge, J. B. Fertig, and J. Burleson, "The Effect of Acute Exercise on Subsequent Cigarette Smoking," *Journal of Behavioral Medicine* 10 (1987): 117–27.

13. J. R. Grove, A. Wilkinson, and B. T. Dawson, "Effects of Exercise on Selected Correlates of Smoking Withdrawal," *International Journal of Sports Psychology* 24 (1993): 217–36.

14. R. A. Faulkner, D. A. Bailey, and R. L. Mirwald, "The Relationship of Physical Activity to Smoking Characteristics in Canadian Men and Women. *Canadian Journal of Public Health* 78 (1987): 155–60.

15. Thayer et al., "Mood and Behavior."

CHAPTER 13 The Practical Psychology of Self-Regulation

1. At present, behavioral scientists are very interested in both the practical and theoretical elements involved in self-regulating emotional states, and a wide variety of approaches have been studied. For a very readable and interesting treatment of many facets of self-regulating emotions and moods see D. Goleman, *Emotional Intelligence* (New York: Bantam Books 1995). For a more technical analysis of this subject see D. M. Wegner and J. W. Pennebaker, eds., *Handbook of Mental Control* (Englewood Cliffs, NJ: Prentice-Hall, 1993).

2. E. Goffman, *The Presentation of Self in Everyday Life* (Garden City, NY: Doubleday, 1959.)

3. D. J. LaPorte, "A Fatiguing Effect in Obese Patients During a Partial Fasting: Increase in Vulnerability to Emotion-Related Events and Anxiety," *International Journal of Eating Disorders* 9 (1990): 345–55.

4. R. E. Thayer, "Energy, Tiredness, and Tension Effects of a Sugar Snack Versus Moderate Exercise," *Journal of Personality and Social Psychology* 52 (1987): 119–25.

5. L. Christensen and R. Burrows, "Dietary Treatment of Depression," *Behavior Therapy* 21 (1990): 183–94.

CHAPTER 14 Overcoming Tense-Tiredness by Increasing Energy

1. As I stated earlier, these predictions are dependent on general variables such as health, physical condition and age and on more immediate variables such as time of day and nutritional status. They also are related to one's overall tension level. Higher levels of tension, for example, may require more exercise to reduce that tension.

2. R. E. Thayer, D. P. Peters, and A. M. Birkhead-Flight, "Mood and Behavior (Smoking and Sugar Snacking) Following Moderate Exercise: A Partial Test of Self-Regulation Theory," *Personality and Individual Differences* 14 (1993): 97–104.

3. R. E. Thayer, "Energy, Tiredness, and Tension Effects of a Sugar Snack Versus

Moderate Exercise," *Journal of Personality and Social Psychology* 52 (1987): 119–25.

4. H. A. de Vries and G. M. Adams, "Electromyographic Comparisons of Single Doses of Exercise and Meprobamate as to Effect on Muscular Relaxation," *American Journal of Physical Medicine* 51 (1972): 130–41.

5. Steve did this study to test the results of my earlier research comparing moderate exercise and a sugar snack. See Thayer, "Energy, Tiredness, and Tension Effect."

6. Thayer et al., "Mood and Behavior."

7. S. N. Blair, H. W. Kohl III, R. S. Paffenbarger, D. G. Clark, K. H. Cooper, and L. W. Gibbons, "Physical Fitness and All-Cause Mortality: A Prospective Study of Healthy Men and Women," *Journal of the American Medical Association* 17 (1989): 2395–2401.

8. R. B. Bassin and R. E. Thayer, "Self-Reported Depression, Moderate Exercise, and Arousal Level," paper presented at the Western Psychological Association, Seattle, 1986.

9. This is somewhat comparable to the advice of Alcoholics Anonymous to recovering alcoholics to avoid drinking only one day at a time because the thought of not drinking for the rest of one's life may be overwhelming.

CHAPTER 15   Reducing Tension to Overcome Tense-Tiredness

1. See, however, H. Benson, *The Relaxation Response* (New York: Avon Books, 1976), who offers a plausible and biologically based explanation.

2. T. George Harris suggested an interesting combination of focused attention and exercise: Together with short brisk walks, you should "count each time your foot hits the ground. Or repeat your favorite song title in time to your steps." See his "The Grand-Time Striders," *Saturday Evening Post*, March/April 1992, 46.

3. J. L. Hager made this point. She studied respiration patterns of people subjected to either a stress-inducing film or a short period of vigorous exercise. Both created arousal, but the two groups' respiratory patterns were quite different. The exercisers breathed more deeply, involving more of the lungs in the gas exchange, whereas those who were stressed breathed quickly but with shallow breaths. See J. L. Hager, "The Human Respiratory Response in State Anxiety" (Ph.D. diss., Cornell University, 1976).

4. This assertion has strong theoretical support, but as far as I know, no scientific studies have been conducted in such a way as to prove the point.

5. E. Jacobson, *Anxiety and Tension Control* (Philadelphia: Lippincott, 1964.)

6. For example, D. L. Watson and R. G. Tharp, *Self-Directed Behavior: Self-Modification for Personal Adjustment* (Pacific Grove, CA: Brooks/Cole, 1993).

7. K. M. Dillon, "Popping Sealed-Air Capsules to Reduce Stress," *Psychological Reports* 71 (1992): 243–46.

8. See T. Field, "Message Therapy for Infants and Children," *Developmental*

and Behavioral Pediatrics 16 (1995): 105–11; and T. Field, C. Morrow, C. Valdeon, S. Larson, C. Kuhn, and S. Schanberg, "Message Reduces Anxiety in Child and Adolescent Psychiatric Patients," *Journal of the American Academy of Child Adolescent Psychiatry* 31 (1992): 125–31.

9. In this brief survey of techniques to reduce tension and raise energy, I have not commented on a wide variety of other things that might well be employed. For example, students in my mood classes have conducted self-studies of mood changes following singing. This activity consistently results in increased energy and reduced tension. Dancing has also been a favorite self-study topic, and a similar pattern of calm-energy usually derives from this activity. These findings are not surprising considering that both singing and dancing combine music, a good mood enhancer, with a kind of exercise and breath control. The activities that influence mood are endless, as might be expected, if we think of mood in its general biological context. Even pleasant odors have been found to reduce tension and increase energy. See S. S. Schiffman, E. A. Sattely-Miller, M. S. Suggs, and P. G. Graham, "The Effect of Pleasant Odors and Hormone Status on Mood of Women at Midlife," *Brain Research Bulletin* 36 (1995): 19–29; and S. S. Schiffman, M. S. Suggs and E. Sattely-Miller, "Effect of Pleasant Odors on Mood of Males at Midlife: Comparison of African-American and European-American Men," *Brain Research Bulletin* 36 (1995): 31–37.

CHAPTER 16   Moods at Different Times of Day

1. Alternatively, an interesting literature seems to show that depressed people have a more accurate perception of many personal characteristics than do those not depressed. See L. B. Alloy and L. Y. Abramson, "Depressive Realism: Four Theoretical Perspectives," in *Cognitive Processes in Depression*, ed. L. B. Alloy (New York: Guilford Press, 1988), pp. 223–65. It is beyond the scope of this discussion to deal with the positive and negative aspects of these conclusions. But in my experience, tense-tired times are not ones in which self-perception is most accurate. Also see C. R. Colvin and J. Block, "Positive Illusions and Well-Being Revisited: Separating Fiction from Fact," *Psychological Bulletin* 116 (1994): 3–20.

2. It is no accident that in a demanding economic system, most employers require their employees to be at work during the high-energy times of the day.

3. J. Rubadeau and R. E. Thayer, "The Relationship of Self-Esteem and Self-Reported Activation Level over a Seven-Week Period," paper presented at the Western Psychological Association, Los Angeles, 1976.

4. Contrary to many popular views, students often live the most stressful life-styles. I know many who have a full-time job and a full course load and are trying to maintain some sort of social life as well. Sleep is one of the first things to go, and bodily stress reactions are common. Furthermore, there is nothing mysterious about the observation that students are among the most depressed groups.

5. W. Masters and V. Johnson, *Human Sexual Response* (Boston: Little Brown, 1966); and M. Zuckerman, "Physiological Measures of Sexual Arousal in the Human," in *Handbook of Psychophysiology*, ed. N. S. Greenfield and R. A. Sternbach (New York: Holt, Rinehart and Winston, 1972) pp. 709–40.

6. Masters and Johnson, *Human Sexual Response*

7. Using this model of mood, Retha Evans and I are conducting systematic research on the relationship between mood and sexual satisfaction.

CHAPTER 17   Systematic Self-Observation

1. C. S. Carver and M. F. Scheier, "Control Theory: A Useful Conceptual Framework for Personality—Social, Clinical, and Health Psychology," *Psychological Bulletin* 92 (1982): 111–35.

2. As a reminder when you do your self-ratings, you could use an inexpensive watch that beeps every hour.

3. W. Gaylin, *Feelings: Our Vital Signs* (New York: Harper and Row, 1979), 102.

Index